Critical Making in the Age of AI

Critical Making in the Age of AI

Emily K. Johnson and
Anastasia Salter

AMHERST COLLEGE PRESS
AMHERST, MASSACHUSETTS

The complete manuscript of this work was subjected to a partly closed ("single
anonymous") review process. For more information, visit https://acpress.amherst.
edu/peerreview/.

Published in the United States of America by Amherst College Press
Manufactured in the United States of America

Library of Congress Control Number: 2024940628
DOI: https://doi.org/10.3998/mpub.14510509

ISBN 978-1-943208-95-1 (paperback)
ISBN 978-1-943208-96-8 (open access)
ISBN 978-1-943208-97-5 (hardcover)

Cover illustration created by Emily K. Johnson and Anastasia Salter using
OpenAI DALL-E 2.

Contents

Acknowledgments

Writing a book inspired by our own pedagogical journeys would be impossible without our amazing students. We especially thank those who have allowed us to share their work with you as examples throughout this book, but we are grateful for all the students who have experimented and explored with us in every iteration of these courses. Concepts from this work have been shared with our research communities, including the Electronic Literature Organization, Society for Cinema and Media Studies, Modern Language Association, and many others: we appreciate the feedback and support those communities have offered.

We would like to thank our editor, Hannah Brooks-Motl, for her enthusiasm and support of this strange project; the editorial team at Amherst College Press; our families; our faculty support group (Mel Stanfill, John Murray, and Anne Sullivan); our colleagues across the country joining us in conversations around AI in the digital humanities (Sherry Rankins-Robertson, Edmond Chang, Paul Shovlin, Leonardo Flores, Elizabeth Losh); our colleagues in English and in the Texts and Technology program; our dean, Jeff Moore, for his support of our work; and the amazing students who worked with us through some of the most challenging semesters of instruction we have ever experienced. Anastasia would particularly like to thank the current and former members of the English faculty writing group for their insights (including James Campbell, Bill Fogarty, Stephen Hopkins, Anna Jones, Veronica Joyner, Tison Pugh, Mel Stanfill, and Pavithra Tantrigoda). And always, thanks to our mentors (Stuart Moulthrop, Rudy McDaniel, Matthew Kirschenbaum, Noah Wardrip-Fruin, and many others).

Preface: Yet Another Crisis

The humanities classroom of today has been irrevocably transformed: whether using Zoom to run class in the exhaustingly uneven modality of hybrid, managing the changed expectations of students in a physical room, or struggling to define the term for a course modality (Johnson et al.), the long-term impact of the pandemic pivot cannot be ignored. We are at a crossroads: talking about the "digital humanities" evokes a bigger tent than ever, with the increasing accessibility to powerful digital tools, especially digital tools for learning. Simultaneously, with the great pandemic pivot, colleagues who had steadfastly refused to convert to slides, much less embrace course management systems, abruptly found themselves caught in a push for instant, radical change. Seemingly overnight, departments with minimal history of social media interaction established Discord and Slack channels or were converted to Microsoft Teams. The sudden required use of several complex technologies, often without moderation or time spent to build familiarity and understanding, left many faculty, staff, and students exhausted.

The last few years have in many ways served as a powerful reminder of just how inaccurate the myth of the digital native is: persisting from

Mark Prensky's claims over 15 years ago, the concept refers to the assumption that today's students "are all 'native speakers' of the digital language of computers, video games and the Internet" (Prensky 29). Anyone watching students and faculty struggle with the online pivot, captured in the memes of "You're still muted," must recognize the fallacy in that claim. Furthermore, as faculty who for years have taught programming alongside critical algorithm studies and procedural tools, we must note that the "digital language" of computers underlies the interface and is designed to evade the user's gaze. Even as our collective struggle underlines the exhausting realities of our reliance upon constantly changing interfaces and software, the larger social consequences of algorithmic feeds and the amplification of misinformation loom over the very platforms on which we teach, research, and share. The gradual but inescapable integration of even more advanced algorithmic manipulation, such as generative AI tools, into our everyday software risks pushing students and faculty even further into the role of users without meaningful control (or understanding) of our tools.

The same transformations continue to impact all scholarly communication, even as the ubiquity of generative AI promises a next transformation of equal impact. We also lost the foundations that bolster many of our fields: academic conferences were cancelled in many instances and moved awkwardly (and hastily) online in others. As part of the leadership teams assisting in the online pivots of two conferences, we found ourselves confronted with the impossibility of balancing a desire for the traditional conference experience with the realities of digital tools. The best of those virtual events drew attention to the possibilities of alternative communication to create accessible and unusual experiences: the worst are perhaps best forgotten, but often involved attempts to keep everything that in the end left their participants and hosts exhausted. A world of vanished travel opportunities (and budgets that may never return) left us fitting conference talks on Zoom between the usual schedule of meetings, classes, and care. Even as conferences have been attempting their return to "normal," they, like our classrooms, cannot regain familiar footing: many faces are missing, with scholars denied funding, medically unable to risk travel, dealing with new long-term care challenges, or simply exhausted. The long-promised "return to normal" is not coming, especially not in humanities departments already under siege.

Out of observing those frustrations, failures, and challenges, we collaborated on a previous book—*Playful Pedagogy in the Pandemic: Pivoting to Game-Based Learning* (2022), which is in many ways a chronicle of failure: the fatigues of Zoom; the acceleration of educational technology adoption; and the destructiveness of increased surveillance culture extending into our students' (and our own) homes and lives. We searched for some signs of hope, and found it in experimental, collaborative digital pedagogy existing outside commercial platforms and educational technology auspices: practices that inform the approaches and methods in this volume. Along the way, we read *How to Make Art at the End of the World*, Natalie Loveless's manifesto for reshaping the university by way of the classroom—written prior to the pandemic, it is a call for innovation in scholarship that resonates deeply in our current landscape of under-resourced and perpetually struggling departments. Hope again emerged, as we found additional ways to diminish the feeling of being powerless in the face of new technologies and ways to restore the feelings of agency through making.

The act of making, described as "research-creation" by Natalie Loveless, is a way to "ask questions differently"—to, as Loveless describes, encourage "modes of temporal and material attunement within the academy that require slowing down...[and] finding ways, through aesthetic encounters and events, to persuade us to care and to care differently" (107). This book is an encouragement to slow down, to care, and to make differently. Indeed, with apologies to Lin Manuel Miranda (and perhaps also with regrets to Hamilton), we wonder if the way forward for our students and ourselves is to "Write Less. Make

More." With the declining "real world" applicability of confining and—for many of our students—uninspiring forms of traditional academic writing as digital modes of communication and personal expression proliferate, we advocate the need to provide different opportunities for students to *make*: to create works that reflect research, critical thinking, and procedural literacy.

We acknowledge that we are particularly fortunate as holders of what might be among the few remaining tenure line jobs, with the time and resources to devote to the writing of this book, and classrooms typically small enough to allow for the continual experimentation in pedagogy that has informed this work. However, we are also writing this volume as faculty at an institution in a state, and country, where the very tenets of humanities education are under scrutiny and attack. Our positions, fields, and departments are increasingly precarious, and the recasting of our work politically as a "public threat" cannot be ignored (Mangan).

In the face of such hostile labeling, this work is intentionally political: we see developing our collective understanding and knowledge of digital making as a means towards building creative, compelling arguments for social justice. The historical gatekeeping and assumptions around the procedural have continued to limit who makes, and whose making is valued. By modeling and adopting inclusive and expansive approaches to making in our research and teaching, we can perhaps shape the humanities of the future. This work provides patterns for using and understanding a variety of digital tools with a focus on beginners, and with the goal of providing structure for work that is both meaningful and achievable with limited resources and time.

Works Cited

Johnson, Emily K., and Anastasia Salter. *Playful Pedagogy in the Pandemic: Pivoting to Game-Based Learning.* Taylor & Francis, 2022.

Johnson, Nicole, et al. "Defining Different Modes of Learning: Resolving Confusion and Contention Through Consensus." *Online Learning*, vol. 26, no. 3, Sept. 2022. *olj.onlinelearningconsortium.org*, https://doi.org/10.24059/olj.v26i3.3565.

Loveless, Natalie. *How to Make Art at the End of the World: A Manifesto for Research-Creation*. Duke University Press, 2019.

Mangan, Katherine. "Is Higher Ed a Public Good or a Public Threat?" *The Chronicle of Higher Education*, 19 Oct. 2022, www.chronicle.com/article/public-good-or-public-threat.

Prensky, Marc. "Digital Natives, Digital Immigrants." *Gifted*, no. 135, pp. 29–31.

INTRODUCTION

Provocations for Making

Write Me an Essay...

As the sophistication of machine learning as a tool for mimicry has grown, speculation as to the fate of the undergraduate essay has unsurprisingly risen with it. Both academics and popular media have noted that students are already using generative AI tools like OpenAI and Moonbeam in the writing of assignments, an inevitable outcome of a software shift that has brought chat-style interfaces for using large-language models to widespread use. Since the resulting text cannot be detected by plagiarism software, it can pass as original—if not yet particularly imaginative or always coherent—writing (Woodcock). The OpenAI playground encourages rapid generation of writing based on prompt—take, for instance, this early response to "Write a defense of the essay as a scholarly form, with an emphasis on the historical role it has played in education" from ChatGPT, which has become the ubiquitous exemplar of generative AI:

> The essay is a time-honored form of scholarly communication, and it has played an important role in education for centuries. Essays allow scholars

to share their ideas and research in a concise, well-organized format. They can be used to communicate complex ideas, and they can be used to spark further discussion and debate.

The essay has also been used as a teaching tool. In the classroom, essays can be used to help students learn to think critically and to express themselves clearly. Essays can be assigned on a variety of topics, and they can be used to assess a student's understanding of a topic.

The essay is an important form of scholarly communication, and it has a long history of helping students learn.

Ignoring the rather painful repetition of "the essay..." in each topic sentence and noting that here we restrained the generative AI to a minimal output rather than allowing it to ramble on, the result is at once readable and familiar, trained as it was on similar discussions of the essay defined in textbooks and Wikipedia entries. This is in keeping with OpenAI's promise to give us a future of "AI writing assistants," a promise that for many sends the same chills as the idea of automated writing feedback—a promise of convergence on uniformity. It is easy to look at these changing technologies and dread a future of automated writing graded by automated systems: a readerless, writerless classroom to round out our educational dystopian nightmares.

However, this headline-driven, faculty-center-led emphasis on generative AI as a plagiarism tool holds in it echoes of many previous panics inspired by technology: the not-so-distant past has seen faculty argue over the need for bans on citing Wikipedia; disagreeing over the presence of laptops in classrooms; and so forth. What Lev Manovich refers to as "softwarization" has fundamentally shifted the practice of writing and imploded our historical practices of composition (Manovich). The integration of generative AI tools into our creative software, coding practices, word processors, and search engines will similarly proceed forward, becoming eventually less transparent. The arrival of ChatGPT caused such consternation because of the accessibility of its interface when compared to prior generations of generative AI, which required programming to manipulate: the next generation will require even less literacy to use, and thus will require educators to contextualize and mediate.

Preparing students to navigate a landscape of rapidly changing software and platforms requires thinking beyond the essay, and even beyond text, as on our misinformation-laden digital platforms text is but one component of any message: Walter Ong's promise of the "secondary orality" of the web has become a true cacophony of memes, GIFs, TikToks, games, visualizations, and more (Ong). Against this onslaught of imagery and overwhelming media we place digital literacy, a means for developing what Eshet has referred to as "survival skills" for an interface-driven, nonlinear, rapidly changing world (Eshet). Generative AI's potential to reshape these interfaces and systems has similarly raised concerns in our field on the need to develop "critical AI literacy" for both faculty and students, which the MLA-CCCC Joint Task Force on Writing and AI defines as "literacy about the nature, capacities, and risks of AI tools as well as how they might be used" (Byrd et al. 7). Building that critical AI literacy demands a historically cognizant approach to these tools and their impact on all forms of digital making.

This book is a response to those calls, and a path forward for thinking about humanities classrooms in an age of AI and "content." The tools and platforms driving communication forward are founded upon dismissing and trivializing the work of the arts and humanities. Digital labor's historic undervaluation amplifies existing patterns of marginalization; as feminist lenses on the web remind us, the web is built on, and of, "free" labor (Terranova). Machine-authored essays are but one of many warnings of what is to come, and indeed, their authorship is not so much "machine" as it is an uncredited remix of that labor—a critical distinction for fostering the next generation of digital literacy. As the procedural outsourcing of "content-making" becomes an increasing site of debate and tension, we need new emphasis on procedural literacy and algorithmic critique and understanding of both the generative and the "content."

This book is a provocation for addressing the overwhelming landscape of these shifting technologies and the already-happening shift to new media and multimodal composition as an alternative to the essay. It is an invitation to rethink both faculty and student practices of composition and making. And yes, it is a book, which might seem like a contradiction in terms: however, we see this book as part of a conversation about what our books might look like. This book is open access, and inherently composite. While it might exist in a printed format, it is not designed to be read through: like any craft book, it is a manual, meant for skimming, revisiting, excerpting, and, hopefully, inspiring practice and pedagogy.

Make It Digital

This is not to say that in digital literacy, or digital platforms, we expect to easily find solutions to the crisis of the humanities scholarship and communication. Attempts to reinvigorate and reimagine the scholarly essay in light of digital affordances have been ongoing for decades, and are critically intertwined with the digital humanities practices. In 2012, the Modern Language Association published their guidelines for the evaluation of digital humanities scholarship. Ten years later, this type of document pushing for the recognition of born-digital scholarly practice as an essential form of humanities work is no longer particularly controversial, although many departments still value the traditional monograph above all other forms of production. Spaces for the evaluation and support of this type of digital project have helped amplify this type of work: for instance, *Reviews in Digital Humanities*, edited by Dr. Jennifer Guiliano and Dr. Roopika Risam, now includes over three years of discussions of projects inclusive of "digital archives, multimedia or multimodal scholarship, digital exhibits, visualizations, digital games, and digital tools" ("Reviews in Digital Humanities"). However, such work is most visibly embraced when it falls under recognizable practices in the digital humanities: institutionally endorsed, traditionally structured, and reminiscent of textual forms and practices. We have in digital humanities typically not fundamentally reimagined the essay, but instead more pragmatically remediated it, often within platforms and intentionally constructed frameworks of scholarly-ness that resist the more personal, remixable, and transformative expressions of the web.

The standouts of scholarly expression that truly break the essay need not even be digital. One powerful example, Nick Sousanis's 2015 comic monograph *Unflattening*, models a practice of humanities inquiry through image-text: throughout, he both illustrates and reflects upon the limitations of text as a means of scholarly communication, as well as the consequences of an education system where text remains central (Sousanis). His work is one of many attempts to push towards formal reflection in the humanities, and it is certainly one of the more exemplary, if hard to imitate, examples: not many of us bring a professional illustrator's knowledge and skill to the task of scholarly communication. *Unflattening* is thus a physical book, bound and distributed by an academic press in the usual fashion, but also is an example of creative practice in scholarly communication, falling in conversation with practices of critical making and public scholarship.

Some of the oldest venues for digital scholarship are also the most welcoming of experimental work that falls outside these frameworks: *Kairos*, for instance, is home to sections including "Inventio" and "Disputatio" that offer space for reflexive engagement with the webtext's very form, as well as the sharing of "mini-manifestos." Other new venues build from the influence of electronic literature, a form of born-digital narrative experimentation, on the making of scholarship: *The Digital Review* features both reflective and critical works in this category across a range of platforms and modalities.

This type of working creates opportunities for the combination of computational and systems thinking required to develop what Michael Mateas describes as procedural literacy: "the ability to read and write processes, to engage procedural representation and aesthetics, to understand the interplay between the culturally-embedded practices of human meaning-making and technically-mediated processes" (Mateas). The skills of procedural literacy are at the heart of both critical making and games studies methods including critical code studies, software studies, and platform studies. Procedural literacy is to some extent a necessary rejoinder to the teaching of digital literacy: if digital literacy is indeed about mechanisms for survival, procedural literacy gets to the heart of resistance.

However, that resistance can be difficult to achieve when the procedural is so deeply embedded in a white, cisgender, straight digital humanities: as Tara McPherson's work reminds us, "code and race are deeply intertwined, even as the structures of code labor to disavow these very connections" (McPherson). McPherson makes an essential call to action for greater procedural literacy:

> We must have at least a passing familiarity with code languages, operating systems, algorithmic thinking, and systems design. We need database literacies, algorithmic literacies, computational literacies, interface literacies. We need new hybrid practitioners: artist-theorists, programming humanists, activist-scholars; theoretical archivists, critical race coders.

Such changes in pedagogy and graduate training are easier said than done: in the program we teach in, the Texts and Technology PhD at the University of Central Florida, we have recently implemented a structure that integrates procedural literacy across the curriculum. Multiple exposures to iterative creative and analytical technical skills throughout the core coursework culminate in a procedural literacy course in either critical making or humanities data analysis. That curricular change was itself not without resistance and challenges, both on the part of faculty and students: some of those problems in turn shaped this volume, in which we hope to provide one pathway into the "hybridity" McPherson seeks.

More Hack, Less Yack?

This book owes a great debt to the spirit of THATCamp, an early digital humanities initiative driven by collaboration and making. THATCamp was an informally linked series of unconferences, usually featuring workshops and conversation, intended to resist the hierarchical model of speakers and conference fees in favor of collaboration and outcomes. That spirit of making is perhaps summed up in part by the early motto Dan Cohen notes as a riff on a local rock station: "Less talk, more grok" (Cohen). THATCamp fizzled in part due to a sense of familiarity—that is to say, how many more bootcamps and conversations did we need around entry points to the digital humanities?—and pragmatically due to a lack of ongoing funding and support. However, it made quite an impact on the field along the way, with over 320 events and over 8,000 people participating, according to former coordinator Amanda French's retrospective (French).

In another reflection on the camps, Trevor Owens noted another challenge: it "feels like we've lost a lot of the optimism that surrounded those events, I think in part as it feels like the community became more aware and engaged with how problematic the values at play in digital technology ideologies are" (Owens). We see a similar challenge alongside any attempts to foster the hybrid practitioner: while an emphasis on playful making has infused the field since the days of THATCamp, the platforms involved have become more complex, barriers to making have grown, and the hazards involved in simply being present and crafting scholarship online continue to rise. We still need "yack"—for theory, and interrogation, of what we "hack"—but we also need to interrogate how we "yack," and, to riff on Dan Cohen, who gets to grok, talk, and be heard.

As other spaces and digital humanities practices have emerged to fill some of the gaps THATCamp left behind, we see promise in work that sits at the fusion of "hack" and "yack." Critical making combines the concepts of critical thinking and physical production, focusing on the act of creating as an avenue for reflection. Critical making in the digital humanities is expanding through playful and experimental work: from Matt Kirschenbaum's BookLab for material text-making (University of Maryland) to Quinn Dombrowski's Textile Makerspace for fiber digital humanities (Stanford). However, these opportunities to break out of the essay are frequently subject to the availability and support of well-funded centers, where materials, workshops, and mentorship can be more easily found.

Similarly, makerspaces, or spaces designed for rapid prototyping of physical or integrated physical-digital objects with the assistance of computation, have become an increasingly common part of campuses since their first introduction approximately two decades ago (Barrett et al.). A survey of such spaces conducted in 2015 noted that most universities either had or at the time of the study were in the process of developing this type of space, typically including 3D printers, laser cutters, and other electronics, usually with wood or metal shops and more rarely with access to textile or fiber arts equipment (Barrett et al.). Such spaces continue to be primarily associated with engineering and computer science despite their humanities leanings and the fact that they frequently include affiliation with libraries and, more rarely, digital humanities centers. The opportunities for humanist work in these spaces are well-documented. Jentery Sayers's *Making Things and Drawing Boundaries: Experiments in the Digital Humanities* collects cutting-edge humanist work from across the field, and in doing so points to the important impacts that "making" things in the digital humanities can have for how we understand technology and what we know about it, advocating a praxis in which work is "not made from scratch but in media res; not transparent platforms but patchworks of memory and practice" (Sayers). However, Sayers's collection is also a reminder of how difficult it is to get started, with participation demanding layered expertise that is constantly changing.

The frequent inaccessibility of this skillset to humanist scholars means that the "DIY" approach to reinventing humanities academia is only possible for those with substantial training, as represented in recent publications in this area. This is particularly unfortunate because this type of approach would have the greatest impact for those at institutions lacking in more traditional structures for support of digital humanities. The advantages of making can be seen in the introduction to the *Hyperrhiz* special issue on "Kits, Plans, Schematics," which centers critical making as scholarship and notes that, "compared to print- or text-centric approaches to DH, developed oftentimes in partnership with university libraries, this alternative approach to DH constitutes itself from a wide range of media and materials and is born oftentimes out of partnerships with digital media arts and theory," and thus represents an opportunity to engage "novel forms of 'small data'" (Rieder). Examples of projects featured in the issue demonstrate the range of what this type of digital humanities can be, from an origami-powered work of interactive fiction exploring the migrant crisis to a queer feminist craft response to mediation focusing on embroidery and cross-stitch. Such work demonstrates how, when making (digital or otherwise) moves into the classroom, it can be intentionally scaffolded with principles of critical analysis and attention to inequality.

Daniel Chamberlain defines work grounded in this way as critical making, a practice which "extends beyond critique into artistry: in making, design and function are not separate. The message (or story) of a work is intertwined throughout its making." This places the emphasis not on learning tools for their own sake, but on thinking through the relationship of our tools (and our code) with our disciplines and scholarship. It is not enough to learn how to use a tool or software program. A critical maker reflects on the tool itself, and rejects, supplements, extends, and critiques it as part of the process of making.

Moreover, a critical making approach helps answer the call to make more slowly and thoughtfully, in contrast with the "move fast and break things" mentality of Silicon Valley and other computer-science oriented making. This "slowness" is centered in Loveless's approach to "research-creation:" making becomes a means to reflect, interrogate, and intervene (Loveless). As Matt Ratto contends, the products of critical making are "a means to an end…[to] achieve value through the act of shared construction, joint conversation, and reflection" (Ratto). Accordingly, as scholars and students seeking procedural literacy, we must engage with a variety of ways to make both physical and computational things (and physical-computational things) as well as ways to critically examine the assumptions built into technologies, how to make more inclusive technologies, and how to use making as a mode of research.

Make It Matter

Incorporating materials outside of text, and indeed outside the digital, into our scholarly making builds on Bethany Nowviskie's notion of harnessing the "resistance in the material," a challenge she notes has been transformed as we've moved from the crafty days of digital humanities—the days of small-scale, direct projects and personal tools—into a massively corporate landscape of digital opportunity and challenge: to a time of 3D printing, wearable devices, mixed reality, and new tools. Nowviskie asks what the humanities will do with these opportunities, but also warns of the challenges of realizing any of this potential:

If we fail to invest institutionally and nationally in full-time, new-model, humanities-trained scholarly communications practitioners, devoted to shepherding and intervening in the conversion of our cultural heritage to digital forms and the new manifestations of digital culture—and if we permit our institutions to convert a generation of scholars to at-will teaching and digital humanities labor—humanities knowledge workers of all stripes will lose, perhaps forever, control over Morris's crucial triad: our material, our tools, and our time.

(Nowviskie)

Nowviskie's words particularly resonate in a moment when time has been disrupted, budgets cut, departments threatened, and lives upended in the wake of the pandemic and international moves towards fascism and white supremacy. Drawing on Natalie Loveless's "manifesto for research-creation," *How to Make Art at the End of the World*, and the digital humanities-infused practices of critical making in the post-THATCamp era, we hope to imagine alternative futures, and consider the power of a turn (or return?) to the models offered by craft.

In the current landscape where academia is under attack for every aspect of our work, it can be easy to feel powerless and to miss the ways that making can empower. It is harder still not to wonder how much of the dystopian future is already here: even as we are accused of indoctrination of students by politicians around the world, humanities scholars lament across social networks the continual difficulties of engaging students in reading and discussion. Generative AI tools have added fuel to these debates, and given frustrated educators a technology to blame: headlines label it "CheatGPT" and offer warnings to humanities faculty—"if the work of grappling with complex ideas can be automated—what's left for liberal-arts professors to do?" (Lewson). These headlines and a hyper-focus on plagiarism can inhibit the development of understanding, which is in turn impeding the much-needed work of developing critical AI literacy in the humanities.

Likewise, students—who are bearing the brunt of wide-ranging political attacks in the form of a diluted education and vanishing student services—are left even less supported to evoke change in these systems, and struggling with building literacy across a technological landscape that is more critical to their lives than ever before. The urgency of digital literacy broadly is that of the triad Bethany Nowviskie evoked: both students and faculty are losing control of our classroom material, our digital tools, and our educational time. The acts of creation this book shares invite students to experiment, but more importantly they demonstrate the ways in which students can control and understand technology through a humanities lens. Building, prototyping, testing, evaluating, and iterating all spark creativity but more importantly expand students' understanding of their potential to reshape the technologies that are shaping our communities and conversations.

Overview and How to Use This Book

This book is imagined as both a survey of methods of alternative scholarly communication and a pattern book, inspired by the craft traditions of textile arts. Patterns in this space frequently serve as starting points, designed to be reimagined and remixed by the maker even as one acquires new skills: the many dog-eared quilting pattern and recipe books that have shaped our own making are often consulted piecemeal, and almost never followed to the letter. Similarly, *Critical Making in the Age of AI* invites readers to explore the practice of making as scholarship, grounded in the humanities, that interweaves design, function, and theory towards born-digital scholarly practice. Engaging in scholarly communication through digital platforms demands attention to code, software, and hardware: all practices traditionally connected to communities of technology that can be exclusionary and difficult to engage. Our work is guided by three principles:

1. Procedural literacy, digital literacy, and critical AI literacy go hand-in-hand, and must be developed through a combination of **theory and practice**. To support this work, we develop examples and guidance for getting started with ten different critical making platforms alongside frameworks for critiquing and understanding those genres. All the examples can be accessed through our GitHub repository (and we obtained permission from each of the named students whose projects we describe and share). Patterns are intended to be usable: we hope you will bring them into your classrooms, transform them, and build upon them.

2. This project centers **free tools and platforms**, offering models for exploring critical making without investing in proprietary software, dedicated lab space, or expensive creative tools. While many universities have invested in software subscriptions (such as the Adobe suite) and may provide access to employees and students, such subscriptions are ultimately prohibitive to long-term use and hostile to precarious creators. While these tools can be precarious, they represent types of making that will endure: as resources for a particular tool potentially vanish, our GitHub repository accompanying this project will preserve accessible, working versions of examples wherever possible, and is intended as a resource to support faculty in continuing to use the patterns even as tools themselves shift.

3. This work centers critical making through a **design justice oriented, feminist lens**, and is thus attentive to drawing on practices of communal making inspired by textile arts, cooking, and other traditionally domestic and feminine crafts. We also acknowledge that this work builds constantly on the practice of others, and throughout place an emphasis on learning from communities already engaged in this work.

This book follows the authors' experience that learning is best approached as a hands-on, collaborative effort between novice and expert, and that the role of the instructor is one of an instigator and guide rather than a droning lecturer. We subscribe to the socio-constructivist learning theory that views knowledge as something that learners construct with other learners through experience: a well-designed learning environment includes a community of learners, interesting ill-defined problems, and readily available resources. Thus, we seek ways to engage, motivate, and challenge learners in ways that will foster learning through exploration and creation.

We seek assignments and experiences for our students that prioritize active learning over passive learning, creation over consumption, and process over product. The activities we emphasize therefore fall on the higher level of the (now antiquated) Bloom's taxonomy. The patterns in this book, however, are not requirement-empty, free-for-all assignments. They are not digital solely for the sake of using digital tools. All patterns necessitate traditional research where peer-reviewed scholarly sources are consulted and cited. However, they go beyond the traditional written essay and ask students to use their unique voices and authentic experiences to intelligently critique some aspect of society, while thinking about the role technology plays in reshaping that expression. The examples included from both scholars and our own students demonstrate how these same tools can be leveraged towards meaningful work across audiences and contexts.

In keeping with these goals of making our materials as reusable and remixable as possible, each chapter is structured with the same four parts:

- **Critical [Tool]**—Discusses the theoretical and pedagogical framework; geared towards an instructor preparing for an undergraduate lecture/discussion, or scholars and graduate students wishing to learn more about the context and capabilities of a given tool or modality.
- **Pattern [Tool]**—A walkthrough of a single platform, written in the voice of an instructor to their students, so that readers can

copy and paste assignment descriptions and tool explanations into their own course materials, or for the reader to follow specific instructions. These patterns are intentionally general and can be remixed to suit a particular course objective.

- **Applications**—Explains and links to student and professional examples, which can be provided to students and used by the instructor to demonstrate possible applications for the tool to different disciplines.
- **Futures**—Discusses the impact of AI and other platforms on the tool and work mentioned in the chapter, and provides suggestions for extensions, iterations, and additional assignments using the tool discussed.

In a graduate course discussing both students' goals in their individual scholarly work and pedagogical applications, chapters might be assigned in their entirety, while in an undergraduate course, the pattern is intended to be removable and remixable to suit the course objectives.

For examples of this in action, please refer to the GitHub repository that accompanies this book: this includes both the undergraduate and graduate syllabus for the courses referenced throughout, as well as examples of adapting the patterns into course assignments. Several full, working examples of completed work are also archived on the repository. To view the web version of these resources, visit: https://anastasiasalter.net/CritMakingAgeOfAI/. To access files and code for specific examples directly, use the GitHub repository itself at: https://github.com/AMSUCF/CritMakingAgeOfAI.

By resisting traditional entry points into these modes of digital making and instead turning to craft for inspiration, we hope to enable more inclusive work in critical making, drawing on digital humanities discourse, intentional design, minimal scripting tools, and multimodal development as part of scholarly communication. The procedural literacy skills we have described are of growing interest in transdisciplinary humanities, but still often seen as the domain of STEM programs, and the rhetoric of code and code education remains exclusionary. Throughout, even as we use code, we seek to interrogate those assumptions and systems, emphasizing process over product, and reimagining familiar genres, such as the "game."

This places the emphasis not on learning tools for their own sake, but on thinking through the relationship of our tools (and our code) with our disciplines and scholarship. A critical maker reflects on the tool itself, and rejects, supplements, extends, and critiques it as part of the process of making. Patterns (drawing on techniques from crafts) offered in each section will provide launching points for creating playful, creative digital scholarly objects ranging from 2D games and generative bots to visualizations and hypertext essays. Through these patterns, we invite you to develop an understanding of both procedural literacy and design research methods, as well as practical insights drawn from the diverse born-digital scholarly experience of the instructors. We emphasize free and, wherever possible, open-source tools, with attention to sustainable and scalable solutions that can be brought to research or the classroom without external funding. Similarly, we turn towards open-access scholarship for models of the future of our communication, imagining a not-too-distant future in which the traditional printed journal might well dissolve.

Our first chapter, **Selfie**, explores the possibilities of material making as a form of scholarly communication while producing our own material "selfie" capturing a personal relationship with the act of making. Drawing on the history of explorations of the self-portrait / selfie (as framed by Jill Walker Rettberg's work on making the self-image), this chapter contextualizes this practice as an entry point to thinking about how the "self" is at stake in the classroom, and indeed in academia. We introduce the concept of computational craft or play at the intersection of traditional material objects and digital forms, while building on Matt Ratto's observations on the need to connect "lived experience to critical perspectives." Next, we explore the limitations of text as a means of scholarly communication by exploring the possibilities of **Comics**, which sit at the intersection of image and image-text, and which speak to the intentional juxtaposition of graphics and text to create meaning. Drawing on the work of Nick Sousanis, whose graphic novel dissertation offers a new way of thinking about the act and form of scholarship, and Jason Helms, whose digital comic-esque book on digital rhetorics explores similar frontiers, we consider how such projects challenge our assumptions of what types of communication are valued. Through making a comic using a mix of materials and both existing and original images, we challenge and rethink the text as default.

As we shift into digital making, we find ourselves in more direct conversation with a common visual shorthand of the internet: **GIFs**, or images in motion. Through these moving images, users of digital platforms communicate rapidly, and shows and films that are otherwise forgotten live on because of an isolated and well-selected moment. GIFs are thus an excellent starting point for exploring new media composition that allows us to consider the role of motion and intertextuality in scholarly discourse. As the reaction GIF's decontextualized communication becomes the norm not only in informal spaces but also in classroom Discord channels, deconstructing it provides an opportunity to rethink web social norms and challenges. While critiquing existing GIFs provides its own opportunity for referential discourse, we also argue that rethinking our libraries of GIFs and building our own allows for correction of historic silences, gaps, and exclusion in digital spaces.

Continuing in our examination of digital humanities practices, we turn to **Maps**, which frequently center in settler imaginings and disputed histories. As GPS technology expands, Geographic Information System (GIS) mapping has become a prominent feature in much critical making work. Recreational geocaching and AR games like

Pokémon Go helped to introduce the public to the possibilities of location-based technologies, but the development of AR (augmented reality) itself, along with VR (virtual reality) and ever more advanced telecommunication tools complicates the concepts of place and space. The accessibility of Google Earth has allowed it to be incorporated into classrooms to understand topographic geography, chart the journeys of historic figures and literary characters, and to note the physical changes to specific neighborhoods over time. Interactive maps such as the Native Land Digital Map make apparent contested histories and invisibilities (Temprano). This chapter provides a pattern for using Google Earth layers to add new perspectives to—and to critique the dominant perspective of land ownership of—a given landscape.

Shifting from geospatial visualization to procedural play, we consider **Hypertext** and the importance of interaction, particularly given the historical interest in hypertext as a key component of multimodal scholarship and the "webtext." Such experimentation is in the face of an underlying contradiction: even as hypertext has become the default for content creation on the web, most scholarship still resists its capabilities. However, journals such as *Kairos* and hypertextual scholarship from authors such as Chloe Milligan, Jim McGrath, Stuart Moulthrop, and Lee Skallerup Bessette blend influences from electronic literature with criticism. Twine, an open-source platform for building hypertexts and the subject of a previous volume in this series, *Twining*, offers a means to explore this type of making thanks to its capacity for constructing choice and argument; crafting autoethnography and reflection; and exploring through simulation and representation (Salter and Moulthrop).

Next, we continue to interrogate mechanisms of code, describing the ways that personal or independent **Games** (games created by independent authors or groups rather than commercial studios) have often a history of critiquing and interrogating various aspects of society: some examples made with Bitsy include cecile richard's *Endless Scroll*, Fred

Bednarski's *The World Has Been Sad Since Tuesday,* and Molleindustria's *A Prison Strike.* With the expansion of game development platforms that require less technical knowledge and the accessibility and free game hosting and publishing available on sites like itch.io, indie games are becoming easier to create and publish. This chapter explores some of these theories and themes that existing indie games have focused on and gives an example critical making pattern for the open-source platform Bitsy. Bitsy is a game creation platform that has unique constraints, requiring thoughtful design planning while also freeing the designer from the choice paralysis of other game development platforms that have more options. The graphics, colors, and mechanics are all limited, but this platform can easily be used to make compelling critiques of society that also allow us to re-examine play itself.

Building on basic structures of code, we next explore the creation and use of text procedurally generated by **Bots**. This chapter delves into the methods of pre-AI procedural generation as a critical making process and looks ahead to the consequences of large-scale generative futures. By laying out a pattern for a program to follow, the author of a generative work becomes a coauthor with the machine. The resulting text or art is often absurd, humorous, or nonsense—and usually a compelling commentary on society and the ways that we rely on machines and technology that are still rather primitive. Projects created with this human–machine task sharing investigate and critique ideas about what it means to be human, how our society views different populations, and more. The pattern this chapter lays out uses an open-source, scaffolded, procedural generation platform built by Kate Compton called Tracery, where the coding language JSON is used to generate short stories, poems, and tweets. Tracery also powers a variety of bots that can be incorporated into other platforms as sources of noise, commentary, and art on social media.

Delving into the textual–visual data opportunities and challenges, **Analysis** considers the ways that computer-assisted analysis (sometimes referred to as machine-reading or distant reading) has altered the landscape of literary study, cultural studies, and more. With the ability to quantify terms and word counts across millions of texts has come different ways to understand writing of any genre— from Shakespeare's works to celebrity tweets, across and between authors. This analysis informs critical making projects and, in some cases, produces critical making projects itself, with the ways that the tools incorporate data visualization tools like word clouds, bubble-lines, scatterplots, and graphs. The pattern in this chapter uses the computer-assisted analysis tool Voyant to demonstrate the methods and potential uses of this type of analysis and the ways that it can create and contribute to critical making projects through offering new ways of seeing and exploring text.

Finally, we explore the emerging tools of AI in **Generation**. With the rapid growth in this technology, it is vital we understand the potential risks and possibilities of working with these tools. The aggressive pace of developments coupled with the widespread public accessibility of OpenAI's ChatGPT raised many eyebrows in academia—and a few lawsuits elsewhere—fueling ongoing debates around authorship, plagiarism, intellectual property, and the purpose of writing assignments. With AI famously passing MBA (Needleman) and bar exams (Cassens Weiss), many faculty are re-examining their methods of teaching and assessment. Though AI chat-based language models and art generators emerged and progressed over the course of writing this book, our pattern provides examples created by students as optional, minor assignments in one author's technical writing course, and we present other example assignments and perspectives on these tools.

Together, these patterns reflect how we might move forward with a crafty—and craftivist—digital humanities. Current digital humanities work has been shaped by the pursuit of grants and an emphasis on large-scale projects bringing prestige to institutions. As those opportunities continue to be concentrated, and perhaps even dwindle, an approach to sustainable, personal digital humanities offers a way of renewing our engagement with technology and community. We turn to craft, and the communities that have sustained crafting traditions, for inspiration on how to build a future for digital humanities work outside of large-scale infrastructure, and indeed for how to sustain our classrooms in a time of increasing precarity, burn-out, defunding, and political attack. Whatever future the humanities are to have, we will need to craft it together.

Works Cited

Barrett, Thomas William, et al. "A Review of University Maker Spaces." *122nd ASEE Annual Conference*, 2015.

Byrd, Antonio, et al. "MLA-CCCC Joint Task Force on Writing and AI Members." *Modern Language Association of America*, Jul. 2023.

Cassens Weiss, Debra. "Latest Version of ChatGPT Aces Bar Exam with Score Nearing 90th Percentile." *ABA Journal*, 16 Mar. 2023, www.abajournal. com/web/article/latest-version-of-chatgpt-aces-the-bar-exam-with-score-in-90th-percentile.

Cohen, Dan. "More than THAT | THATCamp Retrospective." *THATCamp*, 26 Feb. 2020, http://retrospective.thatcamp.org/2020/02/26/more-than-that/ index.html00.

Eshet, Yoram. "Digital Literacy: A Conceptual Framework for Survival Skills in the Digital Era." *Journal of Educational Multimedia and Hypermedia*, vol. 13, no. 1, Jan. 2004, pp. 93–106.

French, Amanda. "THATCamp Retrospective | Memories, Critiques, Epiphanies, Comments ...." *THATCamp*, 25 Feb. 2020, http://retrospective.thatcamp. org/index.html.

Johnson, Nicole, et al. "Defining Different Modes of Learning: Resolving Confusion and Contention through Consensus." *Online Learning*, vol. 26, no. 3, Sept. 2022. *olj.onlinelearningconsortium.org*, https://doi.org/10.24059/ olj.v26i3.3565.

Lewson, Simon. "Students Are Cheating. Professors Are Panicking. The System Is Unravelling. Scenes from the AI Revolution on Campus." *Toronto Life*, 16 Aug. 2023, https://torontolife.com/deep-dives/chatgpt-ai-cheating-revolutionizing-university-education/.

Loveless, Natalie. *How to Make Art at the End of the World: A Manifesto for Research-Creation*. Duke University Press, 2019.

Mangan, Katherine. "Is Higher Ed a Public Good or a Public Threat?" *The Chronicle of Higher Education*, 19 Oct. 2022, www.chronicle.com/article/ public-good-or-public-threat.

Manovich, Lev. *Software Takes Command*. Bloomsbury Publishing USA, 2013.

Mateas, Michael. "Procedural Literacy: Educating the New Media Practitioner." *On the Horizon*, edited by Drew Davidson, vol. 13, no. 2, Jan. 2005, pp. 101–11. *Emerald Insight*, https://doi.org/10.1108/10748120510608133.

McPherson, Tara. "'Chapter 9: Why Are the Digital Humanities So White? Or Thinking the Histories of Race and Computation | Tara McPherson' in 'Debates in the Digital Humanities' on Debates in the DH Manifold." *Debates in the Digital Humanities*, https://dhdebates.gc.cuny.edu/read/ untitled-88c11800-9446-469b-a3be-3fdb36bfbd1e/section/20df8acd-9ab9-4f35-8a5d-e91aa5f4a0ea#ch09. Accessed 1 Nov. 2021.

Needleman, Emma. "Would Chat GPT Get a Wharton MBA? New White Paper By Christian Terwiesch." *Mack Institute for Innovation Management*, 17 Jan. 2023, https://mackinstitute.wharton.upenn.edu/2023/would-chat-gpt3-get-a-wharton-mba-new-white-paper-by-christian-terwiesch/.

Nowviskie, Bethany. "'15. Resistance in the Materials | Bethany Nowviskie' in 'Debates in the Digital Humanities 2016' on Debates in the DH Manifold." *Debates in the Digital Humanities*, 2016, https://dhdebates.gc.cuny.edu/read/ untitled/section/c2d3c339-bcf3-47d7-9520-2939c22837f8.

Ong, Walter J. *Orality and Literacy*. Routledge, 2013.

Owens, Trevor. "Growing up with THATCamp | THATCamp Retrospective." *THATCamp*, 19 Feb. 2020, http://retrospective.thatcamp.org/2020/02/19/ growing-up-with-thatcamp/index.html.

Prensky, M. "Digital Natives, Digital Immigrants." *Gifted*, no. 135, 2005, pp. 29–31. *search.informit.org (Atypon)*, https://doi.org/10.3316/aeipt.141401.

Ratto, Matt. "Critical Making: Conceptual and Material Studies in Technology and Social Life." *The Information Society*, vol. 27, no. 4, Jul. 2011, pp. 252–60. *Taylor and Francis+NEJM*, https://doi.org/10.1080/01972243.2011.583819.

"Reviews in Digital Humanities." *Reviews in Digital Humanities. reviewsindh. pubpub.org*, https://reviewsindh.pubpub.org/. Accessed 18 Oct. 2022.

Rieder, David M. "Introduction." *Hyperrhiz: New Media Cultures*, 2015, https:// doi.org/10.20415/hyp/013.i01.

Salter, Anastasia, and Stuart Moulthrop. *Twining*. Amherst College Press, 2021.

Sayers, Jentery. *Making Things and Drawing Boundaries: Experiments in the Digital Humanities*. University of Minnesota Press, 2017.

Sousanis, Nick. *Unflattening*. Harvard University Press, 2015.

Temprano, Victor. "Native Land: Social Media Education and Community Voices." *Digital Mapping and Indigenous America*, Routledge, 2021.

Terranova, Tiziana. "Free Labor: Producing Culture for the Digital Economy." *Social Text*, vol. 18, no. 2, 2000, pp. 33–58.

Woodcock, Claire. "Students Are Using AI to Write Their Papers, Because of Course They Are." *Vice*, 14 Oct. 2022, www.vice.com/en/article/m7g5yq/ students-are-using-ai-to-write-their-papers-because-of-course-they-are.

CHAPTER 1
Selfie

This first chapter explores the history of scholarly self-image and the relationship between scholar and work, offering a pattern for the design of a material "selfie" to invite students to explore a personal relationship with the act of making. Drawing on the history of explorations of the self-portrait / selfie as a construction in visual culture, this process offers ways to think about image production and art as scholarly communication. Critically, this chapter foregrounds the role of the personal maker in the context of a world of image generators, which reflect and amplify existing stereotypes and perceptions of who counts as a scholar.

Critical Selfie

In 2023, tools for automatically generating images from text became ubiquitous, often offering free trials and browser-powered interfaces to make it easier than ever to turn thoughts into words. A meme emerged out of the extremes these tools could generate, focusing on asking AI image generators to "make it more" and through this process revealing what the dataset might see as the essence of the request (Lanz). One professor, Tomer Ullman, decided to try out this meme on an image of a professor (see Figure 1), resulting in first a fairly mundane image of a white man in tweed in front of a chalkboard, and, several images later, steampunk bearded librarians from the prompt "even more of a professor" (Ullman).

There is a lot to say about these images, including the most obvious note that, to generate a woman-presenting image, Ullman had to add the modifier "female" to the prompt and start again. The resulting image was still white, in iteration after iteration, and in both cases usually surrounded by books (and eventually, galaxies, which invites all sort of fascinating interpretations).

This type of experiment doesn't just tell the viewer what DALL-E thinks a professor is: it reveals the biases in the underlying dataset, where this reductive image of a professor is so engrained and normative. A viral Reddit post similarly captured this trend using another machine-learning image-generation tool Midjourney, prompting the tool to draw professors based on their departments and creating a sea

Figure 1: Tomer Ullman's iterative image of a professor, generated by ChatGPT and DALL-E.

of mostly white, predominantly male portraits (entrendre_entendre). This type of manipulated image reflects back an aggregation of the images that are already available, and thus such exercises reflect the biases already noted in the image datasets (Wang et al.) such as stock photosets that in part power these tools. These biases in turn reflect existing inequities in promotions, hiring, and educational access— inequities that have presented a challenge in the digital humanities particularly, as the intersections with computational fields and resources tend to exacerbate them.

Those same tools have been trained on the collective visual imaginary, and thus offer insights into cultural values as well as the future of cliches such as "a picture is worth 1,000 words." During the 2023 AI boom, a study of image generation across popular platforms offered the following alarming data: "In total, more than 15 billion AI-created images have been generated using Stable Diffusion, Adobe Firefly, Midjourney, and DALLE-2. That's more than Shutterstock's entire library of photos, vectors, and illustrations, and one-third of the number of images ever uploaded to Instagram" (Valyaeva). At this moment of widespread rapid image creation, fueled by existing cultural archives, the making of images by hand is at risk of being rapidly devalued. In turn, this devaluing makes its role in the humanities classroom more critical than ever, particularly as a reminder of what— and who—generative imagery leaves out.

Every educator is to some extent called upon to be image-producers for the classroom and as a scholar: from the ubiquitous job of filling PowerPoint slides to the classic task of diagramming on a whiteboard, to more digital-humanities aligned work such as data visualization, images can illustrate, complement, and complicate understanding of text—and now, thanks to text-to-image generators, they can visualize with far less guidance than 1,000 words. Take, for instance, the prompt "a visualization of a bulletin board completely covered with overlapping and dissonant images, all related in some way to teaching," shown in Figure 2 with its initial result set in the Adobe Firefly public beta (Beck). This tool and others, which Adobe has already integrated into its Creative Cloud, will quickly become an inescapable part of image generation for many educators and students: a convenient shorthand. Similar models are already integrated into popular platforms like Google Slides, offering the alluring convenience of generative imagery with the prompt "Help me visualize."

Given the growing power and allure of convenient tools to "help" visualize, resistance to critical drawing and image-making is likely to be heightened. The framing of technology as a means for bypassing a lack of formal training and expediting the "work" of image creation illuminates an opening tension between the material and the world of software that is the heart of this process of critical making—a process that is, by necessity, far slower than the use of digital tools.

Image generation hides the process of reflection and design intention: it is very easy now to fill the digital equivalent of a blank piece of paper than its real-world counterpart. Filters and generative styling

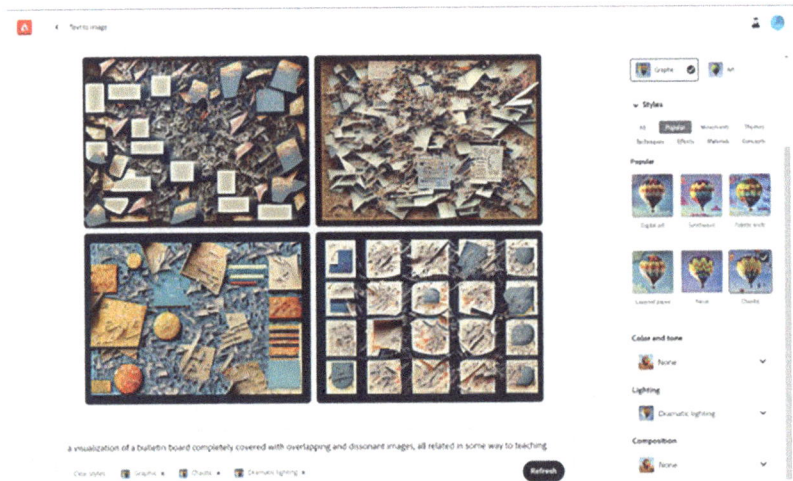

Figure 2: Adobe Firefly with the added values of graphic, chaotic, and dramatic lighting guiding the image generation.

for imitating the materiality of physical drawing are readily available, even if their simulation is rarely fulfilling. The discourse of graphic software for "non-artists" has been part of the marketing and even educational adoption of such tools since the 1990s (Crawford), though studies have noted self-identified non-artists often use such tools differently (Sheng et al.). In the case of AI generation, that might mean getting trapped in a world of defaults and stereotypes, as simple queries often result in the most reductive output—a lesson demonstrated by the results of the "more professor" example above. This is of course to say nothing of the potential devaluing of original artistic labor resulting from the use of machine-learning methods of image generation by prompt, which are also generating understandable concern for their impact on the field (Yanisky-Ravid).

As John Berger extolls in *Ways of Seeing*, an enduring staple in introductory visual culture and art history classrooms, "It is seeing which establishes our place in the surrounding world; we explain that world with words, but words can never undo the fact that we are surrounded by it" (Berger 7). Images are at the heart of Berger's 1990 book, which is itself a multimodal text that embeds painting and photography as part of examining the gaze. However, Berger spoke to a world of images still primarily "made" by people. The human relationship with the image as a form of communication has fundamentally changed since Berger's writing: the ease with which people can reproduce, remix, and share image has only increased with every platform. On every social media platform, people constantly use the images of others to articulate emotions (including the reaction GIFs in Chapter 3's pattern), and visual culture has slowly made its mark on even traditional print academic publishing (as in the comic dissertations and monographs noted in Chapter 2).

The image is one of the few additional modalities available to scholars even in the most traditional artifact: the screenshots included throughout this volume are a static reflection of the tools and objects under discussion, and as the web changes, those records often must serve as a historical role in preserving moments of past digital imaginaries. This static approach is a reminder of how fundamentally authorial use of images tends to shift from the expressive capacities of networked image sharing when moving into scholarly communication: once images become figures, the capacity for using them as illustrative, emotive, and communicative gestures shifts.

Cognizant of the power of images, and the ways in which software shapes the process of making images, this pattern for a "selfie" or self-portrait asks students to reflect on these intersections while engaging materially in their own slow creation alongside the machine's filters and visions. Revisiting the material, and becoming aware of artistic relationships to that material, is part of what scholar and artist Pedro Ferreira describes as a practice of "rematerializing" that can change our relationship with technology by focusing our attention on how the digital is not immaterial: it is actually hybrid, as the outputs of AI generation remind us, and reflects back to us much of our physical world and space (Ferreira 146). These spatial dimensions, and the fundamental relationship between material and digital making (which filters and the generative styles of Firefly and its peers are built upon imitating), are more visible as part of material labor.

The slow making practices this pattern encourages often create an "amateur" aesthetic that is easy to deride. Projects embracing slow, personal image-making by scholars and students thus invite dismissal and a critical gaze, as Michael Dieter and Geert Lovink reject in their own critical making zine: "Our goal now is to move beyond the conventional teardown. Instead, we prefer the positive contribution of the many" (Dieter and Lovink 1).

It is that "positive contribution" that slow making encourages. Opening this first pattern in scholarly critical making with an emphasis on the image's materiality puts personal contribution, and the act of making, at the forefront. The focus is on using materials at hand and engaging in reflexive practice aligned with what Alex Saum-Pascual terms "critical creativity," a practice of resistance that pushes back at the ways "the themes of creativity, innovation and the imagination are being coopted by the creative industries of neoliberalism" (Saum-Pascual). At a time when the humanities are more political (and perhaps too often focused on negativity and teardowns) than ever, such resistance is powerful.

That resistance can take the form of another "un" coined by Cathy Davidson: unlearning. Davidson defines this as a way of rebuilding our relationship with education: "The process of unlearning in order to relearn demands a new concept of knowledge not as a thing but as a process, not as a noun but as a verb" (Davidson 19). Cathy Davidson is a pivotal thinker in the thoughtful fusion of arts, technology, and humanities education and creator of HASTAC (Humanities, Arts, Science and Technology Alliance and Collaboratory), which holds an annual conference where critical making is often practiced: this is fitting, as an emphasis on process is a recurring theme of critical making. Unlearning the creative anxiety that comes with the blank page can be an important stage of this process.

Cartoonist and teacher Lynda Barry has a particularly powerful, and simple, way of encouraging students to unlearn both their fear of drawing and their own expectations of perfection: she takes attendance in her courses through a self-portrait drawn in only a few minutes (Barry). This act is a starting point for writing and creativity that goes beyond drawing, reflecting one of the opening provocations from her syllabus: "What do ideas look like when they are taking physical shape?" (4). Barry's own work is particularly inviting because her style plays with informality and materiality, with drawings that have not been noticeably digitally processed. Her volume is also a powerful example of rethinking scholarly communication and pedagogical design, in line with the next pattern in Chapter 2: the comic, which places images into context and allows for the building of arguments that move towards multimodal design.

Lynda Barry's opening exercises provide a provocation that informs this pattern, which will focus on a readily available, frequently observed object: the self, or selfie. To again recall John Berger's *Ways of Seeing*, "We are never looking at just one thing: we are always looking at the relation between things and ourselves" (Berger 9). Berger sees portraiture and the self-portrait as an opening frame for building a relationship with images, which this pattern embraces. In examining the self-portrait, James Hall evokes a similar connection through the works of Plotinus, "For Plotinus (Greek—204–270), the self-portrait is produced not by looking out at a mirror, but by withdrawing into the self. Here he uses a sculptural metaphor that would be resuscitated in the Renaissance" (Hall 19), quoting him at length as he describes the process of sculpting.

This sculptural metaphor and encouragement to "look" holds possibilities both for thinking about the work of image-making through materials, and also more broadly of scholarly work as material. A reflection on physical self-representation inherently calls to mind a non-scholarly performance, but scholarly identity is in fact profoundly embodied. Katie Manthey's "Dress Profesh" project was designed to use the selfie to interrogate that relationship, providing "a digital space for embodied multimodal rhetorical action, where people come together to interrogate, challenge, and teach each other what it means to embody professionalism" (Manthey). Engaging in this type of space and claiming room as a scholar is itself an act of critical making, as well as a reminder of how much of scholarly identity and "professionalism" is itself a performance drawing on the materiality of textiles.

Tara McPherson called out this trend over ten years ago in an essential critique of the digital humanities whiteness (both in theoretical orientation and composition), pointing out the challenges an embedded history of "modularity" brings from the construction of software and calling for greater meaningful communication between fields that perpetuate a "divide-and-conquer mentality" (McPherson, 153). That type of modularity is an attribute of coding, but it is also a mindset of siloing that the digital humanities, and indeed any call for publicly engaged scholarship, must necessarily reject. Similarly, critical making as a field of practices pushes against any artificial separation of self from scholar, making visible the self behind the production. Introducing this concept to students through their own self-images and self-representations can facilitate their understanding of these concepts by highlighting the dissonances where the "common" vision of an aspect of themselves or their lives often does not line up with their lived reality.

The framing of digital humanities around the production of, and engagement with, the type of public-facing work that Bonnie Stewart refers to as networked scholarship is also part of its challenge to inclusivity: "Networked scholarship, at its core, is the social, public, relational practice of engaging online as a scholarly identity, about issues of scholarly as well as personal interest" (Stewart 349). Historically, this has meant that newcomers to the digital humanities have been directed towards Twitter, a platform that has undergone dramatic changes since its original inception as a key site for the work of public scholarship (Ross et al.)—changes that have made it even more hostile to the embodiment, and work, of many scholars in our field. Marcia Chatelain, curator of the #FergusonSyllabus, documented some of the challenges of hate mail and abuse stemming from her critical work but also noted the resulting outreach and value of her public scholarship: "digital platforms have allowed us to bring a black feminist voice to policymakers and the public at large. As support for digital organizing projects and the digital humanities expands, I'm hopeful that academic women of color can sit securely in our seats as we travel across intellectual boundaries" (Chatelain 183). Chatelain's work and influence is but one of many reminders of the impact and reach networked scholarship can have, but such reach is not without risks.

Networked scholarship exists on the same platforms where the self is continually on display, as collectively we have moved away from the era of the self-portrait to that of the selfie—and further, to the AI manipulated, filtered, or reimagined selfie. The form of the selfie is decidedly a digital construct, as such images are recognizable through their intentional design to be shared on digital platforms and invite reaction: "selfies need to be understood as a social practice, the result of a long and thoughtful process governed by three mechanisms: social calibration, social probing, and social feedback" (Svelander and Wiberg 34). The emphasis on reaction encourages the association of selfies with vanity and femininity, making it easy to dismiss them as "frivolity" in spite of their noted potential for subversion (Abidin). Mark Marino and Adeline Koh's "Know Thy Selfie" assignment, a playful digital humanities example of critical making and reflection in the classroom, offers a framework for supplemental self-reflexive examination of selfies, framed around the questions "How do your selfies produce or obscure a sense of your identity? How do we create our selves?" (Marino and Koh). This type of questioning pushes students towards a thinking-through of their intention that invites them to think not only about their images, but their scholarly selves, as the result of an always-in-process act of creation.

One answer is that, traditionally, users create their self-images in a way designed to fit in with the network: the "Selfiecity" project, led by Lev Manovich, draws the reader's attention to sameness and repetition across selfies when viewed at a large scale while also revealing smaller trends and influences (Tifentale and Manovich). While Manovich's project focuses on the traditional selfie image as a social media object, Jill Walker Rettberg's book on the history of the selfie decontextualizes the form with attention to the other ways people use technology to see themselves. She notes that people typically engage in three types of self-representation: "written, visual, and quantitative"—all methods now popular digitally, but with material precursors that we can explore through the "selfie" (Rettberg 1). Material self-portraits, when brought into this conversation, can have a powerful relationship with their material: "SELFIE," a pottery exhibition of Saskatchewan ceramic artists, included works ranging from sketchy, outlined faces staring up from large flat pottery to abstracted objects covered in text—such works inspire the viewer to see both the material, and the selves being represented, as in conversation (Kurz). They also resist the easy manipulation of image generation, and thus embed a fundamental digital-material tension that this pattern invites students to explore.

Working back and forth between the digital and the material links this pattern to computational craft practices, like those modeled by Anne Sullivan and Gillian Smith in their fusion of textile and handcrafted materiality with digital games and play (Sullivan and Smith). Anne Sullivan's own work includes the powerful selfie quilt shown in Figure 3: hand-stitched and digitally designed, this quilt embodies a material representation that was accompanied by Anne Sullivan's Twitter thread describing the motivation, with the resonating question: "Can you hear my anger now?" (Anne Sullivan Ḥ [@annetropy], "I Finished the Last..."). Anne Sullivan's work speaks to the incredible resonance a material image can bring to a moment, as well as the possibilities of the textile medium for feminist interventions and critique. It is also, quite simply, a testament to the communicative and creative power of an unconventional selfie.

This pattern demonstrates the applied approach that this volume takes: it offers one path for shifting between digital "selfies," AI generation and filtering, and material making to craft a meaningful self-representation. The directions focus on giving students both structure and freedom to create, emphasizing using whatever is at hand. This is in part a nod to Matt Ratto's observations regarding the "role of

Figure 3: Anne Sullivan's middle finger quilt, designed from a self-portrait (Anne Sullivan [@annetropy], "Also for Those Interested in the Design…").

investment in connecting lived experience to critical perspectives" as a part of critical making practice—that is, the time apparently "wasted" in materiality informs a critical perspective on texts and technology (Ratto 258).

Pattern: The Selfie

Many of us take selfies all the time: the desire for self-representation is older than our mobile phones. You might even have ventured further into self-portraiture, particularly if you've taken art classes along the way on your educational journey. For this pattern, you will start with the digital and use it to fuel your slow making. Start by finding a selfie, or taking a new one, using whatever device you have at hand. Selfies are typically characterized by angles and positioning that indicates the device is being directed by the user: this is an essential part of the process and composition, as it makes the "selfie" a result of your own gaze, amplified by the already-algorithmic lens of most modern cell phone cameras. Note the results of using different settings: many phones have some version of a "Portrait" mode, which will typically blur the background to put the emphasis on the figure, resulting in more dramatic results.

Next, load that selfie into any image-augmenting or filtering software, and save at least ten different iterations exploring different directions. Think of this process as generating a gallery of reimagined, altered, glitched, and even "beautified" selves, and particularly notice how different types of filters employ standards of thinness, whiteness, or other critical gazes when modifying your image. Be cognizant of the policies of free image modification apps: if your university has a subscription to Creative Cloud, Adobe's tools are generally safer for use, and offer both conventional (algorithmic) filters as well as augmented (AI) tools for reimagining the images. Note the distinction between the two: what stands out in each model? In your results? In the remixing and mash-ups as your image moves through the hands of different digital "makers"?

Once you have a result that you find both compelling and simple enough to "make," think about the relationship between the generated image and the material. Many filters are intended to mimic physicality: you might try using a "cut paper" lens if you want to build your material version in collage, for instance. Don't get caught up in representational accuracy: think about how the material manipulation requires a different way of thinking, and working, than the rapid process of re-generation digital tools offer. Think about how your process of drawing, making, or transforming the selfie works with and against the algorithmic, and particularly consider the way that the AI filters start to reshape the image at a more fundamental level. As you craft the image, remember to:

- **Explore the relationship between the digital and the material.** What do the different filters make you notice about the image of yourself? How do they distort or exaggerate your features, or perhaps even move the image towards the surreal or unrecognizable? Try a wide range of different options and compare and layer their results to see the most interesting and unexpected emergent changes.

- **Use materials you have on hand.** As you move into making the physical version of the digitally reimagined selfie, I encourage you to craft your "selfie" using materials and knowledge you already have. Think broadly about what that might look like: anything, from a Lego mosaic to macaroni art to Sculpey clay that might be on your table, and bring with it a sense of familiarity and return to physical manipulation that for humanities scholars is not necessarily a strong part of our day-to-day practice. The relationship between the self-representation and the material need not be straightforward: consider how you might use your digital or physical material unexpectedly.

- **Embrace failure and mistakes.** Work to resist the urge to go back, redo, and extend your time beyond these suggested guidelines: this is an ephemeral exercise intended to help us build the mindset for critical making. Digital filters work fast, but the process of slow making can be more frustrating: consider how

> this material resistance shapes the resulting image, and your
> relationship to it—a shift from "selfie" back to "self-portrait."

Journaling this process will increase its value: documenting the work, not just the outcome, can make the material labor more visible and provide context for talking about these practices with others.

Applications

The "slow" selfie is, pedagogically, particularly useful in the context of online classes: it provides an opportunity for making visible the students on the other side of the screen and encourages the building of community. The relationship between selfies and the online class-room, and their potential as a form to explore through pedagogy, has even inspired "The Selfie Course" and a corresponding edited collection documenting those ideas (Albury). This riff on that opportunity for sharing a selfie can in many ways result in something very particular to the student, and draw on interests outside the classroom. When confronted with this challenge (particularly when working from home, and encouraged to use the materials at hand), students have deployed everything from Lego blocks to feathers to plant leaves to embroidery stitching towards the end of making some version of themselves visible to their classmates.

One example shown in Figure 4, created by graduate student Alessandra Zinicola Lopez, demonstrates the potential of crafting to make visible elements that the digital flattens. Lopez describe the process of being influenced by Nick Sousanis's work (discussed in Chapter 2):

> It was around this point where I started thinking about Nick Sousanis' Unflattening book and about perspectives. Earlier, I sort of envisioned that this would be a flat-clay image with just minimal dimension to it where I had to layer certain different colored clays onto the face (eye-balls, lips, etc.), and that just adding color to it would bring a new perspective

Figure 4: Alessandra Zinicola Lopez's polymer clay self-portrait.

to it. But as I played with the clay I realized I could really expand on the profile photo, not just by bringing color to it, but by shaping the clay to attempt to represent my face's shape from perspectives that aren't available when just viewing the image head-on online.

Alessandra's clay selfie allowed her to share her expertise in a medium she was already familiar with from making jewelry and representations of objects such as food and plants, but also involved a lot of experimentation to craft something very different in scale and style from that work. Other examples included in the GitHub repository for this book demonstrate similar play with crafting: Mónica G. González Burgos uses diamond painting to recreate a selfie in an impressively detailed pixel art grid, pictured in Figure 5, and Ashley Zirkle worked with a different grid through building a cross-stitch portrait augmented with details from other fiber arts.

To set the stage for this assignment and provide a similar introduction while teaching online, Anastasia approaches this assignment with a self-demo: this example (Figure 6) began as a basic selfie, which was then manipulated by both Snapchat filters, designed to flatter based on a pre-determined sense of aesthetic appeal, and by an application for Android entitled "Glitch Lab," which was conversely designed to fragment, fracture, and distort the image. Anastasia describes the process in a reflection offered as a sample for students, excerpted here:

> I explored the pre-built filters until I found one that offered a distortion that offered a retro feeling that reminded me of the algorithmic distortions of glitch art broadly. The resulting image was already mostly unrecognizable, a bright pink and yellow cacophony drawing attention to my glasses and removing much of the sense of place.
>
> However, I realized as I moved to the next step that I'd set myself a challenge of materiality: the vibrant colors of the unnatural, processed image were poorly matched by my collection of quilting cottons. But rather than backtrack, I decided to embrace the muted palette and acknowledge that the transformation from tech to textile is perhaps appropriately a type of "softening"—while quilting fabrics can include the more intense hues of the screen, such saturated fabrics usually bleed and fade over time, drawing our attention to their material limitations and wear. Some of the

Figure 5: Mónica crafts a detailed and colorful portrait using diamond painting.

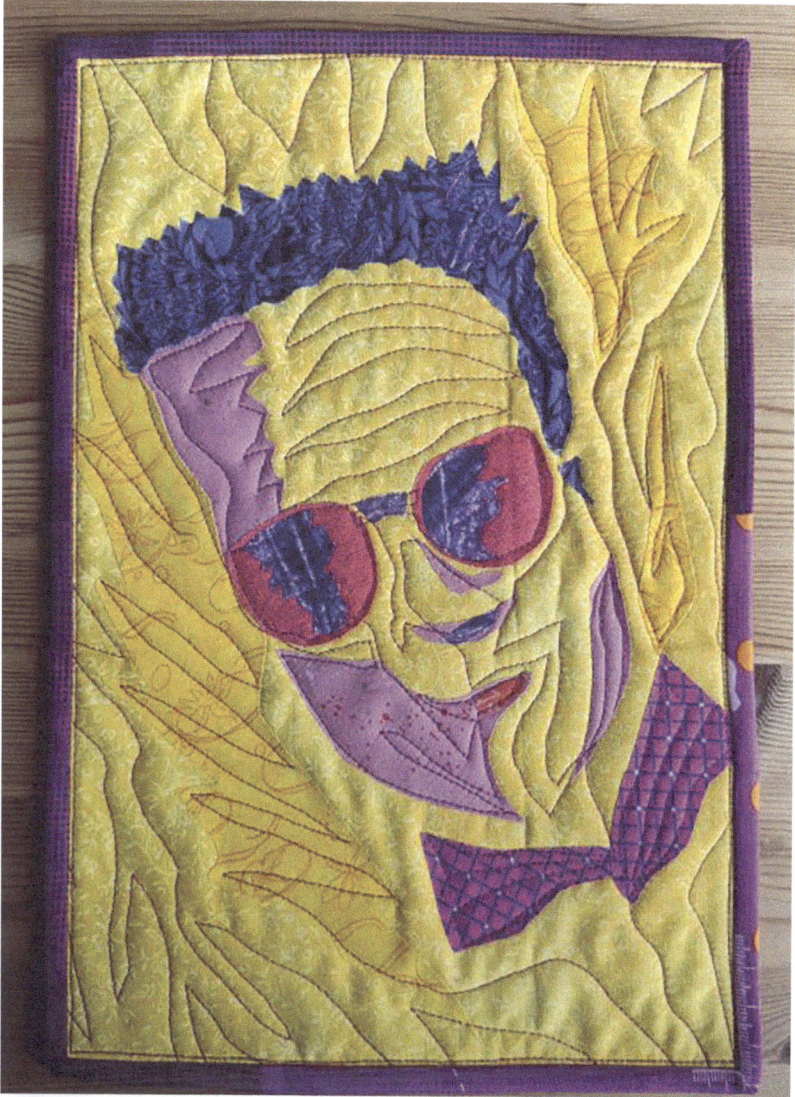

Figure 6: The last iteration of Anastasia's rapid quilted "selfie."

fabrics I pulled had dates listed on their selvedge going back to the 90s, and thus might already be faded: my fabric collection is its own archive reflecting back phases of my work in ways that are themselves layered with memory—for instance, one of the purples I pulled is a remnant from a baby quilt patterned off Eric Carle's illustrations.

I've never quilted a selfie before, and I've been wary of trying to do anything human-looking because the precision is so demanding. That wariness is part of the process that often grips us in any type of making: it can be paralyzing, whether confronting a blank page or an uncut piece of fabric. But for this, I wanted to play with impressions. Once everything was cut and ironed down, I moved to the sewing machine to add the "quilting"—the lines that hold everything together.

The final mini-quilt, as shown in Figure 6, is something not particularly human (the vote in my group chat was "remotely human"), but in the process of blending the procedural artist input of the app's glitched lens with the fiber materiality I see the potential for exploring how we negotiate the tech-text-textile. I could imagine revisiting this as part of thinking through feminist lenses on manipulated photography, which is frequently associated with vanity and performance of artifice. The outcome is perhaps more than a little unrecognizable, but the process demonstrates the filtered gaze of digital and material that is the intention of this pattern.

As a practice, we highly recommend similarly trying the patterns yourselves (and altering them to fit!) before you teach them: regardless of the results, the act of thinking through the relationship of making to your own work makes it much easier to bring into the classroom.

Futures

As the integration of large-language-model generative AI tools into almost every creative software package is ongoing as we write this book, the range of options for algorithmic filtering and image manipulation will only grow. A discussion of the outcomes of different tools can be particularly revealing for understanding the datasets of these models as, themselves, a mirror: prompting students to see the differences in how skin tones, bodies, eyes, and other features are reimagined across tools can be particularly compelling. There can also be some compelling, if dismaying, results that come from trying to describe oneself to a generative tool—if attempting this in class, warn students that the results are unlikely to be familiar!

At the time of writing, the five tools that are easiest to bring into this practice are Adobe Firefly, OpenAI's DALL-E (as of writing, on its third iteration), Midjourney, Snapchat AI, and Microsoft Bing's Image Creator. Of these, some of the most flexible options are those that allow the direct manipulation of existing images: many of these tools are still in their early stages, but this assignment offers a way to explore their limitations, biases, and assumptions.

Works Cited

Abidin, Crystal. "'Aren't These Just Young, Rich Women Doing Vain Things Online?': Influencer Selfies as Subversive Frivolity." *Social Media+Society*, vol. 2, no. 2, 2016, p. 2056305116641342.

Albury, Kath, et al. "The Selfie Course: More than a MOOC." *Massive Open Online Courses and Higher Education*, Routledge, 2017.

Anne Sullivan Ḥ [@annetropy]. "Also for Those Interested in the Design: I Took a Self Portrait, Taught Myself How to Do WPAP Design, Created the Design, Converted It to English Paper Piecing Templates, and Cut Them out Using My Silhouette Cameo." *Twitter*, 20 Jan. 2021, https://twitter.com/annetropy/status/1351953216330674177.

———. "I Finished the Last of Countless Tiny Stitches Early This Morning and Finished This Quilt Top. I Have Been Hand Sewing It for the Last Four Years. Women Are Taught to Please People, to Provide Comfort. We Are Taught to Be Silent, and Not to Get Angry. Can You Hear My Anger Now? Https://T.Co/RwzwkmMt3F." *Twitter*, 20 Jan. 2021, https://twitter.com/annetropy/status/1351943064554766339.

Barry, Lynda. *Syllabus: Notes from an Accidental Professor*. Illustrated edition, Drawn and Quarterly, 2014.

Beck, Cassandra. "Adobe Unleashes New Era of Creativity for All with the Commercial Release of Generative AI." *Adobe*, 13 Sept. 2023, https://news.adobe.com/news/news-details/2023/Adobe-Unleashes-New-Era-of-Creativity-for-All-With-the-Commercial-Release-of-Generative-AI/default.aspx.

Berger, John. *Ways of Seeing: Based on the BBC Television Series*. First edition, Penguin Books, 1990.

Chatelain, Marcia. "Is Twitter Any Place for a [Black Academic] Lady?" *Bodies of Information: Intersectional Feminism and the Digital Humanities*, edited by Elizabeth Losh and Jacqueline Wernimont, University of Michigan Press, 2019, pp. 172–84.

Crawford, Walt. "Graphically Speaking: Graphics Software for Non-artists." *Library Hi Tech*, vol. 12, no. 1, Jan. 1994, pp. 93–112. *Emerald Insight*, https://doi.org/10.1108/eb047915.

Davidson, Cathy N. *Now You See It: How Technology and Brain Science Will Transform Schools and Business for the 21st Century*. Penguin, 2012.

Dieter, Michael, and Geert Lovink. "Theses on Making in the Digital Age." *Critical Making*, edited by Farnet Hertz, Concept Lab, 2012, pp. 15–20.

entrendre_entendre. "What Midjourney Thinks Professors Look like, Based on Their Department." *R/Midjourney*, 28 Apr. 2023, www.reddit.com/r/midjourney/comments/131ebyk/what_midjourney_thinks_professors_look_like_based/.

Ferreira, Pedro. "Rematerialising Digital Technologies through Critical Making." *Proceedings of the 10th Conference on Computation, Communication, Aesthetics & X*, 2022, pp. 134–47, https://doi.org/10.24840/xCoAx_2022_42.

Hall, James. *The Self-Portrait: A Cultural History*. Illustrated edition, Thames & Hudson, 2016.

Kurz, Larissa. "'Selfie:' Ceramics Exhibit at Cultural Centre Showcasing Saskatchewan Potters." *MooseJawToday.Com*, 17 Dec. 2020, www.moosejawtoday.com/local-news/selfie-ceramics-exhibit-at-cultural-centre-showcasing-saskatchewan-potters-3193863.

Lanz, Jose Antonio. "The 'Make It More' ChatGPT Trend—And How to Play Along at Home." *Decrypt*, 29 Nov. 2023, https://decrypt.co/208002/make-it-more-chatgpt-trend-and-how-to-play-along-at-home.

Manthey, Katie. "Dress Profesh: Deconstructing Power through the Clothing." *Hyperrhiz: New Media Cultures*, no. 21, 2019. *hyperrhiz.io*, https://doi.org/10.20415/hyp/021.m03.

Marino, Mark, and Adeline Koh. "Know Thy Selfie." *Hyperrhiz: New Media Cultures*, no. 21, 2019. *hyperrhiz.io*, https://doi.org/10.20415/hyp/021.t03.

McPherson, Tara. "Why Are the Digital Humanities So White? Or Thinking the Histories of Race and Computation." *Debates in the Digital Humanities*, vol. 1, 2012, pp. 139–60.

Ratto, Matt. "Critical Making: Conceptual and Material Studies in Technology and Social Life." *The Information Society*, vol. 27, no. 4, Jul. 2011, pp. 252–60. *Taylor and Francis+NEJM*, https://doi.org/10.1080/01972243.2011.583819.

Rettberg, Jill W. *Seeing Ourselves through Technology: How We Use Selfies, Blogs and Wearable Devices to See and Shape Ourselves*. Springer, 2014.

Ross, C., et al. "Enabled Backchannel: Conference Twitter Use by Digital Humanists." *Journal of Documentation*, vol. 67, no. 2, Jan. 2011, pp. 214–37. *Emerald Insight*, https://doi.org/10.1108/00220411111109449.

Saum-Pascual, Alex. "Digital Creativity as Critical Material Thinking: The Disruptive Potential of Electronic Literature." *Electronic Book Review*, 2 Jul.

2020, https://electronicbookreview.com/essay/digital-creativity-as-critical-material-thinking-the-disruptive-potential-of-electronic-literature/.

Sheng, Heping, et al. "Where to Draw the Line?" *PLOS ONE*, vol. 16, no. 11, Nov. 2021, p. e0258376. *PLoS Journals*, https://doi.org/10.1371/journal.pone.0258376.

Stewart, Bonnie. "Academic Influence: The Sea of Change." *Disrupting the Digital Humanities*, edited by Dorothy Kim and Jesse Stommel, punctum books, 2018, pp. 347–56. *library.oapen.org*, https://doi.org/10.21983/P3.0230.1.00.

Sullivan, Anne, and Gillian Smith. "Designing Craft Games." *Interactions*, vol. 24, no. 1, Dec. 2016, pp. 38–41, *ACM Digital Library*, https://doi.org/10.1145/3019004.

Svelander, Angelica, and Mikael Wiberg. "The Practice of Selfies." *Interactions*, vol. 22, no. 4, Jun. 2015, pp. 34–38. *ACM Digital Library*, https://doi.org/10.1145/2770886.

Tifentale, Alise, and Lev Manovich. "Selfiecity: Exploring Photography and Self-Fashioning in Social Media." *Postdigital Aesthetics: Art, Computation and Design*, edited by David M. Berry and Michael Dieter, Palgrave Macmillan UK, 2015, pp. 109–22. *Springer Link*, https://doi.org/10.1057/97811374 37204_9.

Ullman, Tomer. "Asking for an Image of a Professor and Asking to Make It 'More Professor', a Thread." *Bluesky Social*, 30 Nov. 2023, https://bsky.app/profile/tomerullman.bsky.social/post/3kfgsvoxvco2v.

Valyaeva, Alina. "AI Image Statistics: How Much Content Was Created by AI." *Everypixel Journal*, 15 Aug. 2023, https://journal.everypixel.com/ai-image-statistics.

Wang, Jialu, et al. *Are Gender-Neutral Queries Really Gender-Neutral? Mitigating Gender Bias in Image Search*. arXiv:2109.05433, arXiv, 12 Sept. 2021. *arXiv.org*, https://doi.org/10.48550/arXiv.2109.05433.

Yanisky-Ravid, Shlomit. "Generating Rembrandt: Artificial Intelligence, Copyright, and Accountability in the 3A Era: The Human-like Authors Are Already Here: A New Model." *Michigan State Law Review*, vol. 2017, 2017, p. 659.

CHAPTER 2
Comic

The second chapter positions the significant role of image-text in the history of multimodal scholarly communication, positioning it as a non-digital intervention that draws attention to the limitations of text alone. The most recognized form of image-text, comics, is unjustly historically marginalized and under-valued in academic discourse. Drawing on the work of Nick Sousanis, whose graphic novel dissertation offers a new way of thinking about the act and form of scholarship, and Jason Helms, whose digital comic-esque book on digital rhetoric explores similar frontiers, this chapter examines how such projects challenge collective assumptions of what types of communication are valued. Through making a comic using a mix of materials and both existing and original images, this chapter invites readers to consider the construction of image-text and its relationship to changing tools of generation and remix.

Critical Comics

In 1990, Larry Gonick published *The Cartoon History of The Universe* with Broadway Books. This first collection of what would become an epic endeavor spanning subjects from history to physics and statistics was also a formative read for millennials demonstrating the power of comics to engage: later, "cool" teachers would rely upon the "Introducing [Subject]" series, with its graphic novel approach to introducing theorists and concepts. These graphic guides to topics and theorists often featured humorously remixed photos and visual explainers in between sequences of background text (Collins). Educational graphic novels were briefly cool, and Gonick's first endeavor had a Mel Brooks feel with a professorial avatar of a narrator, operating as a type of remixed self-representation (akin to the pattern featured in Chapter 1) providing both comic relief and insights across the volumes. Gonick's self-inserted character is complete with a tweed jacket and elbow patches, using the visual shorthand of academic stereotypes to his advantage, and adorns the covers of multiple volumes in his series.

Even prior to Gonick's work, comics were making their mark on academic discourse. One of the more famous "rules" in media studies comes to the field by way of a comic by Alison Bechdel from 1985: The Bechdel Test. This test notably requires three things from a piece of media and sets a very low bar: "(1) it has to have at least two women in it, who (2) who talk to each other, about (3) something besides a man" (Bechdel). The comic was not intended to become a foundational test for media studies, but its visual resonance and clear communication has made it an enduring fixture in both popular reviews and academic discourse: a database of nearly 10,000 movies and counting reflects how frequently films fail to pass this low bar ("Bechdel Test"). The test is also misnamed—Liz Wallace originated it—but because of the comic's resonance, the name has stuck (Resmer).

A year after Gonick's first cartoon guide was released, Molly Bang wrote a book called *Picture This* that set out a series of principles for thinking through the composition of pages, choice of shapes, and the ways images communicate everything from stability to danger (Bang). Bang's work is particularly helpful for thinking through the fundamentals of image structures as communicated through images: the text in the book is relatively minimal, and her gradual retellings of "Little Red Riding Hood" instead do the work of demonstrating everything from how a pastel-eyed wolf becomes less threatening to how the scale of Red (visualized as a triangle) can impact our assessment of her power (Bang). The book thus serves as an illustration not only of how to illustrate, but of why images can be just as, if not more, critical in communicating ideas about visual culture through meaningful juxtapositions and intentional design.

Bang's structures are not marketed as comics, nor is her volume immediately recognizable through the structures of panels and gutters that might be familiar from newspapers, webcomics, or superheroes: instead, it falls into a broader category of image-text juxtapositions. We can recognize image-text as any mode where the two types of communication "appear separate yet integrated in both semantics and form" (Martinec and Salway 338): this juxtaposition can be equal or unequal and yield different results, as Radan Martinec and Andrew Salway offered in their system for considering image-text status relations (349). The line between comic books and other types of illustrated texts is thus very blurry, particularly in children's literature, which Bang's work evokes. The recognition of meaningful image-text communication in children's literature has often been ignored in the broader humanities, in part because of the challenges in getting the field taken seriously in the first place, as children's literature scholar Charles Hatfield observes: "The default position for many recent comics researchers has been to reject entirely the link between comics and childhood, as if to jack the form up to some higher standard of seriousness" (Hatfield 376). This emphasis on "seriousness" can also lead scholars to ignore the history of meaningful educational picture books and other works that take advantage of image-text's possibilities.

The meaning-creation on display in some of the first sequenced image-texts young readers encounter is worth revisiting, as scholars can find inspiration for their own work in these early formative books. Maria Nikolajeva and Carole Scott offer a guiding set of frameworks for thinking through the relationships of works and pictures in picture books, noting that most are complementary, "with words and pictures supporting one another by providing additional information that the other lacks" (226). Much more elaborate dynamics are possible, including counterpointing, "where words and images collaborate to communicate meanings beyond the scope of either one alone," or even contradictory, "where words and pictures seem to be in opposition to one another" (Nikolajeva and Scott 225). Such juxtapositions can be particularly provocative for scholarly work, offering opportunities to convey complexity that text sometimes obscures.

There is perhaps an argument to be made that any academic article with figures falls somewhere on this spectrum, though such images usually lack the intentional placement of the picture book or the comic. Certainly, figures are critical to understanding the argument, but often the author has very limited control over the placement and design of the page. Erin Kathleen Bahl defines comics scholarship as marked by more intentional arrangement: "text within image discourse in which the words, images, and layout all contribute substantially to the argument (rather than, for example, a primarily alphabetic text accompanied secondarily by images as illustrations)" (Bahl 178). This definition puts the focus on the image–text relationship. By excluding this more generic type of scholarship, Bahl brings the focus to texts that offer more experimentation and play.

A historical example of that type of play drawing on graphic design approaches is the 1967 collaboration between Marshall McLuhan and designer Quentin Fiore, *The Medium Is the Massage: An Inventory of Effects.* This very short book contains few words and takes on the changing landscape of broadcast media with attention to their impact on human attention spans, communication, and culture: sections like "electronic circuitry, an extension of the central nervous system" accompanied by arrows pointing in all directions are still provocative, even as the conditions of media environments have changed dramatically since the page was composed (McLuhan and Fiore 41). Books like this one serve as a reminder that formal experimentation has been a part of media scholarship for some time, although the expense of production made it more difficult to afford and circulate such works.

To return to Larry Gonick's work for a moment, image-text scholarship also broadly describes the type of composition he excels at through using a recognizable style of comics to do the work of a more traditional textbook (Gonick). This is academic labor that itself warrants note: Erin Bahl warns would-be authors that "comics take an incredible amount of work to compose, and regardless of interest, the majority of academics do not have the time, training, or resources to fully flesh out an argument as a thoroughly composed comic"—words not intended to dissuade, but to caution readers on the amount of work involved (178). However, this doesn't mean that the language of comics and the broader spectrum of image-text composition should be abandoned in scholarly work: instead, it serves as a warning that authors (and tenure, thesis, and dissertation committees!) need to recognize our limitations as well as the labor and costs involved when scholars do take on more ambitious visual projects. And indeed, these limitations are perhaps changing with the increased availability of AI image generation, addressed at the end of this chapter.

In 1993, the most famous and enduring example of such an ambitious work as comic-on-comics was published: Scott McCloud's *Understanding Comics*. This book remains the must-assign textbook of the comics classroom, and introduced his flexible definition of the form by way of his own cartoon avatar: comics are "juxtaposed pictorial and other images in deliberate sequence, intended to convey information and/or produce an aesthetic response in the viewer" (9). This broad definition puts McCloud's work in line with the academic discussions around image-text, and foreshadows ideas he would explore in later work. McCloud would follow up this book with two others exploring the form using his comic avatar to communicate: one, *Making Comics*, takes the principles he's observed and moves them into a more instructional space and can serve as a good reference for thinking about approaching the page (McCloud, *Making Comics*). The other, *Reinventing Comics*, speculates on the intersection of comics and technology in ways that have mostly not proven popular, but remain fascinating for thinking about the future of media design (McCloud, *Reinventing Comics*).

Comic books are still an object of academic suspicion, although the field has grown substantially over the last two decades: as Hatfield describes, "Rhetorically, the 'comic book' has traditionally served, and to an extent still continues to serve, as a kind of last glaring example of the unassimilated and unassimilable, a marker of the boundary between literature and mere 'reading'" (Hatfield 365). Thus the "cartoon" guides mentioned earlier are often marketed as a shortcut or a way to engage people reluctant to read traditional scholarship. The case of *Understanding Comics* offers an alternative proposition demonstrating the value of comics on comics: other works in this tradition, like Paul Karasik and Mark Newgarden's fantastically detailed *How to Read Nancy*, would make use of similar methods by dissecting comics visually to build a nuanced critique of the visual language at work in a single three-panel classic Nancy comic (Karasik et al.).

McCloud's influence on the field is not without its criticism. In an introduction to a special issue on "*Understanding Comics* at 30," Rachel Miller and Daniel Worden capture some of the tensions of revisiting McCloud in current discourse:

> …many of McCloud's assumptions about the comics medium feel unnecessarily limited. The book is very white, very straight, and very male, not just in its color palette and interlocutor, but also in its accounts of art, comics, and literary history. McCloud's notions of iconicity, evolutionary

development, human cognition, media history, and universal symbols are all based on narratives of implicit progress, in the book's account, as comics become increasingly abstract, cerebral, and in tune with the tradition of Western fine art throughout their history.

(Miller and Worden 236)

This read of iconicity is particularly critical, and McCloud's work favors a decidedly Western approach to comics while minimally engaging alternatives from other practices, such as manga. At the same time, McCloud's work opened the door for others to expand on his ideas, and he is frequently acknowledged as an inspiration for comics-creating scholars. As Nick Sousanis described in an interview, McCloud's initial forays in the form proved "that comics could tackle all kinds of subjects and not be limited to narrative genres, and really it showed both how much thought went into making comics and how much thinking could be conveyed through them" (Jenkins). Nick Sousanis would take that inspiration to create a comic book dissertation speaking to and expanding on that capacity.

Nick Sousanis's *Unflattening*, a more recent exemplar of the possibilities of a dissertation as comic, builds on and defies these traditions: less concerned with the on-page avatar and more with abstraction, Sousanis's work pushes back intently at not only the textual default but also the confining and "flattening" aspects of the education system's historical industrial ties. As the comic introducing his dissertation project explains in a fragmented series of boxes, "Comics hold multiple threads together—a literal means of lateral thinking—creativity. / To make good thinkers / see from other sides / which means good seers / able to access all of who we are and can be / the promise and power of comics" (Sousanis, "The Shape of Our Thoughts" 5). Sousanis holds text's centricity up for scrutiny, suggesting that "In relying on text as the primary means of formulating understanding, what stands outside its linear structure is dismissed, labeled irrational," as demonstrated in Figure 1 (Sousanis, *Unflattening*).

Figure 1: A page from Nick Sousanis's *Unflattening* depicting the limitations of boxes.

Others brought McCloud-influenced methods to approaching pedagogy in related fields. In 2013, *Understanding Rhetoric: A Graphic Guide to Writing* created by a team led by Elizabeth Losh took advantage of some of those assumptions by demonstrating how a "graphic guide" could offer a resonant approach for the teaching of first-year composition (Losh et al.). The book has been reprinted in several editions, and ten years later is still a frequent choice for its engaging approach. Anastasia has been calling for comics in the classroom since 2012, writing at the time in ProfHacker (a blog launched out of THATCamp dedicated to "Teaching, tech, and productivity") about the importance of teaching a form that requires we "structure visual and textual data with intention" (Salter, "ProfHacker: Comics in the Classroom and Beyond"). A conversation on "Expanding Forms of Scholarly Inquiry" with Nick Sousanis, Anastasia Salter, Paul Tritter, and Tom Neville, who at the time were all working on different ways to "hack" and reimagine the dissertation, sought to broaden engagement and bring in a range of disciplinary perspectives to that work.

That same year, collective enthusiasm for critical making was heightened by Garnet Hertz's *Critical Making* volume, published as a zine—while mostly textual, the format's flexibility and potential for illustrative and design-driven work allows for experimentation along the lines Sousanis advocated. The project also held a strong material component that Hertz valued: the project was printed, bound, and made by Hertz, who asked himself the question: "Why do things the hard way? What's the value of doing something yourself as an amateur?" (Making Critical Making). Zines are a form of production that decidedly falls into Bahl's definition of the image-text, as, in their making, a scholar, artist, or writer is asked to make many decisions centering intention and form—the value Hertz gestures to is in that control, and the learning and opportunities that type of making presents.

In 2015, fellow digital humanist Roger Whitson and Anastasia edited a special issue of *digital humanities quarterly* dedicated to the possibilities of "Comics as Scholarship:" in the introduction, they noted the importance of considering "the scholarly process that is on display and the opportunities we have in the digital humanities to embrace and refine these processes" (Whitson and Salter). In this same tradition of critical making and reflecting on intention, they later collaborated with one of the featured authors and wrote "Making 'Comics as Scholarship,'" a multimodal reflective text which included a note on the importance of process:

> Ultimately, we see this webtext as a way to reveal the invisible labor and process behind work that might otherwise not be seen. We believe comics offer us a way of seeing and thinking about our scholarship, but that way of seeing is as much about the process as the results.
>
> (Salter et al.)

Such web image-texts (discussed more in Chapter 5) are one of many scholarly formats owing a debt to the examples of McCloud,

Losh, and others: these forms are in turn being continually reimagined by new scholars engaged in extensive image-text authorship.

This chapter's pattern is designed to present students with suggested "steps to get you moving" rather than a scripted, linear set of directions to follow exactly, and thus can suit very different levels of familiarity with image-text broadly and comics specifically. This is the second assignment in Anastasia's graduate course, so students at this stage often still need the reminder that these are experimentation exercises, the emphasis is on the process rather than the product resulting from the making, and that the point is to engage rapidly, without getting stalled by the search for perfection. It could easily be integrated into an undergraduate critical making course; followed by a digitization process for Emily's digital tools course; or adapted to focus on a specific style of rhetoric, creative writing, or other type of content area.

This pattern is influenced by a prompt from Nick Sousanis, and draws on his Making Comics course, which takes a much more extensive look at the practice and composition of comics (Sousanis, "Making Comics S2021"). The broader practice guiding this exercise is the mini-comic, which is frequently approached as a means for exploring the format within material limitations that keep the exercise from becoming overwhelming in scope.

Pattern: Remix Mini-Comic

Whether you've encountered comics online, circulating through platforms such as Instagram and Reddit, or on paper, the basic structures are the same: comics rely upon panels, or framed images, often with text in or below, separated by gaps, or gutters. These structures are recognizable but incredibly flexible: take for instance Figure 2 from ChatGPT4 and DALL-E, based on the prompt "create a generic stick figure conversation newspaper comic, with six panels:"

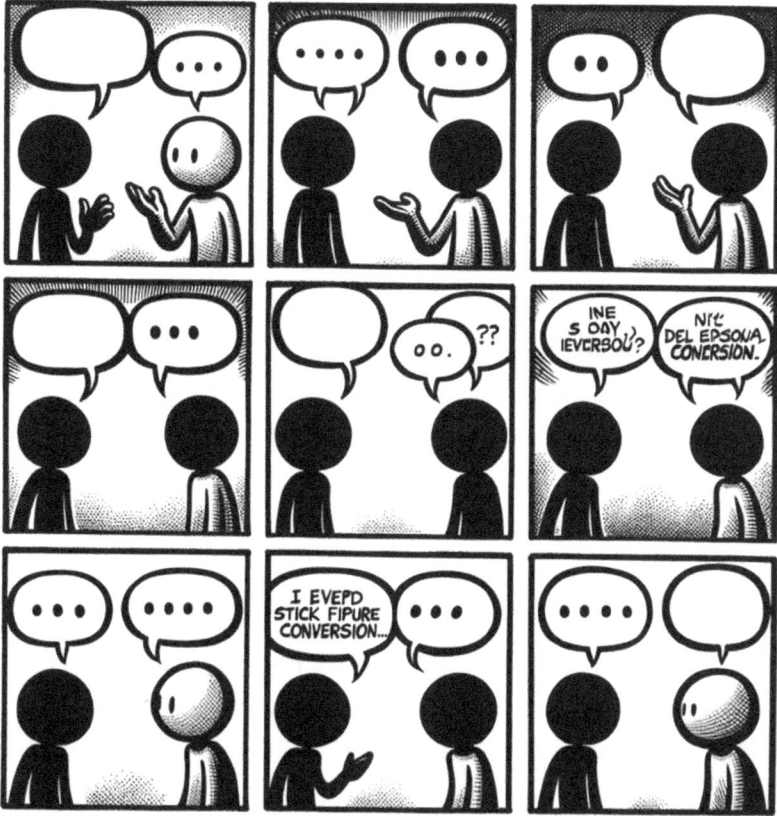

Figure 2: A slightly odd comic book page as generated by AI.

Notice the conventions that reflect what the visual essence of a comic book is, at least according to the training materials DALL-E has consumed: these conventions of speech bubbles, juxtapositions, and transitions can get you started in understanding the comic page.

As you make your comic, try to:

- **Unify form and intention.** Note how scholarly comics build an argument, commentary, or critique through the juxtaposition of the visual and the textual. For this pattern, start to think about your communicative intention: will the comic you make critique an object relevant to your research? Connect with a frustration you have about text or its usual assumptions and structures?

- **Focus on visual exploration, not stress over your drawing ability.** Make "found" images your base, and draw or annotate within your comfort zone. Think about how images serve as a lens for exploring thoughts and expanding metaphors for thinking and criticism: exploring your thoughts through comics can be as simple as annotating on top of the images being remixed, or as complex as building new images out of layering and juxtapositions with your own drawing and commentary.

- **Keep it short and work slowly.** Working physically and remixing images takes time, and once you cut out a section or write something in marker, you're usually stuck with it! There's no undo button in physical cut and paste, so this process encourages slowing down and working on a smaller scale.

To build a workable foundation, start by folding a page into eight parts: this can easily be converted into a booklet by cutting a line between the two sets of center panels, and thus becomes "book-like" in a way that encourages thinking through sequence and juxtaposition. This is a basic way to use the page and keep your scale manageable. However, you can also look at work that uses more experimental formats for ideas: folding the page differently, for instance, can yield new juxtapositions like those at work in Andy Poyiadgi's expanding origami comic, with images that are disrupted and remixed as you refold (Poyiadgi). Experimentation is part of the goal: to quote a great guide on making mini-comics, the answer to "How Do I Make Mini-Comics?" is "any way you want" (Spurgeon).

Next, gather images and combine them on the page: mix your own material with that of relevant archives and your area of interest. Think about how selecting images intentionally and "remixing" them into your comic can create new meanings through juxtapositions. If you've ever seen an old-school Xerox zine, that's a good starting point: using a scanner, or printing out images from the web, can give you small images to work from. As you combine the images, consider trying several approaches to image-making and manipulation. Tracing can be particularly helpful if you want to represent but adapt a specific image: for example, the comic sections of the "Alice in Dataland" experiment started as a retracing of a Tenniel illustration recast through a digital lens (Salter, "Alice in Dataland"). Try "filtering" through your own physical edits and think about the similarities of that work to the digital tools offered by software such as Photoshop.

This type of remix, tracing-to-create, and play is the focus, and the act of creating and manipulating images will open new possibilities for understanding and exploring them in the future. Reading comics by imaginative creators who remix and rethink the page, such as Bryan Talbot's *Alice in Sunderland* on the links between Lewis Carroll and the port city of Sunderland (Talbot), can inspire new approaches in your own design.

Applications

Students in Anastasia's graduate classes complete this pattern early in the course, and often return to the comics form for other projects. As students bring in different backgrounds with art and design, the resulting comics often include a mix of hand-drawn and found imagery to tell a story or craft an argument. One compelling example of using the format to tell a story comes from Karen Tinsley-Kim, who focused on the instructional potential of comics to make visible options in digital accessibility. As she described in her reflection:

> This interactive comic is a mini choose your own adventure with unfolding by taking one of two choices. There are four resulting keyboard descriptions and their uses, starting either in Traditional or Specialized Keyboard categories. The character of Key is intended to lighten up the topic as well as be a guide introducing his "Keyboard Family."

The result (shown in part in Figure 3) uses remixed photos of the actual keyboards, and introduces a wide range of specialized keyboards through unfolding and following the paths of the physical comic.

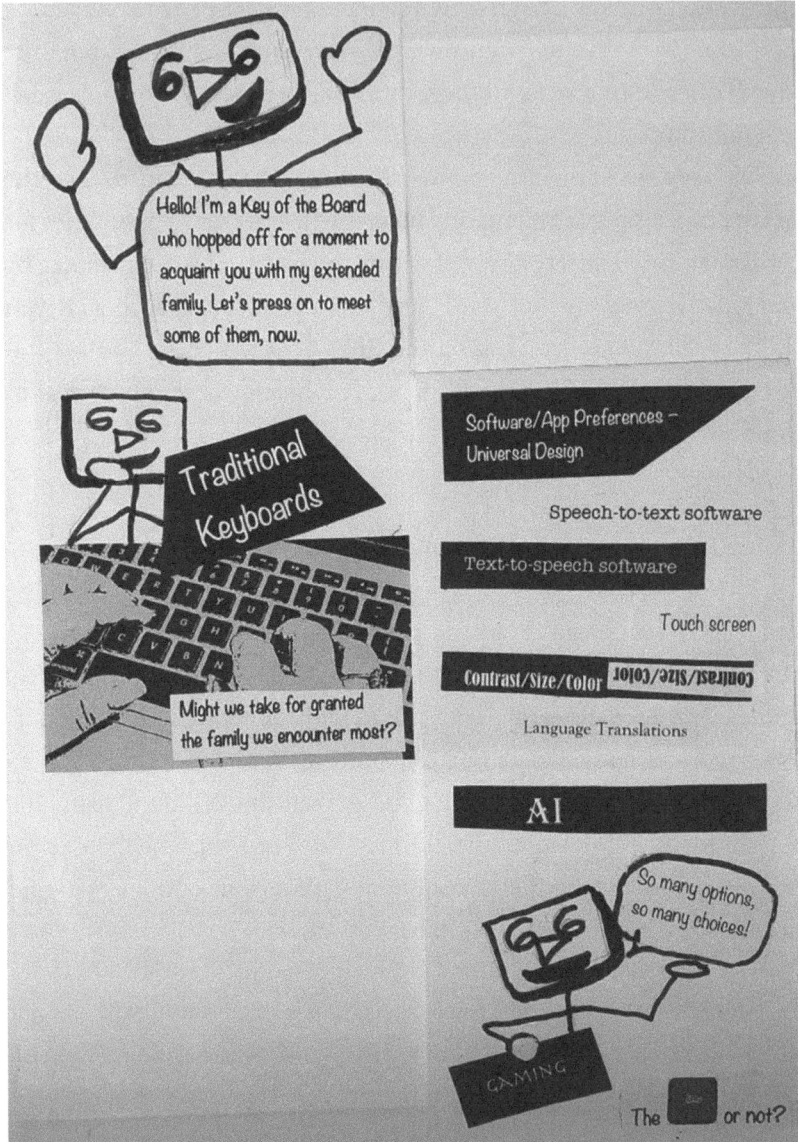

Figure 3: Karen Tinsley-Kim's "Key" explaining traditional keyboards.

Taking this pattern's work as a starting point, a group of students collaborated on an image-text-inspired zine building on this pattern and their work in class for the DIY Methods Conference ("DIY Methods 2022 Conference Proceedings"). These proceedings open with the promise of providing "A Mostly Screen-Free, Zine-Full, Remote Participation Conference on Experimental Methods," and the materiality they center is in line with the practices explored in this pattern. Nikki Fragala Barnes, Farrah Cato, Keidra Daniels Navaroli, and Abigail Moreshead, all Texts and Technology PhD students at the time, collaborated on "Resisting In and Through the Material—or, critical making at the end of the world."

One of the pieces documented in the zine is Keidra Daniels Navaroli's reflection on this pattern's comic collage, shown in Figure 4:

> I started the project by collecting and cutting magazine pages, reducing images, in a René Descartes-inspired fashion, to bodies and body parts. I plotted the designs of the composition with mockups that included four distinct but interconnected vignettes—Africa, Europe, The Middle Passage (Atlantic Ocean), and the U.S. I purchased watermarked paper and painted an ocean to connect each story. The vignettes are formatted to resemble a Mesoamerican codex and meant to be read from right to left.
>
> ("DIY Methods 2022 Conference Proceedings" 391)

The entire zine is an incredible display of this form of image-text, with a wide variety of experiments and design approaches that also push at the assumptions of what conference proceedings might look like.

Nikki Fragala Barnes explores mapping as a method, using the images of maps as material in a process "reframing maps and mappings as collage / assemblage, leaning in to the making [read: pieces and layering] of zines as research method" ("DIY Methods 2022 Conference Proceedings" 385). Drawing on textile materiality, Farrah

Figure 4: An excerpt from Keidra Daniels Navaroli's comic in the zine.

Cato's "Craftivist Tool K(n)it" documented images and explained the steps involved in dyeing threads as a process for thinking through resistance both material and immaterial ("DIY Methods 2022 Conference Proceedings" 389). Finally, Abigail Moreshead's exploration of typewriters layers new text upon typed pages, treating text as image and exploring the fixed materiality of traditional "print" and the anxieties that come with it—as well as the history of labor erased by more current methods of textual production ("DIY Methods 2022 Conference Proceedings" 395). Collectively, these works engage feminist productions of image-text towards a collaborative "mini-comic"-inspired zine.

A compelling scholarly formal experiment by Jason Helms, *Rhizcomics,* is a digital comic that also draws attention to the challenges of defining the form: as Helms describes, "Comics must be approached as rhizomes with middles everywhere and no center to be found. This project attempts just that—to work in between scholarly and popular modes, between readers and writers, between disciplines, between media, between comics" (Helms). Helms operates over a much broader set of styles in image-text composition than Sousanis or McCloud, in part thanks to the affordances of motion and hypertext (as we'll be discussing more in Chapters 3 and 5 respectively), and in part because he is not operating as strongly in the classic vocabulary of a "comic," but instead thinking through the intersection of a number of the modalities discussed in this book.

Helms's book defies simple reading, and reflects an intentional use of the qualities that Johanna Drucker describes: "Digital environments increasingly depend upon a whole series of contingent texts, transient documents, that are created on the fly" (Drucker 22). She suggests that, in time, "we will 'publish' our data trails as guidebooks for the experience of reading, pointing to milestones and portals for in-depth exploration of stories, inventories, and the rich combination of cultural heritage and social life in the global world" (26). This type of annotation builds on the tradition of earlier texts, recalling marginalia, but it also reflects a type of communication that comics already excel at: the building of trails and meaning through both spatial and chronological juxtapositions that can meander as needed. (A similar type of "sequence" with an emphasis on nonlinearity will be described in Chapter 5.)

For more inspiration and examples of this method of scholarly communication writ large, Nick Sousanis maintains a list of comics as scholarship (among other examples of alternative scholarship) as part of his blog (Sousanis, "Comics as Scholarship & Alternatives"). As more graduate students are introduced to these possibilities early, the flexibility of comics for scholarly communication is driving even more experimentation with the form. Such works are particularly valuable to explore before starting a major textual endeavor, such as the dissertation—these examples are a reminder that students at institutions around the world are continuing to push back at the traditions and structures of that form, not unlike Nick Sousanis's own pointed attacks on the "boxes" of educational norms and structures (Sousanis, *Unflattening*).

Futures

The work of professional artists such as Larry Gonick, Scott McCloud, and Nick Sousanis featured here can make the process of comic-making appear quite daunting: while the remix approach centered in the pattern allows for a more accessible modality, the future of generative tools suggests even greater ease for would-be scholarly comic creators. Scholars, coders, and artists interested in procedural generation participate annually in Darius Kazemi's National Novel Generation Month (Kazemi): several have used generative tools to craft comic books, such as Zach Whalen's "VAUDn oc HORRRR" pictured in Figure 5 (Whalen).

Whalen's example (created in StyleGAN2, a generative image model requiring a code-driven interface and training preceding the now-popular web-based generative image models) demonstrated the similarity of AI to the remix approach taken in this pattern: Whalen trained the model on EC Horror comics and used a limited set of cover images to craft the oddly-familiar shapes shown in Figure 5. Looking back at this type of experimentation is also a powerful way for students to understand how image generation models are changing in their understanding of text and composition: a version of this cover generated as of this book's writing (using the tools shown in Figure 2) would already be more legible than Whalen's exemplar, and each generation promises a potential increase in fidelity.

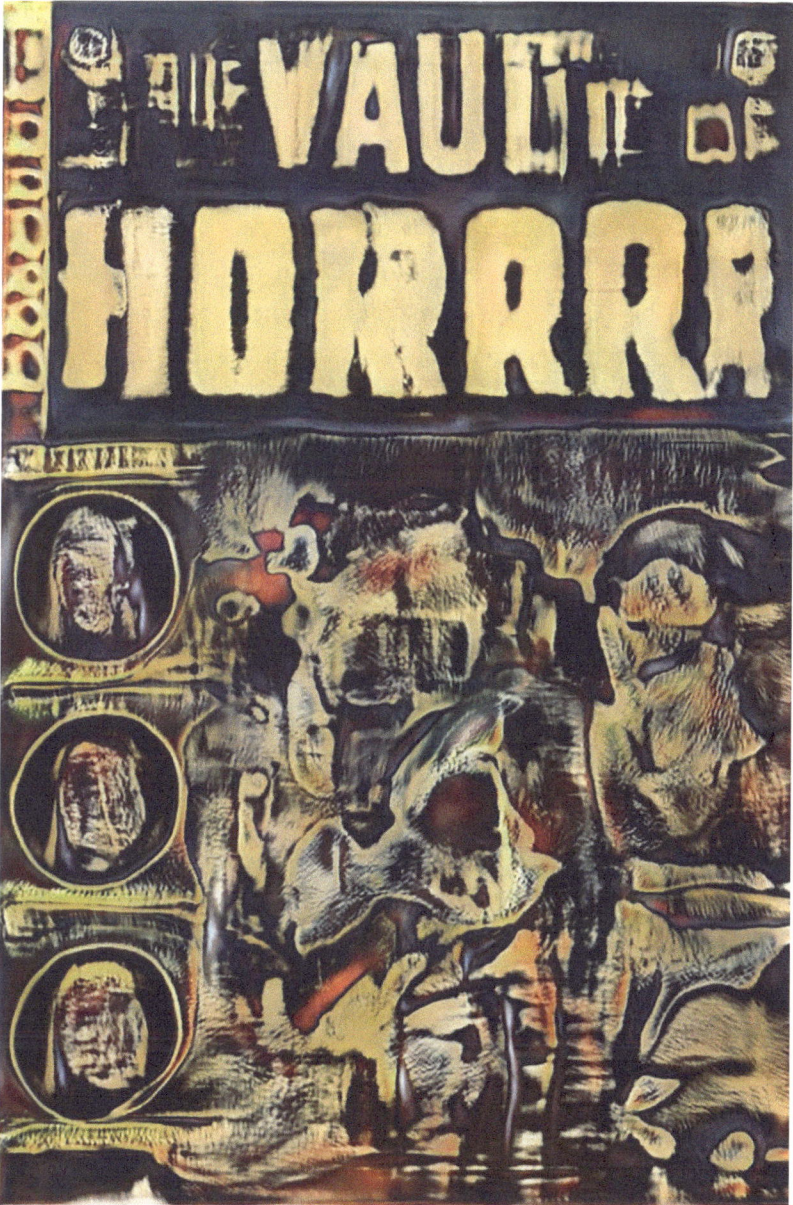

Figure 5: Zach Whalen's National Novel Generation Month comic, released December 2020.

While it may be out of reach due to time or skill constraints for humanities students to train their own AI models to produce a critical making work, AI tools are evolving rapidly enough to be useful for generating images for students to remix into their material or digital comics. Students could also involve generative AI and use non-AI means to represent their prompt-and-response "conversation" with the digital tool. The very process of text to image generation, discussed in Chapter 1, creates "image-text" where the model remixes and layers existing imagery towards an attempt to illustrate the written prompt: the juxtaposition offers space to think about authorial control and intent.

Works Cited

Bahl, Erin Kathleen. "Comics and Scholarship: Sketching the Possibilities." *Composition Studies*, vol. 43, no. 1, 2015, pp. 178–82.

Bang, Molly. *Picture This: How Pictures Work*. Anniversary, Expanded edition, Chronicle Books, 2016.

Bechdel, Alison. "The Rule." *Dykes to Watch out For*, vol. 22, 1985.

"Bechdel Test Movie List." *Bechdel Test*, 2023, https://bechdeltest.com/.

Collins, Jeff. *Introducing Derrida: A Graphic Guide*. Icon Books Ltd, 2014.

"DIY Methods 2022 Conference Proceedings." *DIY Methods 2022 Proceedings*, 2022. *hcommons.org*, https://hcommons.org/deposits/item/hc:48563/.

Drucker, Johanna. *Graphesis: Visual Forms of Knowledge Production*. Illustrated edition, Harvard University Press, 2014.

Gonick, Larry. *Cartoon History of the Universe Volumes 1–7*. First Edition, Crown, 1990.

Hatfield, Charles. "Comic Art, Children's Literature, and the New Comic Studies." *The Lion and the Unicorn*, vol. 30, no. 3, 2006, pp. 360–82. *Project Muse*, https://doi.org/10.1353/uni.2006.0031.

Helms, Jason. *Rhizcomics: Rhetoric, Technology, and New Media Composition*. University of Michigan Press, 2017, https://doi.org/10.3998/mpub.7626373.

Hertz, Garnet, editor. *Critical Making*. Telharmonium Press, 2012. https://www.conceptlab.com/criticalmaking/.

———. "Making Critical Making." *Critical Making*, edited by Garnet Hertz, Telharmonium Press, 2012, pp. 1–10. http://www.conceptlab.com/critical making/PDFs/CriticalMaking2012Hertz-Introduction-pp01to10-Hertz-MakingCriticalMaking.pdf.

Jenkins, Henry. "Geeking Out About The Comics Medium with Unflattening's Nick Sousanis (Part One)." *Pop Junctions*, 21 Sept. 2015, http://henryjenkins.org/blog/2015/09/geeking-out-about-the-comics-medium-with-unflattenings-nick-sousanis-part-one.html.

Karasik, Paul, et al. *How to Read Nancy: The Elements of Comics in Three Easy Panels*. Illustrated edition, Fantagraphics, 2017.

Kazemi, Darius. "NaNoGenMo." *NaNoGenMo*, 1 Nov. 2013, https://nanogenmo.github.io/.

Losh, Elizabeth, et al. *Understanding Rhetoric: A Graphic Guide to Writing*. Edition Unstated, Bedford/St. Martin's, 2013.

Martinec, Radan, and Andrew Salway. "A System for Image–Text Relations in New (and Old) Media." *Visual Communication*, vol. 4, no. 3, 2005, pp. 337–71.

McCloud, Scott. *Making Comics: Storytelling Secrets of Comics, Manga and Graphic Novels*. First edition, William Morrow Paperbacks, 2006.

———. *Reinventing Comics: The Evolution of an Art Form*. First edition, William Morrow Paperbacks, 2000.

———. *Understanding Comics*. Perma-Bound Books, 1993.

McLuhan, Marshall, and Quentin Fiore. *The Medium Is the Massage*. First edition, Gingko Press, 2001.

Miller, Rachel, and Daniel Worden. "Understanding Comics at 30: An Introduction." *Inks: The Journal of the Comics Studies Society*, vol. 6, no. 3, 2022, pp. 231–37. *Project MUSE*, https://doi.org/10.1353/ink.2022.0019.

Nikolajeva, Maria, and Carole Scott. "The Dynamics of Picturebook Communication." *Children's Literature in Education*, vol. 31, no. 4, Dec. 2000, pp. 225–39. *Springer Link*, https://doi.org/10.1023/A:1026426902123.

Poyiadgi, Andy. "Origami Comic." *Andy Poyiadgi*, 2013, www.ajpoyiadgi.com/comics.

Resmer, Cathy. "Dykes to Watch Out For » Blog Archive » The Rule." *Alison Bechdel*, 16 Aug. 2005, https://dykestowatchoutfor.com/the-rule/.

Salter, Anastasia. "Alice in Dataland." *20.1, Kairos: A Journal of Rhetoric, Technology, and Pedagogy*, 15 Aug. 2015, https://kairos.technorhetoric.net/20.1/inventio/salter/index.html.

———. "ProfHacker: Comics in the Classroom and Beyond." *The Chronicle of Higher Education*, 25 Jun. 2012, www.chronicle.com/blogs/profhacker/comics-in-the-classroom-and-beyond.

Salter, Anastasia, Roger Whitson, and Jason Helms. "Making 'Comics as Scholarship': A Reflection on the Process behind DHQ 9.4." *23.1, Kairos: A Journal of Rhetoric, Technology, and Pedagogy*, Aug. 2018, https://kairos.technorhetoric.net/23.1/inventio/salter-et-al/index.html#f.

Sousanis, Nick. "Comics as Scholarship & Alternatives." *Spin Weave and Cut*, 2023, https://spinweaveandcut.com/comics-alternative-scholarship/.

———. "Expanding Forms of Scholarly Inquiry within the Academy." *Imagining America 2012*, 2012, http://expandscholarship.selfloud.net/.

———. "Making Comics S2021." *Spin Weave and Cut*, 10 Jun. 2021, https://spinweaveandcut.com/making-comics-s2021/.

———. "The Shape of Our Thoughts: A Meditation On & In Comics." *Visual Arts Research*, vol. 38, no. 1, 2012, pp. 1–10.

———. *Unflattening*. Harvard University Press, 2015.

Spurgeon, Tom. "Making Mini-Comics." *The Comics Reporter*, 10 Oct. 2004, www.comicsreporter.com/index.php/all_about_comics/all_about/77/.

Talbot, Bryan. *Alice in Sunderland*. First Edition, Dark Horse, 2007.

Whalen, Zach. "This Comic Does Not Exist · Issue #55 · NaNoGenMo/2020." *GitHub*, 1 Dec. 2020, https://github.com/NaNoGenMo/2020/issues/55.

Whitson, Roger Todd, and Anastasia Salter. "Introduction: Comics and the Digital Humanities." *Digital Humanities Quarterly*, vol. 009, no. 4, Dec. 2015.

CHAPTER 3

GIFs

GIFs, or images in motion, have become the shorthand of the web. On nearly every platform, including text messaging, options abound for inserting GIFs that include everything from familiar moments caught on camera to strange characters laughing or dancing. GIFs offer a way for using other people's imagery and experiences as a major form of communication. They are a powerful, if fragmented, archive, and shows and films that are otherwise forgotten live on because of an isolated and well-selected moment. GIFs provide an entry-point for understanding new media composition and introduce motion and intertextuality. Working with GIFs can build perspective on the usage of these images for reactions, as well as an understanding of where they come from.

Critical GIFs

GIFs are one of the older native file formats of the web, designed intentionally for compression in 1987, when any color image risked taking up far too much space (and bandwidth) for web shareability

(Boissoneault). The term stands for "Graphics Interchange Format," and since its introduction it has been used for both animated and static images, taking advantage of the compression to enable exchanges at scale: even now, the relatively small size enables GIF essays to load quickly despite their image-dense design. Many GIFs—both memes and animated GIFs—fall into what Nick Douglas calls the "internet ugly aesthetic," or "the aesthetic of the mundane conversation and idle doodlings that have always existed, but which the internet makes shareable by default" (Douglas 337). This aesthetic owes a debt to a wide range of sources, spanning image boards, early web-comics, web shows or animations, and other low-res, often amateur-created, graphics. "Internet ugly" is not always amateur, however: sometimes, it is intentional, drawing on the styling of comics and cartoons for exaggerated impact.

Most things that are "internet ugly" find their way into GIFs, even if they are not originally found in that file format. Kate Miltner and Tim Highfield go so far as to position "the GIF at the root of digital cultures," arguing that the form affords "the opportunity to provide heightened and layered communication, demonstrate cultural knowledge, and occasionally engage in displays of resistance to certain ideologies and actors" (Miltner and Highfield 9). GIFs add nuance, emphasis, and emotion to online communication, and can both augment and replace text. This complexity is also one of the challenges inherent in deploying existing GIFs in daily use: even when a user believes that they are familiar with the original context in which a GIF was produced, GIFs develop new referential connections and meanings as they travel within communities, and intentionality is hard to judge.

The boundaries between GIF and meme are blurry: at root, both are often recognizable as something akin to a comic, featuring image and text in juxtapositions that recall those of either single-panel cartoons à la Far Side or, more rarely, multi-panel comic strip compositions. Memes are first and foremost a "genre," according to Bradley

Wiggins and G. Bret Bowers, with a sociocultural impact and recognizability that marks them and makes them worthy of documentation in colloquial digital histories such as that of *Know Your Meme*. Limor Shifman's definition emphasizes the status of memes as recognizable through their common form, meta-awareness, and the patterns of circulation and imitation that reshape them (Shifman). Animated GIFs are one option for creation in the broader genre of memes, and at times are simply memes with minimally moving images accompanying a single or multi-line text. Motion defines an animated GIF, which is distinguished by the looping animation plays through a timeline of ordered images. A GIF thus holds many image-texts in a single file and offers them up to the viewer rapidly for consumption.

Classic GIFs are often smaller, and less grounded in screen captures, than those shared now, which often start from media clippings. Jason Scott's "Under Construction" gallery, exhibited as part of the Archive Team's history of the internet and shown in part in Figure 1, is both a history of a practice and a reminder of the perpetually in-progress feel of the early web (Scott). This screenshot cannot capture the rapid motion and flashing of this page, which reflects the usually fairly short and often dramatic animation loops of each image.

Figure 1: A small fragment of Jason Scott's Archive Team exhibit "Under Construction."

As Ian Milligan notes in a history of GeoCities, "Many users never did get past the 'Under Construction' stage of a brand-new site," so these GIFs were a perpetual indicator of an intention to expand and build an online home (Milligan 144). Other GIFs would be a more distinctive marker of GeoCities communities: "there is clear evidence of borrowing and cohesiveness across these communities: the children's community really did have children's pictures, and so forth" (149). In these histories of the web, a shared GIF—like a bouncing Tigger popular in the children-oriented neighborhood of Enchanted Forest—becomes a shared reference point and a sign of how images were saved and reused.

The GIF endures for this usage in part because of its technological affordances. GIFs are not the only type of animation that was a pivotal communication tool for the early web: Macromedia Director, and later Adobe Flash, would play a pivotal role in shaping internet humor. From Homestar Runner's successful humorous shorts to Flash animation hubs such as Newgrounds, Flash was the ideal form for motion in the web. Homestar Runner's vectorized characters communicated substantial emotion and humor through minimal motion, providing a sense of the early web vernacular while moving away from the cost of production associated historically with hand-drawn animated work. However, the rise of mobile platforms dethroned it, and with small screens and cellular network bandwidth native web technologies regained their appeal (Salter and Murray). The animated web of Flash's era is unretrievable, while the affordances of GIFs have ensured a relative longevity.

This modern, resurgent, era of GIF usage often takes advantage of higher resolution than classic GIFs, which originally needed to communicate much more for as little bandwidth as possible. However, it is still a form fundamentally characterized by brevity in both file size and length. An examination of animated GIFs' popularity among users "found that the animation, lack of sound, immediacy of consumption, low bandwidth and minimal time demands, the storytelling capabilities and utility for expressing emotions were significant factors in making GIFs the most engaging content on Tumblr" (Bakhshi et al. 575). Designing for share-ability remains an essential feature for modern GIFs, which are frequently compressed again and again as they are manipulated to new ends: it is not unusual to see a GIF become source material for endless reimaginings. For instance, the iconic Simpsons image of "Homer slowly backing away" exists in forms ranging from the original hedge to walls of pizza: it even made its way back onto the Simpsons as a GIF Homer uses in a text message (Sirucek). The Simpsons writer who created the meta-gag, Cesar Mazariegos, described GIFs in an interview with Vulture as "sampling—little snippets, removed from their original context and repurposed into a whole new creative thing" (Sirucek). That sampling in turn inspires other forms of artistry, both digital and material. Homer backing away has become so immediately recognizable that the meme now has a design life of its own: it has inspired everything from embroidery patterns to an Adidas sneaker (Cheung).

The GIF has been thoroughly decontextualized and colonized. It has shifted from a homemade mechanism for referential in-jokes to a commercial one, to the point where skits "done for the GIF" are common everywhere from Netflix to late-night shows. The corporate GIF is a much more cynical tool than the fan-associated decontextualized frames of Superwholock, a shorthand for the three fandoms most prominent on Tumblr, one of many platforms where GIFs circulate widely (Booth). As a medium, GIFs are distinct from emojis thanks to their complexity: as Jiang et al. have noted, "GIFs, as a new nonverbal media commonly used to supplement text communication, surpass emoji on all these dimensions: GIFs have more details and offer a greater variety of depictions—they are essentially short video clips. The same GIF can also be inventively used in various contexts" (Jiang et al. 4). This is of course a pragmatic shift: with faster modems, higher resolution and denser GIFs are now easily consumed in quantity. GIFs and emojis now coexist as emotional shorthand, easy to search and add to Discord messages, tweets, Facebook posts, and so forth: databases of both media-industry-approved and fan-created GIFs exist as quick searchable fields on those platforms, a fast, decontextualized alternative to the fan archive collections popular in the past.

The usefulness of interrogating the GIF specifically is in the development of digital literacy, with real consequences for behavior on social platforms. As classes and communities are increasing their reliance on platforms where GIF communication is ubiquitous, educators and moderators are faced with the task of managing their implications: consider the options that Discord presents a user who searches for appropriate GIFs for "hate this," for instance. While a search for Hitler returns obviously antisemitic results, it also returns material from *History of the World Parts I and II*—as well as more esoteric references, such as Taika Waititi's *X*. The exemplary case of the challenges of such communication's meaning in the classroom has commonly been addressed through the case of Pepe the Frog—as we discussed in our previous article on Discord in the classroom, this type of white supremacist dog whistle can be used knowingly, in ignorance, and even at times with the intent of subversion or reclamation (Johnson and Salter). However, the reality is that this type of relatively well-known visual reference point is far easier to parse than the much broader world of moving image communication online.

This continuing relationship with materiality is part of what places GIFs here, in a space of transition as we start to think about the digital image-text relationships that can inform our work. Albin Wagener refers to GIFs as postdigital:

> Memes and GIFs fit into the postdigital spectrum—they are indeed messy, unpredictable, both digital and analog, relying on technological tools and non-technological references. Moreover, it is important to assess that they remain informational and biological, inasmuch as they

represent capsules of cognitive and emotional expression, meaning that information, biology, and technological means become strongly entangled and intertwined in a messy process of creation-reception.

(Wagener 848)

It is precisely this "both digital and analog" quality that makes them so compelling and reusable. Anna McCarthy notes that GIFs are satisfying because of their instability: "GIFs are also like zombies and pod people. They may come back, but they're never the same. Something has changed: resolution, aspect ratio, size. Or the image material has become encrusted with memes" (McCarthy 114).

Reconciling scholarly forms or the traditional essay with these online norms and formats isn't easy, but it's a challenge many digital humanities scholars have taken on: from blogging and tweeting to tooting and tumbling, each platform offers potential opportunities for scholarly communication. No collection better exemplifies this in digital humanities than *Buzzademia*, a project focused on experimental and playful scholarship. The editorial team describes this approach as making use of "the Internet Vernacular," or the tools of digital culture, with the goals of "playfulness, approachability, openness, and legibility" (Cong-Huyen et al.). The collection takes its name from BuzzFeed, a company founded in 2006 known for clickbait headlines and listicles, among other retweet and repost-friendly content types. The initial call for the project was aimed at building a print edited collection: however, that idea quickly fell to the wayside in the face of the multimodal materials submitted, none of which could easily be confined to print.

The project instead found a home at *Hyperrhiz: New Media Cultures*, a non-traditional online journal dedicated to academic, creative, and hybrid works—such works often take the form of webtexts, which we will address in more detail with hypertexts in Chapter 5, but the majority of the pieces in *Buzzademia* are focused more on the web's capacity to support multimodal image-text. Several of the works included in the *Buzzademia* special issue focus on pedagogical applications in line with the practices we're engaging here, such as Leonardo Flores's exercise for teaching critical memes as a means of analyzing text (Flores). One of the most relevant to our explorations of motion is Veronica Paredes's "GIF Essay," which asks students to make use of existing "GIFs and annotations to create a coherent whole" (Paredes). This process takes advantage of what GIFs can deliver: meaningful connections and intertextual references that at times endure long beyond the interest in the original object, capturing moments in motion that endure.

As with comics on comics, the tradition of film about film (documentary and otherwise) is well-explored but specialized: such productions are intensive, often expensive, and limited. Exploring those possibilities returns our attention to a still prevalent default of scholarly communication: the screenshot. Why do we represent so many non-static artifacts through static formats? Historically, the justification for this approach has been the need to create printable scholarship, a default that persists even in open access and fully online journals that will never see a physical edition. These defaults seem all the more absurd when they coexist with our new educational norms and even the scholarly communication structures of our other platforms, where the flexibility of multilayered work can be easily realized. Copyright certainly plays a role in cementing that norm: the screenshot is a more protected form, although scholars who have sought to include images from notoriously litigious companies might disagree. The moving image, on the other hand, has become a much more useful means for recovery and capture—particularly in the case of objects that are difficult to access, such as specific sequences from games or works of electronic literature. Journals acknowledging this shift include of course *Hyperrhiz* itself, and many more that we'll be exploring for examples throughout these patterns.

Michael Z. Newman has pointed out the need for more GIFs in film criticism particularly: "GIFs allow us to publish criticism of the moving image using the technology of the moving image, and in a way that is complementary with written language. Amateurs have been using them already for years, as have writers whose work is native to the web. Academic film criticism needs GIFs too" (Newman). The challenges and possibilities of videos as a digital humanities research object are also apparent in what Jason Mittell refers to as "videographic criticism," or "manipulating moving images and sounds to create new audiovisual texts that convey arguments and ideas that would otherwise be impossible to generate or articulate via the written word" (Mittell).

While a film clip, or indeed a looping GIF, may be recognizable in a frozen state or screenshot, this nod to printability is a reminder of the central element that the GIF affords for communication: motion. The exploration of GIFs as a research artifact opens the door to thinking about what motion might add to conveying complex ideas: as one team exploring the form as a way to communicate noted, "each frame, animation, and timing adjustment, as in sketching, also created self-generated push back and asked us to rethink and synthesize our design concepts, aims, and objectives" (Biggs et al. 11). At the same time, the "small temporal loop" that GIFs are limited to—reminiscent of historical and experimental film—creates a distinctive pattern and temporality (Bering-Porter 161).

Incorporating GIF creation into a critical making course is, in part, unexpected due to their ubiquity across social media and popular culture. However, as the above overview explains, this is a media worthy of serious study and critical experimentation, and it is also intentionally disconcerting: it pulls apart the construction of something so familiar that it often goes unremarked in common usage. Additionally, at the graduate level, students are expected to engage with the scholarly conversation, positioning their own assertions and research within a body of literature that is already underway and thinking about making GIFs to better understand the format. The contextualizing aspect of this GIF assignment, then, is an excellent exercise in how to situate their individual work into an ongoing conversation.

Pattern: GIPHY

The range of tools with which we might approach the making of moving images for scholarly communication is far too vast to cover here, and continually changing. We have instead selected one video-driven option for exploring the GIF specifically (and animation more broadly) as a tool for scholarly discourse and communication. By making GIFs and experiencing some of the amateur toolsets for that making, we aim first to build our understanding of the GIF, and its potential for misinformation and misinterpretation, as a constructed and manipulable form, subject to rewriting and remixing like any digital form. Next, we can explore the possibilities of the GIF and animation as an archive, considering their potential for low-investment documentation of interfaces, interactions, and ephemeral works. Finally, we should look to interrogate our cultural usage of GIFs as demanding of increased visual literacy and engagement with image-texts outside of the disciplines traditionally invested in this work.

GIPHY

One of the largest platforms for GIF sharing, GIPHY, also offers free tools for GIF making. These tools are, unlike some of the other methods we'll use, embedded in a sea of internet ugly (thanks to the ecosystem of many, many GIFs) and thus GIPHY also offers a living archive to explore the same content it produces. Accounts are free, and give you access to explore the contents and take inspiration from other

GIF makers. Here are a few things to keep in mind when exploring this form:

- **Explore rapid prototyping.** A GIF's limited looping structure and smaller scale make it an object better suited for rapid thoughts and quick impact than detail and nuance. This is a "fast" form for internet communication—most of the work goes into shaping your source material and coming up with ideas on what to make. Try iterating and refining to make the most of this low-investment form, and use lots of different materials (your own and ones you've found in the archives) to get the most out of the modality.

- **Place your GIFs in conversation.** Many of the "GIF essay" approaches discussed above treat GIFs as beats in a sequence: this larger pattern of motion brings GIFs into an image-text mode of composition. Thinking through your GIF as part of the web can also be a method for exploring and communicating your relationship with it as a technology as we play with two fundamental procedural elements: loops and motion.

- **Focus on aesthetic impact.** Just like with every skill we're experimenting with, there's a lot to learn when taking video or arranging still photos. Play with your camera orientation; closeness to the object; framing; and choice of subject. Think about how you will be isolating the moment: you don't need more than a few seconds of video for an effective loop.

The most flexible way to make GIFs is with Adobe Photoshop, or other high-cost image editing software. Those tools are also overwhelming and support a much broader range of purposes, so we don't recommend using them for this pattern. If you have used a tool of that kind, you'll immediately find GIPHY is not as aesthetically flexible. However, GIPHY does provide a fast way to go from your video fragments to the styling of the internet vernacular, with options for meme styling, text design, and filtering—and the limitations help contextu-alize some of the sameness you might have experienced in amateur web content.

We will make GIFs from video clips: this process can be done with both your own video, and video from other sources. First, try working from your own video clips, which can be a strong method to explore the making components of GIFs through first exploring physical mate-riality and movement, then digitizing and fragmenting the results. For this type of GIF, you'll need low-resolution video: your phone cam-era or laptop's built-in webcam are all you need. If you're comfortable in front of the camera, you might try starring and placing your own "scholarly avatar" at the forefront, as Casey Fiesler does in her academic TikToks—another platform where scholarship is put in motion (@pro-fessorcasey). If you're less thrilled about that, consider objects, pets, places, and moments (the passing of a storm, perhaps) that resonate.

Once you have filmed your source material, the GIPHY editing process consists of two stages: first, crop your clip down to a short timeline that feels appropriate for a loop, as shown in the editing inter-face in Figure 2. Loops are a fundamental structure of the web—recall their importance to the experience of GIFs in motion—and are what make GIFs distinctive for their endless repetition and the motion

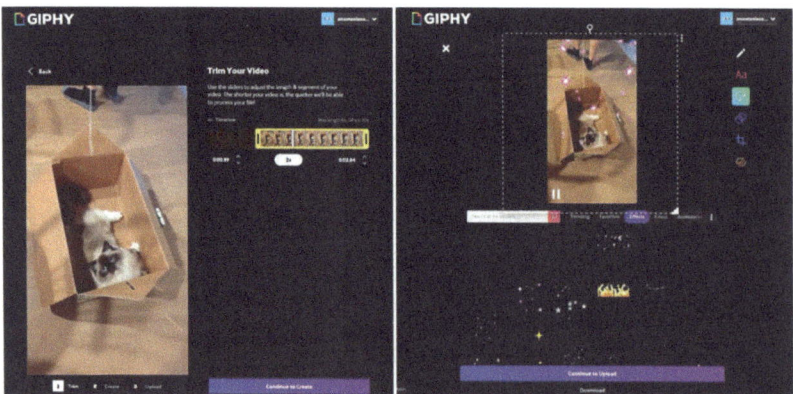

Figure 2: The GIPHY interface for trimming and editing a video clip.

that draws your attention when scrolling a feed. Pragmatically, loops reduce the amount of data required to provide content, and thus allow GIFs to function as shorthand. Usually, this will be shorter than the original clip.

Finish your video to GIF conversion with filters, drawings, stickers, or texts as shown in the options in Figure 2. As you do so, think about layering the different options GIPHY provides and experimenting with combinations. Most tools are drag and drop, with different options available by right-clicking. The "layers" tool at the bottom offers additional control of every element you add. Notice the role of collaboration in many of these tools: the "Stickers" option shown in Figure 2 allows for the selection of both pre-built and user-contributed moving images, emojis, and special effects, like the falling pixel petals shown in the Figure 2 example. These options are continually changing, and often reflect trends in online design or memes for reactions that can be layered upon your design to put it in conversation with the rest of the internet.

It's also possible to make a GIF from a still image: to start this type of GIF, return to the main menu and upload an image instead of a video. The editor will warn you that this initial input isn't in motion and will provide lots of options for adding that motion, using the same interface as the video options shown in Figure 2. Filters are particularly effective on still images: these are designed to offer artificial materiality to the image, and often recreate historic media perceptions through options like a slightly blurred, line-filled "VHS" option. There are many ways to develop such stills with a sense of movement to come: you might take photos of elements arranged using material objects (fabric, paper shapes, clay, LEGO figures) or you can turn to photography, drawings, and screenshots. Large files will often not be accepted: think about the GIFs you've seen and consider imitating the scale for best results. The better composed your source material (in composition, thoughtfulness, timing, etc.), the more compelling the final output will be.

Applications

Most students found success working with video shot on their phones, which allows for easy capture and doesn't introduce additional technology or challenges of import and export into the process. The student approaches reflected a tendency to turn to familiar source material of the internet vernacular—pets and particularly cats can take center stage when reflecting on one's own scholarly working environment and the conditions under which our labor is undertaken. PhD student Farrah Cato made particularly effective use of her dog in a commentary on the importance of play, as shown in Figure 3:

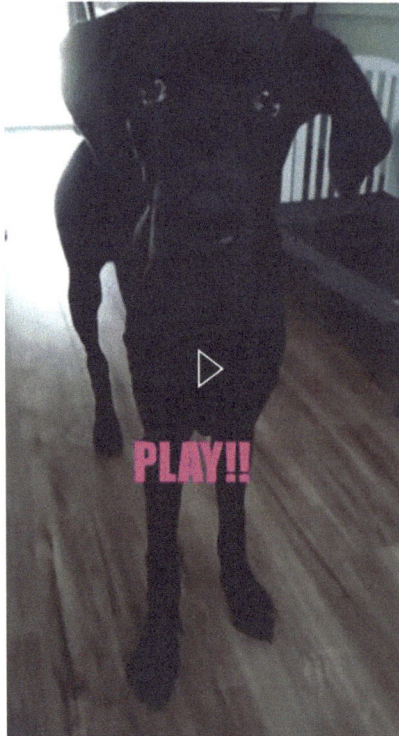

Figure 3: A screenshot of the key moment of text reveal in Farrah Cato's GIF on play. https://doi.org/10.3998/mpub.14510509.cmp1

My first GIF took a short video of Nora barking at me while I was trying to meet a deadline. My stress level was high and her barking was incessant. In a most obnoxious and necessary way, she insisted I stop and take a much-needed break. She wanted to play and I was supposed to play with her. Nora's insistence is not so far removed from the argument made by Shira Chess in her *Play Like A Feminist*. Chess argues in part that play is a necessary and important intervention in our everyday lives. In these "dark times" we live in, she says, the "pleasures of play" are feminist acts of protest and agency (Chess 84, 130)(84; 130). They are also moments with great potential, perhaps because we allow ourselves to look at the world from a different angle or a fresher set of eyes. In other words, the act of play might help "unflatten" our perceptions of the world we live in. There was a better moment of play that I cut out of this video. It was too blurry and, without sound, not easily interpreted, but I got what I wanted most out of the image, which was to present her bark as a command: STOP working; come PLAY; recharge your batteries! I wanted to time her command with her bark, and eventually I was mildly successful at doing so.

Farrah's process reflection speaks to the layered challenges of making in this style: the point of view Shira Chess offers for reframing familiar acts of domestic labor and play through a feminist lens meets with the technical and design challenges of trying to time, capture, and loop imagery and audio. As this reflection and GIF is from a course taught in fall 2021, the use of pets as models and focus on the domestic was particularly common as a response to the conditions of studying during the pandemic: this was the first iteration of Anastasia's graduate course, offered fully online during a transitional period for higher education working through the challenges of the expected return to the classroom.

Students already engaged in media studies work often brought a different lens to the exercise, building on collections of material they were studying and saved. In the GitHub repository, other examples include a commentary on the education and games debate that also features Yingzi Kong's cats, while Kate Loesel comments on disciplinary discourse while manipulating an image from Disney show Phineas and Ferb. Building on video research, PS Berge iterated through several GIFs based on their collection of early consumer advertisements for home virtual reality. As they described in their reflection:

> I'm currently working on a VR-centric project and have a problem where a segment of a video I edited that discussed early consumer-VR advertisements ended up getting cut due to time. The argument was that early consumer-VR ads (especially for Oculus and PlayStation VR) mostly followed a similar trope, and encouraged an "anti reality" ethos that was represented by the trope of destroying users' living rooms onscreen.
>
> So I thought, hey, what about gifs??

They tried different approaches to combining and juxtaposing the imagery of advertising fragments featuring the destruction of the home, as captured in Figure 4, and ultimately ended up creating a large collection of GIFs that would play side-by-side, inviting users to, in PS's words, "enjoy the destruction of a bunch of living rooms via dragon, laser-portal, black hole, and Batman." One of these is featured in full on the GitHub repository.

Other scholars have similarly tried to take on the GIF through nontraditional scholarship and found multiple GIFs effective in sequence. Jason Eppnik's history of the GIF takes the form of a multimodal, image-text essay, as shown in Figure 5: he notes that these GIFs operate as "digital slang, a visual vocabulary unencumbered by authorship, where countless media artifacts are viewed, deployed, and elaborated upon as language more than as art product" (Eppink 301). This framing puts GIFs into conversation with the discussion of comics in the last chapter, and previews some of the hybrid forms that emerge when the different building blocks of these patterns are meaningfully remixed.

Figure 4: PS Berge's exploration of VR advertisement tropes through GIF-making. https://doi.org/10.3998/mpub.14510509.cmp2

Daniel Rourke's essay "The Doctrine of the Similar (GIF GIF GIF)" offers another exemplar of the scholarly GIF essay, although the version included on the journal's website is flattened—"left paralysed by their conversion to PDF format," as the author wryly describes the challenge (Rourke 1). Rourke illustrates several types of GIFs in motion in the original version of the essay: the "classic" style exemplified by website icons and under construction GIFs; "frame capture," drawn from video clips; "art," which works at a higher resolution; "glitch," which can be either intentionally or unintentionally badly encoded and disrupted; and the "mash-up," which draws together any combination of

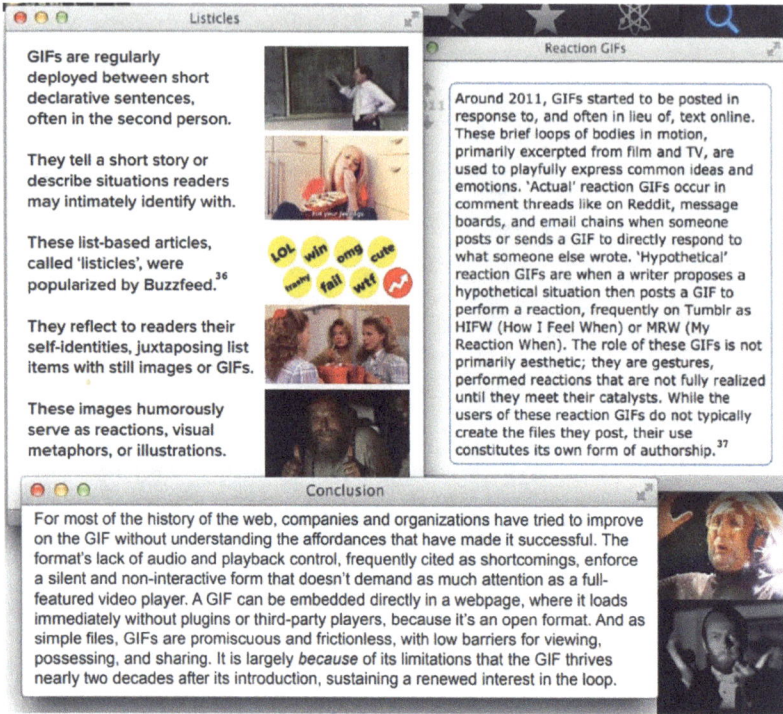

Figure 5: Eppnik's browser window style essay covering usages of the GIF across web history.

these forms (2–4). The flattened version shows but a single frame of the GIF, omitting the looping entirely.

Scholars and creators have been thinking through other ways to explore motion, with tools in the digital humanities powering publications that fit somewhere between GIFs and Flash. One example of this type of tool for playing with motion is Stepworks, a new media motion composition tool that has thus far gone through two iterations: Stepworks Classic and Stepworks Studio. Stepworks was created by Erik Loyer, an electronic literature author, scholar, and developer whose works have often pushed the boundaries of critical making. Stepworks has been described as a digital humanities tool taking a "one-button storytelling" approach distinct from a history of more complex, less remixable platforms: this ease of authoring is part of its value (Tabbi). Stepworks Classic is powered by Google Sheets, and thus draws our attention to another way of seeing the timeline beneath the motion (Loyer). As this platform allows for the embedding of media, it is an ideal tool for importing one's animated GIFs as well as other media artifacts (such as audio and still images). Stepworks has been used to create works such as *Trina*, a mixed reality mediation on future technology that also demonstrates the capacity of web motion to document and recreate an experience originally designed for live interaction (Burdick). These types of dedicated platforms are more intensive to learn but offer important possibilities for exploring this modality in more depth.

Futures

One of the key aspects of GIFs is their use of layering, a function of image-editing software that inherently transforms what is created— Lev Manovich's analysis of Photoshop as a form of media-shifting "cultural software" points out that this type of affordance fundamentally changes image-making (Manovich). In the context of GIFs, layering can function as a "semiotic mode," and thus frequently the single GIF becomes in itself a form of "image-text" that can be used as shorthand (Gürsimsek 339). This layering is at the heart of conversions such as that of Homer Simpson: once a single user made the background transparent, anything was possible. Homer's remixability foreshadows much more powerful motion-creating tools to come. Machine learning interventions in animation, such as Deforum Stable Diffusion and EbSynth, are currently most impactful for abstractions and experimental pieces but likely to become part of the motion creation toolsets moving forward, as we will discuss further in Chapter 9 on generation and artificial intelligence.

Given the popularity of GIFs as an online form of communication, machine learning tools specific to these processes are already under development. One early example, Picsart, uses a similar text-to-image approach as the interfaces for AI image generation discussed in Chapter 1, but outputs an animated GIF influenced by style choices selected by the user. The tool was introduced to the platform as "our latest (and most unhinged) addition," and described as the "next ~~weapon~~ tool for you to bring to the group chat," placing an emphasis on potential usage for highly individualized reactions and social material (Picsart). However, it's hard to imagine these generated GIFs displacing the popular media-centric GIFs in current usage easily, given their lack of connection to the intertextual, reference-heavy cultural discourse.

Works Cited

Bakhshi, Saeideh, et al. "Fast, Cheap, and Good: Why Animated GIFs Engage Us." *Proceedings of the 2016 CHI Conference on Human Factors in Computing Systems*, Association for Computing Machinery, 2016, pp. 575–86. *ACM Digital Library*, https://doi.org/10.1145/2858036.2858532.

Bering-Porter, David. "The Automaton in All of Us: GIFs, Cinemagraphs and the Films of Martin Arnold." *The Moving Image Review & Art Journal (MIRAJ)*, vol. 3, no. 2, Dec. 2014, pp. 178–92. *intellectdiscover.com*, https://doi.org/10.1386/miraj.3.2.178_1.

Biggs, Heidi, et al. "Moving Design Research: GIFs as Research Tools." *Designing Interactive Systems Conference 2021*, Association for Computing Machinery, 2021, pp. 1927–40. *ACM Digital Library*, https://doi.org/10.1145/3461778.3462144.

Boissoneault, Lorraine. "A Brief History of the GIF, from Early Internet Innovation to Ubiquitous Relic." *Smithsonian Magazine*, 2 Jun. 2017, www.smithsonianmag.com/history/brief-history-gif-early-internet-innovation-ubiquitous-relic-180963543/.

Booth, Paul. "Introduction: SuperWhoLock Fandom: Fandoms Crossed." *Crossing Fandoms: SuperWhoLock and the Contemporary Fan Audience*, 2016, pp. 1–27.

Burdick, Anne. "Trina: A Design Fiction." *The Digital Review*, no. 01, 2021, https://doi.org/10.7273/SGDQ-C440.

Chess, Shira. *Play Like a Feminist*. MIT Press, 2020.

Cheung, Adam. "An Iconic Meme Inspires The Simpsons x Adidas Stan Smith Homer Simpson – Sneaker News." *Sole Retriever*, 27 Oct. 2022, www.soleretriever.com/news/articles/the-simpsons-x-adidas-stan-smith-homer-simpson-white-release-date-2022.

Cong-Huyen, Anne, et al. "Editors' Introduction." *Hyperrhiz: New Media Cultures*, no. 21, 2019. *hyperrhiz.io*, https://doi.org/10.20415/hyp/021.i01.

Douglas, Nick. "It's Supposed to Look Like Shit: The Internet Ugly Aesthetic." *Journal of Visual Culture*, vol. 13, no. 3, Dec. 2014, pp. 314–39. *Sage Journals*, https://doi.org/10.1177/1470412914544516.

Eppink, Jason. "A Brief History of the GIF (so Far)." *Journal of Visual Culture*, vol. 13, no. 3, Dec. 2014, pp. 298–306. *Sage Journals*, https://doi.org/10.1177/1470412914553365.

Flores, Leonardo. "Teaching Critical Memes." *Hyperrhiz: New Media Cultures*, no. 21, 2019. *hyperrhiz.io*, https://doi.org/10.20415/hyp/021.t02.

Gürsimsek, Ödül Akyapi. "Animated GIFs as Vernacular Graphic Design: Producing Tumblr Blogs." *Visual Communication*, vol. 15, no. 3, Aug. 2016, pp. 329–49. *Sage Journals*, https://doi.org/10.1177/1470357216645481.

Jiang, Jialun "Aaron," et al. "'The Perfect One': Understanding Communication Practices and Challenges with Animated GIFs." *Proceedings of the ACM on Human–Computer Interaction*, vol. 2, no. CSCW, Nov. 2018, 80:1–20. *ACM Digital Library*, https://doi.org/10.1145/3274349.

Johnson, Emily K., and Anastasia Salter. "Embracing Discord? The Rhetorical Consequences of Gaming Platforms as Classrooms." *Computers and Composition*, vol. 65, Sept. 2022, p. 102729. *ScienceDirect*, https://doi.org/10.1016/j.compcom.2022.102729.

Loyer, Erik. "Stepworks: Classic." *Stepworks*, 2023, https://step.works/index.php/site_2023/classic.

Manovich, Lev. *Software Takes Command*. Bloomsbury Publishing USA, 2013.

McCarthy, Anna. "Visual Pleasure and GIFs." *Compact Cinematics: The Moving Image in the Age of Bit-Sized Media*, edited by Pepita Hesselberth and Maria Poulaki, Bloomsbury, 2017, pp. 113–22.

Milligan, Ian. *Welcome to the Web: The Online Community of GeoCities during the Early Years of the World Wide Web*. UCL Press, 2017. *uwspace.uwaterloo.ca*, https://uwspace.uwaterloo.ca/handle/10012/11859.

Miltner, Kate M., and Tim Highfield. "Never Gonna GIF You Up: Analyzing the Cultural Significance of the Animated GIF." *Social Media + Society*, vol. 3, no. 3, July 2017, p. 205630511772522. *Sage Journals*, https://doi.org/10.1177/2056305117725223.

Mittell, Jason. "Deformin' in the Rain: How (and Why) to Break a Classic Film." *DHQ: Digital Humanities Quarterly*, vol. 15, no. 1, 2021.

Newman, Michael Z. "GIFs: The Attainable Text." *Film Criticism*, vol. 40, no. 1, Jan. 2016, https://doi.org/10.3998/fc.13761232.0040.123.

Paredes, Veronica. "Annotated Series of GIFs." *Hyperrhiz: New Media Cultures*, no. 21, 2019. *hyperrhiz.io*, https://doi.org/10.20415/hyp/021.e01.

Picsart. "Introducing Your New Favorite Unhinged AI Tool: AI GIF Generator." *Picsart Blog*, 27 Jun. 2023, https://picsart.com/blog/post/introducing-your-new-favorite-unhinged-ai-tool-ai-gif-generator.

Rourke, Daniel. "The Doctrine of the Similar (GIF GIF GIF)." *Dandelion: Postgraduate Arts Journal and Research Network*, vol. 3, no. 1, Feb. 2012. *dandelionjournal.org*, https://doi.org/10.16995/ddl.259.

Salter, Anastasia, and John Murray. *Flash: Building the Interactive Web*. MIT Press, 2014.

Scott, Jason. "Please Be Patient—This Page Is Under Construction!" *Archive Team: Under Construction*, 7 Oct. 2009, www.textfiles.com/underconstruction/.

Shifman, Limor. *Memes in Digital Culture*. MIT Press, 2013.

Sirucek, Stefan. "The Full-Circle Journey of 'Homer Simpson Backs Into the Bushes.'" *Vulture*, 24 Jun. 2019, www.vulture.com/2019/06/simpsons-homer-backs-into-the-bushes-meme-gif.html.

Tabbi, Joseph. "Digital Humanities." *The Bloomsbury Handbook of Literary and Cultural Theory*, edited by Jeffrey R. Di Leo, Bloomsbury, 2018, p. 255.

Wagener, Albin. "The Postdigital Emergence of Memes and GIFs: Meaning, Discourse, and Hypernarrative Creativity." *Postdigital Science and Education*, vol. 3, no. 3, Oct. 2021, pp. 831–50. *Springer Link*, https://doi.org/10.1007/s42438-020-00160-1.

Wiggins, Bradley E., and G. Bret Bowers. "Memes as Genre: A Structurational Analysis of the Memescape." New Media & Society, vol. 17, no. 11, Dec. 2015, pp. 1886–906. *SAGE Journals*, https://doi.org/10.1177/1461444814535194.

CHAPTER 4
Map

As GPS technology expands, Geographic Information System (GIS) mapping has become a prominent feature in much critical making work. Recreational geocaching and augmented reality (AR) games like *Pokémon Go* helped to introduce the public to the possibilities of location-based technologies, but the development of AR itself, along with virtual reality (VR) and ever more advanced telecommunication tools, complicates the concepts of place and space. The accessibility of Google Earth has allowed it to be incorporated into classrooms to understand topographic geography, chart the journeys of historic figures and literary characters, and to note the physical changes to specific neighborhoods over time. Interactive maps such as the Native Land Digital Map (https://native-land.ca/) make apparent the fact that any given location has deeper and different meaning for different populations as well as individuals. This chapter provides a pattern for using Google Earth layers to add new perspectives to—and to critique the dominant perspective of—a given landscape.

Critical Mapping

Making maps has allowed us to foster deeper thinking about a variety of issues surrounding place and space. Perhaps because of how little we think about the many layers of a "place" in our daily lives, it seems like this perspective is a new one for many of our students, and it is also a lens that offers us a different way to think about the shape of our scholarship and its relationship to historically contested territories (and even the natural world). The way that any given place can hold multidimensional meaning is something few of us ponder deeply on a regular basis, yet existence of and in any given place holds numerous implications and every physical space we can inhabit holds layers of meaning for each of us that differ from one person to the next. Towns are situated within districts, counties, states, and more, and exist in specific hemispheres on the planet Earth. Each individual person experiences their own combinations of contexts and meanings for any given place. In America and many other colonized countries, physical locations hold additional layers of meaning as the native lands of indigenous peoples, stolen or bartered for, with often deadly consequences for the original inhabitants. Any place can simultaneously hold ancestral ties, happy childhood recollections, and memory of trauma. Place can include a category of things, as well. Just as a hometown would encompass a broad area of land, buildings, etc., the place of a classroom can hold layers of meaning including and moving beyond those layers of a geographical place.

This type of mapping can be an important part of digital humanities practice, particularly when interpreting texts that reflect on the possibilities in this locative relationship. One work that has been the subject of repeated mapping (both physical and digital) is James Joyce's *Ulysses*, a novel whose underlying relationship to Dublin's geography is so essential that it has inspired a "Bloomsday" practice of taking a walking tour to follow Leopold Bloom's own meandering path. An

MAP   93

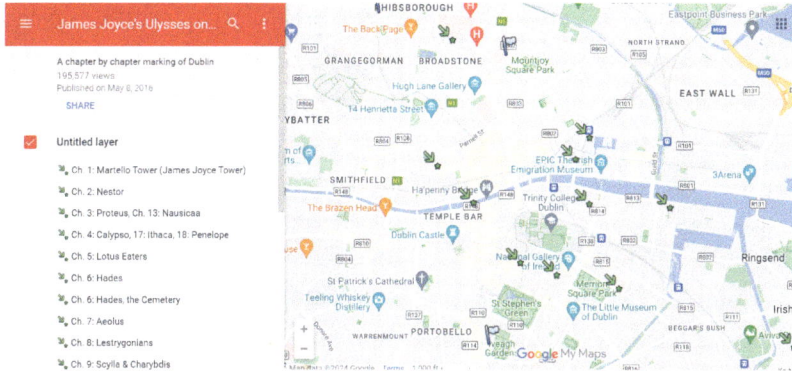

Figure 1: An example of digital humanities mapping centered on Joyce's Dublin.

anonymous Google Maps visualization (Figure 1) allows the viewer to follow the journey digitally, chapter by chapter, and has attracted over 100,000 views as a resource for pedagogy and textual understanding.[1] The project also demonstrates one possibility for the map as a scholarly interface: as Caleb Derven and John Keating note in their observation of the value of a geographically foregrounded digital edition of *Ulysses*, "investigating geographical elements in a computational context becomes another way to both read through the novel and assist in establishing a critical editing function" (Derven and Keating 2). The novel's relationship with the city can be brought to a forefront through mapping in ways other interfaces do not invite.

Mapping also offers us opportunities to rethink the relationship of our work in the humanities with geography more broadly. Looking at the Native Land Digital Map (https://native-land.ca/) reminds us that the dominant perspective of land ownership in the United States runs against the understanding of land ownership of the original inhabitants of the land comprising the country today. This tool displays the

1   Interactive map available here: www.google.com/maps/d/u/0/viewer?mid=1PGlW 4GaoXRaEBdsILVzl8fvCdAk&hl=en_US&ll=53.34547376848066%2C-6.25436 99448242585&z=14

names of the indigenous tribes who lived on this soil for centuries prior
to European colonization. Maintained by a full board of advisees, the
website explains, "Native Land is an app to help map Indigenous territories, treaties, and languages" and provides a link for users to report
errors. Their mission statement is also included on the site:

> Native Land Digital strives to create and foster conversations about the
> history of colonialism, Indigenous ways of knowing, and settler-Indig-
> enous relations, through educational resources such as our map and
> Territory Acknowledgement Guide. We strive to go beyond old ways
> of talking about Indigenous people and to develop a platform where
> Indigenous communities can represent themselves and their histories on
> their own terms. In doing so, Native Land Digital creates spaces where
> non-Indigenous people can be invited and challenged to learn more about
> the lands they inhabit, the history of those lands, and how to actively be
> part of a better future going forward together.
>
> ("Why It Matters")

This interactive map offers an entry point for understanding
beyond contemporary names and boundaries of various locations and
helps remind us that all borders—national and local—are imaginary
and political. It is also in conversation with the principles Catherine
D'Ignazio and Lauren Klein set out for scholars in *Data Feminism* to
value multiple forms of knowledge, and resist over-relying on existing classifications and binaries that may be inherently exclusionary
(D'Ignazio and Klein).

K12 teachers have been using Google Maps and layers in their
classes since the early 2000s (Liang et al.). The ability to display land
formations, country boundaries, and images of the full globe as well
as street views can be beneficial for classes in geography, history, and
literature. Showing students the contemporary path of a historical
journey, for example, can help make the past more concrete and easier
for young students to understand. One site, Google Lit Trips, curates

MAP 95

completed Google Maps journeys that follow characters in books commonly read in K12 classes, describing these as "immersive 3D literary field trips where students virtually become traveling companions with characters in stories commonly taught in grades kindergarten through high school" ("About Google Lit Trips"). Likewise, assigning older students to research and then map out the path of a character in a novel, a journey of a historical figure, and even a wished-for road trip where students calculate a trip budget can add dimension, perspective, and motivation for students of all levels. As with Leopold Bloom's journey, several Google "My Maps" have already been created to follow the journey of the Joad family in John Steinbeck's *Grapes of Wrath*. This novel centers around the journey of a family across America during the Dust Bowl—a widespread drought throughout the United States in the Depression era. One of these, created by an anonymous user in 2015, depicts the journey and includes summaries of the book at each location along with questions to guide student reading and help them think critically about the events in the book and compare them to contemporary events, as well as questions that ask students to evaluate the ethical decisions of the characters and apply the lessons the characters learn to their own lives ("Grapes of Wrath").

Of course, maps do not need any digital technology to be compelling. One example is a map created in collaboration between residents of a specific neighborhood in Detroit and geography faculty at nearby universities in 1971. This map, frankly titled "Where Commuters Run Over Black Children on the Pointes-Downtown Track," displays a black circle on the map at each location where a black child was struck and killed by a white driver. Described in detail in D'Ignazio and Klein's *Data Feminism*, the creators of this map plotted data to create a powerful argument to policymakers what residents of the area had long known: the area was dangerous for pedestrians, especially children. D'Ignazio and Klein contrast this map with the "Residential Security Map," one of the first instances of redlining, created in 1939 by the Detroit Board of

Commerce and the Federal Home Loan Bank Board. Critically thinking about maps and the influences behind them is another way to introduce students to critical making projects around the ideas of place and
space. It can also help bring to the forefront the ways that mapping and
geolocation are used—and misused—throughout society.

Detroit is the subject of another compelling mapping project that
does use contemporary technology. The capabilities of the Google
Maps Street View and its Time Machine feature have been leveraged
to create compelling narratives of various neighborhoods. Alex Alsup
maintains a blog, "GooBing Detroit," that uses current and historical Google Maps and Bing images to display the decline and neglect
of various buildings in Detroit neighborhoods over time (Alsup). The
striking images displayed one after the other, as well as how recently
these homes have decayed—many go from occupied, maintained
homes in 2009 to abandoned, empty lots in 2015—is a call to interrogate the housing systems in this city and our country. This work
reminds us of the systemic racism that remains in these policies and
others that have such a profound impact on the lives of real citizens.
Alsup's work has also been on display in art museums such as the
Prizer Gallery in Austin, Texas, which he hopes will spur change to
the city's rampant foreclosures, driven by a system that is inherently
biased (Abbey-Lambertz; Sheehan). This project and others like it can
convey powerful contradictions to our societal narrative of "progress,"
showing, in sometimes striking juxtaposition, how we treat our buildings, conduct business, and impact one another.

Both of these maps of Detroit point at the same thing: dangerous
systemic racism that is embedded in the housing market of this city
(and the state and country in which it is located). The problems of
redlining, gentrification, and other ways that policymakers control
where and how people can live—and who can live exactly where—are
brought into stark relief through the use of maps and historic images
in these two projects alone. Mapping projects of all types can help

MAP   97

people literally see where injustices and other events are taking place, which can help demonstrate a problem, potential solutions, and therefore call for change.

Maps can also be used to aggregate and visualize data in the service of communicating important issues to an outside audience. One common theme in marginalized communities is how little data is collected and presented to boards or those with authority to improve conditions (discussed at length in D'Ignazio and Klein's *Data Feminism*). One example D'Ignazio and Klein share is the "Feminicidios en México" map created and maintained by a Mexican woman who uses the pseudonym Princesa ("Feminicidios En México"). This map displays the location, name, age, and information known about women who were killed in Mexico. At the time of writing, the map includes thousands of records of murders that took place between 2016 and 2020. The act of mapping the locations of the murders of women in Mexico, along with the victims' names and the circumstances surrounding their deaths, results in a poignant critical making work and call to action against the policies, attitudes, and violence allowing these injustices to occur. Looking at the clusters of crosses on this interactive map is chilling.

Mapping events, businesses, houses, and more can help people more easily notice patterns and trends across a space too large to observe in person or too difficult to visualize as being connected by location. Even reading news reports, research, charts, or other data where these sources are available, is rarely as easy to grasp as plots on a map. Data visualization like this can be truly gripping—especially when overlaid with maps of places that hold meaning to us—our home country, the city where we live, and so forth. Adding a layer of information over the location images and landmarks we commonly see on our phones as we navigate via GPS can allow us to better grasp the overall picture.

Even seemingly banal information, such as the interactive map displaying "education deserts," can highlight cultural values and inequities within populations. For example, the "education desert" map marks places in the United States that are too far to commute to a community college or university (Hillman). The map discussed by Hillman shows the locations of broadly accessible institutions of higher education with the intent of calling attention to places in the United States where it is more difficult for people who live in these places to obtain advanced degrees. While the authors of course are embedded in an institution of higher education and obviously see its merits, it is worth interrogating the perspective: the phrase "education desert" implies that higher education is a lifeforce—like water or a fertile field—necessary for success in our country. This map, therefore, displays a specific and debatable stance on higher education.

Maps are all drawn from a particular point of view, and it is important to draw our students' attention to these aspects of maps and to help them question what principles and values they amplify, and whose objectives they serve. Assessing existing maps—contemporary digital examples as well as historic maps outlining the "conquest" lands of our ancestral colonizers—can help students understand the power of the map and spur ideas for their own critical making map projects.

Beyond geographical locations, the advent of technologies such as VR, AR, and beyond (such as extended reality or XR) stretches our understanding of place and space. The ability to use technology to exist in more than one place simultaneously is more realistic than it was in the past, but VR headsets are being touted as ways to connect with one another—for work and for play—from the comfort of our own living rooms. We can, virtually, tour ancient ruins, deep sea dive, stand beside the Mars Rover, shrink to the size of a molecule, battle aliens, and more, without leaving our homes. We can also sit beside colleagues at a virtual conference table. Indeed, with Meta advertising virtual board rooms, it seems we face an inevitable future of corporate VR, to be followed by corporatized education in VR.

All of this technology was in development long before the COVID-19 pandemic shook the world, but the pandemic and the resulting need for virtual gatherings again stretched public understanding of

MAP 99

the ideas of place. For many, work has regained (or maintained, given that many positions continued to require physical presence throughout the pandemic), but it is likely that at least some aspects of communication remain virtual. Many workplaces found the convenience and other benefits of Zoom and other videoconference technology to outweigh the negatives for at least some types of meetings. Many of our university meetings, for example, have remained virtual despite our campus returning to "normal" in-person policies more broadly. The fact is, more faculty can attend virtual meetings, and many of them prefer it. The distinction between virtual and physical attendance in meetings and classes has, for many (but notably not all) become blurred. The pandemic expanded our everyday definitions of place and space, which can be interrogated further in critical making works.

We encourage students to engage in the critical thought of the duality of what "here" can mean while in VR (or Zoom or Teams, for that matter), what constitutes "presence" in the physical and virtual worlds, and how that impacts communication and perspectives. This thought can be teased out in the mapping projects discussed in this pattern. One student (example two below) merged a virtual world with the "real" world in their map, plotting the birthplaces of fictional video game characters. This mashup works to blur the perception of virtual and real characters: a sort of commentary on the extent to which our physical lives are consumed in the Matrix-esque virtual worlds where we work and play. Having students create maps of fictional worlds that appear in video games, films, and literature could also be an interesting way to think differently about place and space.

Finally, another digital tool we like to use with students for creating critical maps is ArcGIS StoryMaps, which has access to large datasets, includes tools to demonstrate change (before and after views), and allows for elaboration on a website around different maps. For a more material-centric critical mapping project, maps can be created (or printed) on paper and annotated with words, images, and symbols.

Sometimes merely adding data points to a map, like the aforementioned example from 1971 Detroit, can create a compelling argument as collated data makes patterns visible.

Pattern: Google Earth Layers and Maps

With the mainstream application (and reliance on) GPS technology, most of us already spend a lot of time looking at digital maps. You might even have engaged in some annotation, particularly if you've saved favorites or mapped out a road trip in advance. While once GPS devices were reserved for hikers and others engaged in more serious exploration, now we are often carrying multiples on our person—even as I write this, I'm wearing a GPS-capable watch and sitting next to a GPS-capable phone that are broadcasting my location most of the time.

Since we're so familiar with this technology, it feels like a more accessible interface for one of our first patterns engaging in the digital: as you explore map-making, the emphasis will not be on coding, although more advanced forms of this work have the potential to delve into more complexity. The coding is nearly all done for the user, behind a what-you-see-is-what-you-get (WYSIWYG) interface. The process of creating a Google Earth layer is more interface-driven than many of the other patterns in this book; as with all critical making projects, the key here is to create the map around a coherent, informed critique. This pattern is thus an opportunity to think about spatial visualizations using a constrained interface for telling map-driven stories. As you map, think about how you can:

- **Focus on spatial specificity and structure.** Your map will work best with a concrete connection to locations, whether that's on a smaller scale like Joyce's Dublin, or a larger scale like a war history visualization. In some cases, you might be mapping the fictional onto the "real" history or the historical onto landscapes

MAP 101

that have changed vastly, and that juxtaposition can add to the meaning.

- **Try to tell a story.** As the examples we've discussed thus far highlight, one of the distinctions between a critically constructed map layer and a more basic information visualization about a location comes through in the intention. The slide-like structures map layering offer are also well-suited to organizing a narrative, and thus conveying an argument.

- **Explore image-text possibilities.** Google Earth embeds several options for juxtaposing visuals and texts: think about using those elements not just for description but for communication, persuasion, and critique. As maps are themselves a form of image-text, consider how your layering is in line with comics and other image-texts.

Google Earth layers can be created at earth.google.com using a Google or Gmail account: logging in also stores your project for sharing and changes later, just like other Google services. Start by selecting "New" and choosing "Create" under "Drive project." Or, if you want to build from one of the examples, select "Local KML file" and upload the KML file from our GitHub repository.

Once launched, you'll see options for creating title overlays, slides, adding placemarks, paths, and more. As interfaces often change, rather than providing specific direct instructions here, we encourage you to click different icons to see what they do and experiment with the various tool options. Note that the map can be used to display information about various locations—highlighting the similarities, differences, and more between the various locations, as informed by your research and engagement.

However, as a critical making tool, Google Earth works best as a space for commentary and even reflection on the journey you are taking here. Remember, your map must be **interactive**, and it must contain a **critical making statement** that calls attention to, questions, critiques, or celebrates some larger aspect of humanity.

Expect to be frustrated by some of the limitations of the tool: working within constrained interfaces and platforms can limit our expressive potential, but it also helps guide the making and provides limitations that can prevent the possibility space of the entire world from becoming too overwhelming to proceed. This is a particularly good exercise for narrowing your scope and thinking thoughtfully about what is necessary to communicate your intentions—practice that will serve you well in our next pattern, hypertext, which similarly pushes us into path-making that can lead in many directions (Chapter 5).

Applications

Most of the maps discussed here are linked in the GitHub repository with the KML files included: KML files export the annotations and coordinate information from the maps, and thus can be loaded into other interfaces and viewed even if the original map is no longer available. There are two graduate student samples included, reflecting different ways students approached Google Maps to convey arguments drawing on their own work and experience. For instance, Emilie Buckley's "Florida Banned Books" map draws on a dataset encompassing the 200 titles banned across 67 counties.[2] The map allows a Florida viewer to dive into local challenges in their region while seeing the larger scale of the challenges at work. The scrolling data overlaying some counties can be overwhelming in areas with long lists of book challenges, and emphasizes the currency of this trend, complete with the data and results of the challenge at the time the data was collected. Working in the context of game studies, Mirek Stolee worked with the

2   Available at https://earth.google.com/earth/d/1X9Ws99u0LAokFPPMw7GMn_P3hVR7n7js?usp=sharing

MAP   103

Figure 2: Mirek Stolee's map of the mechanics of the game *Mombasa* onto a map of Africa.

mechanics of the 2015 board game *Mombasa*, which centers trading throughout the African continent while using an underlying map to structure the routes of trade. Mirek layers that same map onto the digital interface, analyzing the mechanics and situating their relationship to the physical space (see Figure 2).

Students in Emily's undergraduate course build Google Earth assignments as part of the "Place and Space" unit. For this assignment, students are given three tool options to use for their project, with three options: Google Earth layers, ArcGIS StoryMaps, or SparkAR. Most of them chose Google Earth layers, a small handful created ArcGIS StoryMaps, and no students attempted an augmented reality (SparkAR) project. Therefore, in the syllabus on our GitHub repository (and future sections of the course), we have replaced SparkAR with StoryMapJS,[3] an open-source, user-friendly tool very similar to ArcGIS StoryMaps (though less robust).

While only one section has had these specific options, it does give a slight indication of the level of technological complexity that undergraduates in a digital humanities minor are willing to attempt for one project in a course where four are assigned. It should also be noted that

---

3   StoryMapJS is available at: https://storymap.knightlab.com/

although we mention Google Earth Street View above, this tool was not explicitly listed as an option for students, and none used it. Future sections will include this as an option for students who wish to investigate how specific locations have changed over time, like the GooBing Detroit project discussed above.

The first example of a Google Earth layer is titled simply "LGBTQ+ Persecution and Immigration." This project was created by undergraduate Cody Crittenden.[4] Cody's map includes an impressive 70 individual countries. When viewing in presentation mode, the viewer visits each country around the globe, beginning with Papua New Guinea and two nearby island nations and continues in a more or less western direction from there. At each location, a short paragraph is displayed that describes the legal rights of LGBTQ+ people in the country displayed. Countries are presented in mostly geographical order, rather than in alphabetical order or by extremity of punishment. Viewed in Google Earth's "presentation mode," the reader feels as though they are "hopping" from one location to the next. The United Kingdom, United States, and Canada appear last and are described only as "top three countries for LGBTQ+ immigration." The information for the remaining countries includes the criminal sentences—including death—for being LGBTQ+, expressing gender in a certain way, and more. For example, the text for Saudi Arabia reads:

> Outlaws same-sex relations between men in the form of "homosexual acts." Also criminalizes forms of gender expression. Homosexual acts can result in 100 lashes and banishment for 1 year, or even the death penalty. Forms of gender expression can result in flogging and imprisonment.

Cody's "tour" of the globe displaying the vast number of countries where there are such terrifying consequences for people merely

---

4   Cody gave permission to discuss the project here but has removed the project from Google Maps.

MAP   105

"discovered" as being LGBTQ+ is unsettling. Information about each country's laws on how people can express themselves, love, and live is represented in a matter-of-fact tone, for the most part without much hint of whether or not the author feels the laws are just.

The tone taken by the text in this project notably does not strongly convey Cody's personal stance on these issues. It is not blatantly obvious in this work if the reader is expected to feel that these laws are morally or ethically wrong or right. By refraining from condemning certain countries for their cruel policies towards this population, the map displays policies in a factual way, with the exception of the "top three country" descriptions, which have a moderately positive spin (though admittedly a reader with a homophobic perspective is still free to interpret it as a negative list). Without blatant assessments of these policies being wrong or right, the reader can be left to draw their own conclusions about the perspectives of different nations on LGBTQ+ rights—and potentially consider the issue without first digging their heels in the stance of their preferred political party. This is one approach to critical making work that seeks to engage an audience who may hold a different viewpoint or set of values than the author. Without a heavy-handed message or "moral of the story," presenting facts in this way can often be more effective in persuading people to change their stance on a hot-button issue. Of course, not all projects use this approach, and many if not most critical making projects take a specific, polarizing stance on a topic in order to emphasize the importance or urgency about the subject being presented.

An example on a lighter topic is "Cultural Representation in VALORANT" by undergraduate Sarah Scalisi. This map depicts the "home countries" of 17 different characters in the video game *VALORANT*.[5]

---

5   Available at this link: https://earth.google.com/web/@18.1259561,17.85240426,-1116.03429696a,12869613.24073792d,30.00000017y,0.00071437h,0t,0r/data=Mik KJwolCiExYXl6M2ZaWU55SXpuY3pPSWVl1a29aamo3S2V0bUhtSnYgAQ

Briefly, *VALORANT* is a first-person shooter set in a future version of earth, and most gameplay revolves around team-based battles where each team is assigned a specific objective. Sarah's project focuses on the different characters that players can select as their avatars. The *VALORANT* Wiki mentions this in one of the first paragraphs on the main page, stating: "due to the backstories of these characters, the *VALORANT* team features interesting dynamics as the individuals not only sometimes know each other, but they also come from a wide spectrum of backgrounds ranging from crime to the military" ("VALORANT").

Impressively, this project remains largely legible to readers who are unfamiliar with the video game itself. Context about the game's storyline is included where some locations describe the character's motivation for joining the "VALORANT PROTOCOL." Each location in the map presentation includes the name, image, and a brief background on a character in the game. Sarah's map includes information about the voice actors and concludes many of them with an evaluation of the country's representation. The entry for the Philippines, for example, reads:

> Home to VALORANT agent Tala Nicole Dimaapi Valdez (Neon).
>
> Neon was born and raised in Manila, Philippines. She is the youngest member of the VALORANT PROTOCOL who joined the team after inheriting bioelectricity abilities.
>
> Neon is voiced by Filipino voice actor Vanille Velasquez who is fluent in English, and Tagalog. Her fluency in Tagalog allowed her to incorporate many words and phrases into Neon's voice lines like:
>
> "Ingat ka" (be careful), "Tara na" (Let's go), "lola" (grandma), "Tabla tayo" (we're even),
>
> "Tapos ka na!" (You're done!) and many more.

With the amount of Tagalog lines, words, and phrases incorporated into Neon's character, she represents the Philippines well.

MAP 107

In the example above, Sarah describes the character's full name and alias in the game, her place of birth, and a bit of other game-related information about the character. The entry continues by listing the voice actor for this character, the languages she can speak, and some examples of non-English language that is spoken by the voice actor/character in the game. Based on the information she has been able to find and post here, Sarah concludes with a summative evaluation of the quality of the representation of the Philippines in the game based on how authentic the character's voice is via the voice actor. Unlike the neutral approach to a topic like in Cody's project, Sarah uses evidence from the game and from outside research about the voice actors to make a judgment statement about the voice actors cast to speak for the game characters, clearly taking the stance that diversity in game characters is a positive attribute. The project's evaluative statements go a step further to imply that authenticity in character diversity, especially in matching the home countries of the voice actors to the game characters, is important.

The third undergraduate student example, "Microplastic and Macroplastic Global Distribution," was created by Taylor Rice.[6] The project begins with a definition of microplastics and macroplastics, then provides an introductory page titled "Plastic Pollution Emissions (by Country)." This page adds context to the map and to its sources, stating, "from data collected in 2019, pinpoints on this map depicted in orange or yellow will show locations that emit the highest amounts of plastic waste into the world's oceans."

This page continues in a carefully neutral tone, warning the reader against hasty conclusions:

Plastic production and mismanagement aside, these countries' geographical locations aid in the flow of plastic distribution into oceans across the

6 Accessible at this link: https://earth.google.com/earth/d/1xL0rED_o8MNc5FzrR eJvdph2iJimIMaj?usp=sharing

globe. Whether plastic waste is well managed or not in these locations, it's far easier for plastics (especially microplastics, which are often too hard to see with the naked eye) to—accidentally or on purpose—make their way into flowing water due to geographical layout.

After this informational text, the map moves on to take the viewer on a tour of countries that have emitted the highest levels of plastic waste as of 2019, according to Taylor's sources (Boucher and Friot; Ritchie and Roser; Shim et al.). After touring the six highest contributors to the ocean's plastics, the map displays the United States, with this text:

> For the purpose of putting our current location into perspective, the **United States** is ranked lower on this list with a contributing percentage of 0.25% in 2019.
>
> Though this number appears small, please keep in mind that even if the U.S. isn't the top most country for production/emission of plastics, there is still a large amount of plastics ending up within the region's waterways regardless. This can be due to numerous reasons such as mismanaging waste collection, influx of discarding microplastics, accidental loss of plastic waste during transport of exports, etc.

The map then moves to focus on the oceans themselves, with an informative text screen explaining that microplastics were more difficult to measure and thus likely excluded from the data. The map continues by describing the three oceans with the highest amount of macroplastics, and then the viewer arrives at a page titled "Let's Talk About Sources." Taylor continues in an informal, conversational tone, "By now, I bet you're beginning to wonder what exactly are the main sources of these plastics that are making their way into the oceans." The page continues with facts and quotations directly from the three sources, overlaid on a chart of sources of ocean microplastics. The concluding screen explains the research findings in a matter-of-fact way:

MAP 109

Asia is the highest contributor to plastic pollutions in the world's oceans, especially due to the islands being surrounded by water/having rivers throughout the region.

The Mediterranean Sea and North Pacific Ocean are the regions with the highest abundance of microplastics and macroplastics.

Taylor's tone continues to be one that is free of accusatory language towards any single country or industry. This type of tone may be helpful in engaging an audience with preconceived notions about plastics and pollution, and informs without taking a polarizing stance, but again the tone of the project will vary by topic, message, and maker.

Futures

Extensions of the place and space project with the Google suite include asking students to create more than one layer of the same area, and comparing and contrasting the stories they tell. Even modifying labels on existing map layers could call into question frameworks and systems that we often ignore or perceive to be neutral. Juxtaposing street views can be embedded within another tool to add depth to a critical statement.

Additional tools that a place/space unit could use include ArcGIS tools, as mentioned above, or others. Open-source StoryMapJS and JuxtaposeJS were developed by Northwestern University's Knight Lab ("Knight Lab"). Their page includes a range of additional tools for creating interesting digital humanities projects. Another open-source tool that uses elements of TimelineJS to allow users to create maps from tables in Google Sheets is called TimeMapper (Open Knowledge Foundation Labs), explained in a Loyola Marymount University blog post (Hubbard). The range of how location-based data can be displayed and considered continues to grow with new technologies and

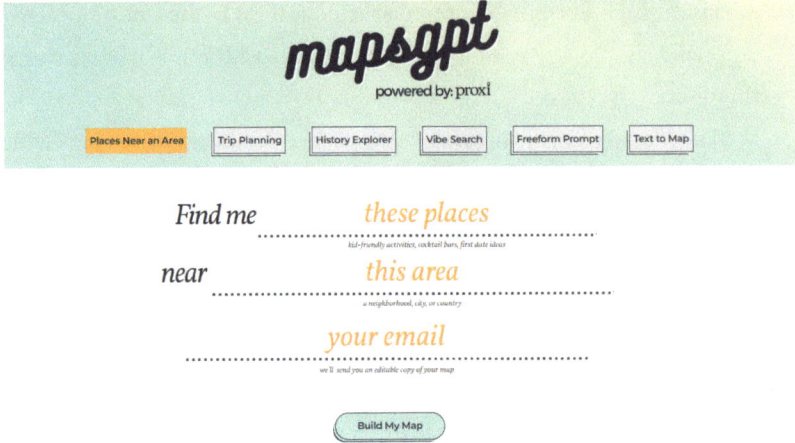

Figure 3: MapsGPT Vibe Search.

tools, and we encourage our students to explore and share with us new tools they find and use throughout our courses.

As with all things AI, as we write this book, tools leveraging these technologies continue to emerge and evolve. One AI-powered mapping tool is MapsGPT (see Figure 3),[7] which has the user fill in the following blanks: "Find me ____ near ____." It does not require an account to sign up, but does require an email address. Additional options include trip planning, history explorer, vibe search, freeform prompt, and text to map. AI at this early stage is almost sure to return incomplete results, therefore likely to produce a compelling critical statement about what and who gets included and excluded.

As AI technology and tools become more ubiquitous, it is likely that they will become more accurate, or at least have less obviously missing data. They do have the potential, however, to become helpful tools for critical making projects.[8]

---

7   www.mapsgpt.com/
8   Available at https://earth.google.com/earth/d/16YTE3MbL6EG6NF-tWpTYx_iGi 6XOU2mA?usp=sharing

MAP   111

Works Cited

Abbey-Lambertz, Kate. "Watch Detroit Neighborhoods Fall into Ruin with Google Street View." *HuffPost*, 26 Mar. 2016, www.huffpost.com/entry/goo gle-street-view-detroit-abandoned-homes-foreclosure_n_56f41be3e4b0c 3ef52183d4b.

"About Google Lit Trips." *GLT Global ED*, www.googlelittrips.org/aboutGLTGE/ aboutGLT.php. Accessed 6 Jan. 2023.

Alsup, Alex. "GooBing Detroit." *GooBing Detroit*, www.goobingdetroit.com/. Accessed 5 Jan. 2023.

Boucher, Julien, and Damien Friot. *Primary Microplastics in the Oceans*. 2017. *policycommons.net*, https://policycommons.net/artifacts/1373068/primary-microplastics-in-the-oceans/1987281/.

Derven, Caleb, and John Keating. "Modeling Place in Ulysses: Ontologies and Pre-Texts." *Digital Humanities 2017*, vol. Session 437, 2017.

D'Ignazio, Catherine, and Lauren Klein. "Data Feminism." *Data Feminism*, Mar. 2020. *data-feminism.mitpress.mit.edu*, https://data-feminism.mitpress.mit. edu/pub/ei7cogfn/release/4.

"Feminicidios En México." *Google My Maps*, www.google.com/maps/d/ viewer?mid=174IjBzP-fl_6wpRHg5pkGSj2egE. Accessed 4 Jan. 2023.

"Grapes Of Wrath." *Google My Maps*, 3 Jun. 2015, www.google.com/maps/d/ viewer?mid=1y1WysAoNA2xYLmev5z7AGOlBWDY.

Hillman, Nick. *Place Matters: A Closer Look at Education Deserts*. Third Way, 2019. *JSTOR*, www.jstor.org/stable/resrep41709.

Hubbard, Melanie. "Getting Started with Digital Tools: Voyant and TimeMapper." *LMU Library News*, 10 Sept. 2015, https://librarynews.lmu.edu/2015/09/ digital-humanities-using-timemapper-to-study-literature/.

"Knight Lab." *Northwestern University Knight Lab*, 31 Jan. 2023, https://knightlab. northwestern.edu/.

Liang, Jianming, et al. "Applications and Impacts of Google Earth: A Decadal Review (2006–2016)." *ISPRS Journal of Photogrammetry and Remote Sensing*, vol. 146, Dec. 2018, pp. 91–107. *ScienceDirect*, https://doi.org/10.1016/j. isprsjprs.2018.08.019.

Open Knowledge Foundation Labs. *TimeMapper*, https://timemapper.okfnlabs. org/. Accessed 30 Aug. 2023.

Ritchie, Hannah, and Max Roser. "Plastic Pollution." *Our World in Data*, Sept. 2018. *ourworldindata.org*, https://ourworldindata.org/plastic-pollution.

Sheehan, Patrick. *Revitalization by Gentrification*. https://jacobin.com/2015/05/ detroit-foreclosure-redlining-evictions/. Accessed 5 Jan. 2023.

Shim, Won Joon, et al. "Toward a Long-Term Monitoring Program for Seawater Plastic Pollution in the North Pacific Ocean: Review and Global Comparison." *Environmental Pollution*, vol. 311, Oct. 2022, p. 119911. *ScienceDirect*, https:// doi.org/10.1016/j.envpol.2022.119911.

"VALORANT." *Valorant Wiki*, https://valorant.fandom.com/wiki/VALORANT. Accessed 10 Feb. 2023.

"Why It Matters." *Native-Land.Ca*, https://native-land.ca/about/why-it-matters/. Accessed 11 Jan. 2023.

CHAPTER 5
Hypertext

As hypertext linking has become the default for content creation on the web, most scholarship still resists its capabilities. However, journals such as *Kairos: A Journal of Rhetoric, Technology, and Pedagogy*, *Computers and Composition Online*, and *The Digital Review* as well as hypertextual scholarship across humanities disciplines from authors such as Jay David Bolter, Chloe Milligan, Jim McGrath, Stuart Moulthrop, and Lee Skallerup Bessette blend influences from electronic literature with criticism, demonstrating the potential of embracing hypertext as a means of both creative expression and scholarly critique. Twine, an open-source platform for building hypertexts, offers a means to explore this type of making thanks to its capacity for constructing choice and argument; crafting autoethnography and reflection; and exploring through simulation and representation.

Critical Hypertext

In 1987, Jay David Bolter and Michael Joyce shared a tool for creating nonlinear novels, dubbed the Storyspace system, with the community at the very first ACM Hypertext conference. They described their new tool as a means for developing interactive fiction incorporating two elements: "episodes and decision points (links) between episodes" (Bolter and Joyce 42). Storyspace continues to be an available creative platform for hypertext to this day, although its cost and closed platform system has limited its use for the classroom and web-focused work: however, at the time of its introduction, it was the essential tool for making literary hypertext, and would capture the attention of novelists looking to imagine the future of the form (Bernstein). Even at the earliest stages in the history of hypertextual electronic literature, the potential for this type of work was exciting: a few years later, hypertext novelist and scholar Stuart Moulthrop pointed to 1987 as the "annus mirabilis of hypertext:" the year Apple's HyperCard would bring cheap hypertext authorship to a wide number of users; Ted Nelson's *Literary Machines* would inspire a greater hypertext imaginary; and of course academics were taking an interest (Moulthrop, "You Say You Want a Revolution?"). Platforms that would further democratize the web were still a few years away—GeoCities, the original home on the internet for many in our generation, would bring its websites for all community-driven model to the web in 1994—but the foundation was finally in place.

Arguably the first large-scale academic work to really take advantage of hypertext's potential was Jay David Bolter's own *Writing Space*, a text now generally taught through its printed book form—a fundamental loss to the work's experience and intention. Writing a few years later, Bolter captured some of the scholarly enthusiasm for hypertext:

> Hypertext suggests new kinds of collective works, and in suggesting new kinds of text, hypertext compels us to reconsider the relationship among the text, the author, and the reader. The computer as hypertext raises fundamental questions of literary theory because it undermines both the fixity of the text and the authority of the author.
>
> (Bolter 10)

Why begin the discussion of hypertext at this moment in the 1980s and 1990s? In part because, even in these early iterations, hypertext was already at the center of imaginations of the future—indeed, Bolter and Joyce were already addressing the potential of AI to transform these systems of choice and authorship in their talk in 1987. Over these 30-plus years, hypertext has moved from novelty to default, and yet it is in the process of being continually flattened: to recall Nick Sousanis's term, the desire to recreate normative forms and structures has continually undermined the potential for "unflattening" that hypertext might hold (Sousanis, *Unflattening*). This is in part a testament to a collective desire for scholarship that can be archived, accessed, and entrusted to print: the monograph remains the default of scholarly societies, despite the efforts of organizations like MLA to promote guidelines for supporting born-digital scholarship—guidelines which note that "born-digital and Web-based projects are often spatial, interactive, iterative, and networked. If possible, they should be viewed in electronic form, not in print or as snapshots of dynamic behavior" (MLA Committee on Information Technology). Written in 2000 and revised in 2012, these guidelines are still more aspirational than commonplace, as anyone who has ever tried to compile a PDF (or worse, print) dossier for tenure or promotion is painfully aware.

These tensions also reflect the challenges of the archive, as the history of hypertext is filled with losses and gaps. While creative works by Stuart Moulthrop, Deena Larsen, Judy Malloy, and many more shaped the experimental landscape of early hypertext novels, those same novels would be rendered unplayable over time, subject to intensive efforts to either document—as with Dene Grigar and Stuart Moulthrop's Traversals and Pathfinders projects (Grigar and Moulthrop)—or recreate, as with Moulthrop's recently rebuilt *Victory Garden* (Moulthrop, "Victory Garden 2022"). Tools built on proprietary platforms have suffered the most, and similar challenges have rendered the full history of hypertextual scholarship difficult to access. The *Kairos* Preservation

Project team notes that the preservation of scholarly webtexts is complicated by the questions raised by these works:

> What should be preserved, and how can we preserve it? What is critical to
> the preservation of a born-digital text? Words, images, navigation, links?
> These questions require critical examination of how digital publications
> enact their contributions to disciplinary conversations and what we consider essential to the integrity of a digital text.
>
> (Lockridge et al.)

These questions are also the questions to ask when setting out to create a scholarly webtext, questions that push authors to think about the materiality of our works even if they can prove daunting. This is perhaps key to why most scholars still do not submit born-digital texts to nearly any academic journal: flattening offers us an ease of access even if it erases meaning in the process. Bolter's print version of *Writing Space* is, after all, the version Anastasia assigns in their media history classes, as no other iteration remains reliable and usable.

However, born-digital essays have maintained their significance on the web, with renewed interest in the form driving shifts in publication standards. In 2020, the newly-launched *The Digital Review* opened its first issue with a call to reclaim the digital essay, noting the form's historical significance on the web:

> In this inaugural issue of *The Digital Review*, the editors have curated a
> collection of works that help us recover a mode of digital writing that was
> prominent in the early days of the web: the born-digital essay. The revival
> of this multi-modal essayism is central to this journal's creation in 2020.
> It is an effort to bring back attention to the personal, idiosyncratic, provocative and experimental forms that fuse "the digital"—discrete, deterministic, algorithmic, constrained—with "the essayistic"—digressive,
> liminal, wavering, exploratory.
>
> (Luers)

The key framing of the digital essay as "personal" is a strong reminder of what has been lost in the structures of Web 2.0 and beyond. Consider the difference between a Facebook page or an essay on The Medium and an old-school web manifesto: the control over the stylesheet, format, and structure has frequently been ceded to a publishing template, offering "users" only the most limited influence over the aesthetics of the web.

The born-digital essay has remained as an artifact of intention and a tool for digital reflection: one of our personal favorites is Paul Ford's "What is Code?", a work particularly relevant to Twine structures and practices that unfolds with embedded animation, interaction, and code itself (Ford). The argument is in line with some of the methods familiar from Nick Sousanis or Scott McCloud's work in image-text, as previously discussed in Chapter 2: that is to say, the form is inherent to the argument, and the illustrations serve to shape the meaning as much as (if not occasionally more than) the text.

It should thus be no surprise that some of the early examples of this type of play are also from Scott McCloud: his series entitled "I Can't Stop Thinking," published from 2000 to 2001 and shown (Figure 1) on the summary page from his website, embodies a fusion of comic and hypertext that McCloud called the "infinite canvas" (Scott McCloud, "I Can't Stop Thinking: 2000–2001"). McCloud's concept is an exploration of the web's visual potential, but it is also inherently a means to explore the nonlinear: if a comic can, in virtual space, move in any direction, it can also defy the ordering principles of a page.

These early works foreshadow other infinite canvas experiments, such as Jason Shiga's *Meanwhile*: a work that begins with a choice of ice cream flavor, and spirals quickly in every direction, which was compiled for print using a tabular system to track the connections between screens (Shiga). In one of the installments, Scott McCloud introduces the term "trail-based comics," suggesting that they allow for an escape

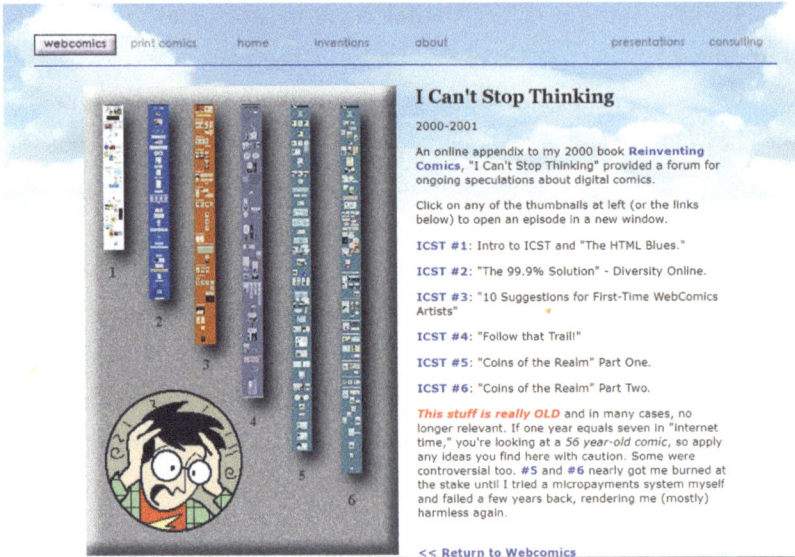

Figure 1: Scott McCloud's overview page with his "I Can't Stop Thinking" experiments.

from "the old left-to-right and up-to-down protocol of traditional printed comics" (McCloud, "I Can't Stop Thinking! #4").

Similarly, Whitney Trettien's dissertation (shown in Figure 2) offers a multi-directional expanding hypertext, using a series of cards that both chronicle and comment upon the practices of combinatory literature and text generation (Trettien). Trettien's method of linking works in unexpected ways while keeping the previous passages visible, allowing the reader to effectively read across those passages to think through the links and decisions—what Trettien refers to as the "art of combination."

Chapter 3's discussion of GIFs and Chapter 4's discussion of mapping each offered starting patterns to take advantage of the "born-digital" web. Twine extends this work to engage the foundational technologies of the web: HTML, CSS, and JavaScript, a trinity of languages that serve to shape the user experience of most websites students encounter. These languages of the native web have thus far

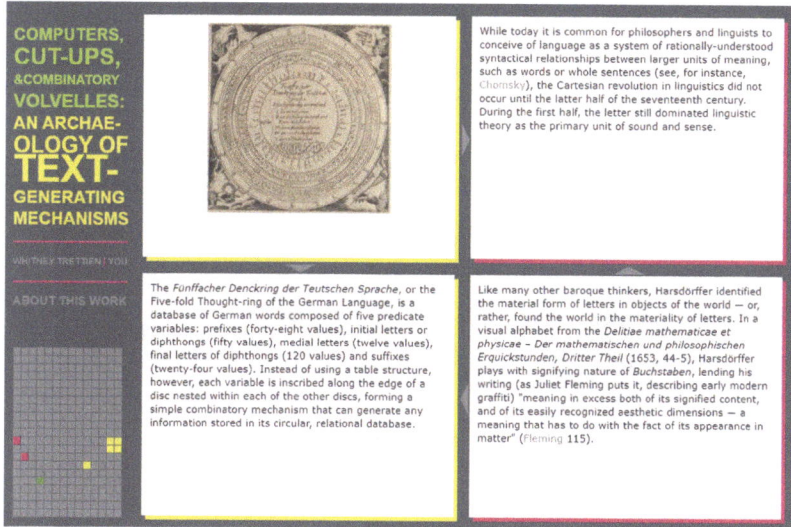

The figure contains the following text panels:

COMPUTERS, CUT-UPS, &COMBINATORY VOLVELLES: AN ARCHAE-OLOGY OF TEXT-GENERATING MECHANISMS

WHITNEY TRETTIEN / YOU

ABOUT THIS WORK

While today it is common for philosophers and linguists to conceive of language as a system of rationally-understood syntactical relationships between larger units of meaning, such as words or whole sentences (see, for instance, Chomsky), the Cartesian revolution in linguistics did not occur until the latter half of the seventeenth century. During the first half, the letter still dominated linguistic theory as the primary unit of sound and sense.

The *Fünffacher Denckring der Teutschen Sprache*, or the Five-fold Thought-ring of the German Language, is a database of German words composed of five predicate variables: prefixes (forty-eight values), initial letters or diphthongs (fifty values), medial letters (twelve values), final letters of diphthongs (120 values) and suffixes (twenty-four values). Instead of using a table structure, however, each variable is inscribed along the edge of a disc nested within each of the other discs, forming a simple combinatory mechanism that can generate any information stored in its circular, relational database.

Like many other baroque thinkers, Harsdörffer identified the material form of letters in objects of the world — or, rather, found the world in the materiality of letters. In a visual alphabet from the *Delitiae mathematicae et physicae – Der mathematischen und philosophischen Erquickstunden, Dritter Theil* (1653, 44-5), Harsdörffer plays with signifying nature of *Buchstaben*, lending his writing (as Juliet Fleming puts it, describing early modern graffiti) "meaning in excess both of its signified content, and of its easily recognized aesthetic dimensions — a meaning that has to do with the fact of its appearance in matter" (Fleming 115).

Figure 2: Whitney Trettien's combinatory, expanding dissertation on text generation.

proven resistant to the cycles of replacement and deprecation that have taken most other platforms, although as the *Kairos* Preservation team notes, even that is no guarantee with changing HTML validation checks, accessibility standards, and support (Lockridge et al.). Our next platform is grounded in this language trinity and allows us to build works with as much resilience as the native web can offer while simplifying the process of creation and allowing us to focus on shaping the work's meaning: Twine. Twine's editing screen is its own form of infinite canvas, offering a portal for exploring the potential of the web for ever-expanding creations.

Anastasia has written about Twine at length elsewhere (Salter and Moulthrop), speaking to Twine's enduring accessibility as an entry point to nonlinear making. However, in most of those conversations, Twine is introduced first as a tool for creative rather than critical work. The popularity of Twine with creators seeking to make games or interactive fiction is immediately clear: it has been adopted in industry prototyping and used to make games available on both Steam and itch.io, two important marketplaces for game distribution on the web. Twine's own description emphasizes its use for "telling interactive, nonlinear stories" ("Twine"), a phrasing that recalls a connection to the history of Nelson's "literary machines" (Nelson). Scholarly webtexts, on the other hand, have been defined by Cheryl Ball (long-time editor of *Kairos* and advocate for multimodal scholarship) as "research-based artifacts that enact an author's scholarly argument through a web-based design" (Ball 53). This inclusive definition opens the door to a wide range of technologies and design choices, but the form must be meaningful, as Ball notes as a key aspect of journal criteria for publication: "A webtext cannot be printed without losing its argument" (Ball 55).

Twine does not at first appear to be an ideal tool for making scholarly webtexts. It does not include mechanisms for citations, and many of its features are patterned around storytelling. However, this emphasis on storytelling can lead to compelling experiences. Several scholars have made compelling use of the personal storytelling aspects of the platform, such as Lee Skallerup Bessette's reflexive hypertext "Moving In and Out of Time," published in *Kairos* (Bessette). Bessette's work is one of only a few pieces published in *Kairos* to make use of Twine: another is Anastasia's own experiment *Alice in Dataland*, which takes a personal, critical making-fused approach to thinking through Alice's influence on the web (Salter).

Bessette's hypertext exemplifies the unprintable, integrating audio to emphasize the experience of ADHD alongside a "self-interview" structure that includes reflexive passages making visible the process of writing, in Figure 3.

In another passage, Bessette notes that she "hated Choose Your Own Adventure books growing up," because of the constant dead ends of wrong choices—her argument here is grounded in the opposite approach, "bringing everything into the narrative, to give as full access as I can to my writing and my ADHD mind" (Bessette). Here, Twine's affordances are brought to the forefront with a minimalist

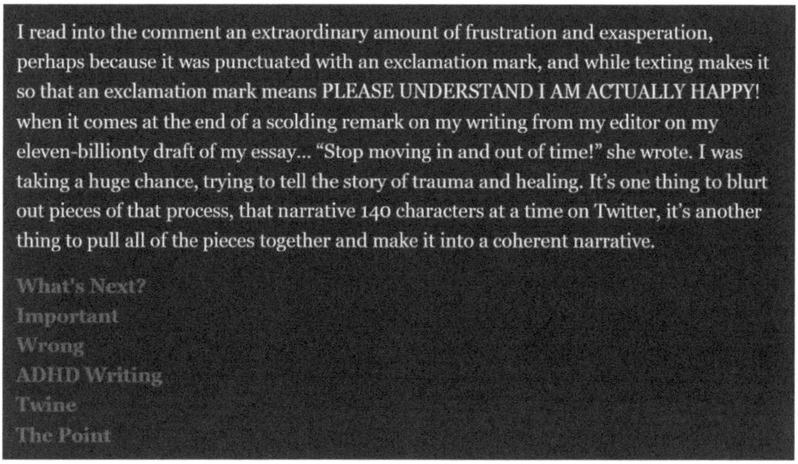

> I read into the comment an extraordinary amount of frustration and exasperation, perhaps because it was punctuated with an exclamation mark, and while texting makes it so that an exclamation mark means PLEASE UNDERSTAND I AM ACTUALLY HAPPY! when it comes at the end of a scolding remark on my writing from my editor on my eleven-billionty draft of my essay... "Stop moving in and out of time!" she wrote. I was taking a huge chance, trying to tell the story of trauma and healing. It's one thing to blurt out pieces of that process, that narrative 140 characters at a time on Twitter, it's another thing to pull all of the pieces together and make it into a coherent narrative.
>
> What's Next?
> Important
> Wrong
> ADHD Writing
> Twine
> The Point

Figure 3: Bessette's passages often feature stream of consciousness.

approach to the making process: many of the essential elements of Bessette's hypertext, such as the return button and the passage structure, are easily created in Twine without diving into the procedural layer. Throughout, hypertext's historical linkage with the representation of the mind and consciousness as brought forth by N. Katherine Hayles's work is made visible, demonstrating the potential for representing neurodivergent experience in the academy through interactivity (Hayles).

That same issue of *Kairos* contains "basic coding," a piece by Stephen Quigley that exposes its underlying code that laments our increased reliance on the interface:

> We find solace in UI design, entrusting it with our functions, which it performs in real-time, at distances that can crisscross continents. It does for us. Makes for us. Knows for us. But while UI design increases usability, it both distances us from the code that performs our functions and the technical literacies we must promote if we wish to attend to the digital divide.
>
> (Quigley)

Twine is a bridge between what Quigley describes as UI design, or making with an interface, and making through code: it is not, as has occasionally been claimed, a tool that eliminates code, but it does simplify its structures and offers a strong starting point for hypertextual making.

This approach offers a means to explore three aspects of hypertextual scholarship's potential: choice and argument; autoethnography and reflection; and simulation and representation. Since branching hypertext allows for links with different valances and direction, interactive essays can employ those choices for emphasis and as part of the scholarly framework. Jim McGrath's "Insufficient Memories" offers an example of this in action as part of an exhibition on memory and materiality where the user is prompted to delete digital objects without full knowledge of their contents and subjected to the erasures of the algorithm (McGrath). Chloe Milligan's "En(Twine)d with Ergodic Rhetoric" employs choice as a means of interrogating the platform itself: the work is in part a call to use the mechanisms of Twine towards "a nonlinear pedagogy...requiring instructor and student alike to interact alongside one another with the composition process in ways that require more embodied participation, more active engagement, and more ergodic play" (Milligan).

Opportunities for autoethnography and reflection in Twine are exemplified by works like Lee Skallerup Bessette's Twine representation of ADHD. This practice is deeply embedded in the Twine tradition: Dietrich Squinkifer's "Impostor Syndrome" uses Twine to place the reader in the position of a conference speaker dealing with increasing audience responses to something going on in social media: the speaker is constantly given the choice as whether to press on, or not (Squinkifer). Fundamental challenges of being present in a gender-marginalized body in tech are brought out through the increasing tension of the choices. Similarly, Cait S. Kirby's series of COVID-19-inspired games capture the academic stress of a moment: the first, September 7, 2020, speaks to the tensions of the return to campus in fall 2020—a time in which every choice felt loaded, and many others were outside of individual control as each institution managed its own response to the pandemic (Kirby).

Kirby's work also takes advantage of an important aspect of Twine that is shared with the worldbuilding structures of games: the capacity for simulation and representation. Twine offers the means for building on a dataset or an area of study in a way that invites the reader to share the experience. As Cait S. Kirby's work is motivated by this type of data-driven representation of reopening policies as well as by autoethnography and reflection, it offers a reminder that many of these elements overlap and intersect in practice. Carly Kocurek and Allyson Whipple's *Choice: Texas* similarly is not built in Twine, but it uses Twine-like mechanics and hypertext structures with similar intent (Kocurek and Whipple). It's also a work that has become even more harrowing to revisit, as it depicts the challenges of abortion access—an updated version would have to deal with nearly insurmountable issues. The most famous Twine creation to date is a work of fiction but also a work of critique: Zoe Quinn's *Depression Quest*, which played a major role in culture wars too vast for discussion here, dives powerfully into the experience of living with depression by representing the challenges of making the right choices without treatment and support (Quinn).

Many of these works engage at a metalevel with the construction of an essay, and through their modality invite us to rethink our expectations. Emma Kostopolus's "Let's Play This Article: A Heuristic for Digital Games and Materiality," published in *Computers and Composition*'s special issue on "Making Games Matter: Games and Materiality," opens with a false choice and explores each mindset:

Do you want to play a game?

Yes

No, I want to read an article

(Kostopolus)

Similarly, Stuart Moulthrop's "The Hypertext Years?" invites the reader into an experience that is "simultaneously essay, talk, and hypertext built in Twine" (Moulthrop, "The Hypertext Years?" 219). Structured with passages that capture moments in time and including audio clips as a significant element (as with Bessette's work), the piece plays itself, embedding generation and humor with asides like "Being esoteric, beans exoteric." Thanks to Twine's affordances, the user can also unpack that generation by diving under the surface and opening the .html file back in the Twine editor—its structures are as visible as the scholarly output.

The variety among these works also reminds us that Twine is a powerful meta-platform: it can be used to incorporate elements of other making. While it offers us a textual default, Twine can easily expand to include images, animation, audio, image-text, and other types of procedural content (including embedded works created using some of the other patterns throughout this book.) Since Twine exports to .html, it builds works that don't rely upon any special system to compile or interpret—this lack of extensive dependencies is one of the best markers of a sustainable tool.

Twine is a flexible authoring platform that is useful for novices and seasoned coders alike. Students can begin with the simple sets of instructions in the user-friendly Harlowe version, then build in additional features by adding code in JavaScript and formatting .css stylesheets. The pattern suggests taking students through two stages, beginning with a physical prototype before moving into code. The physical prototype uses index cards and string, with string serving to represent the "links" between passages on different cards. Obviously, this method cannot replicate a complex computational choice—it doesn't allow for the addition of variables controlling choices, and it fundamentally marks a simple action (a click) without much nuance. This is in part what makes it ideal for prototyping a first nonlinear text: it encourages simplicity and clarity at the stage of imagining, and helps students think about scope visually.

Working with this type of materiality also allows students to step back and think about the limitations of the traditional page: just as Scott McCloud's passages take advantage of the ability to move in any direction behind the window of a browser, so too can the materiality of a hypertext theoretically take readers on as many paths less traveled as an author can imagine. Working physically asks students to take on constraints and notice when a thread is getting out of control—it encourages students to work in patterns that return to central nodes, rather than try to construct paths that would quickly exceed the available space of a classroom table. The first stage of the pattern can be omitted for a shorter lesson or workshop.

The second stage of the pattern uses Harlowe, Twine's current default format. Note that Twine story formats are very different in their code.

Pattern: Twine

Hypertext is, fundamentally, linked text: the structure of the link is the most meaningful innovation the web offers us, as it offers both a way of crafting internal structures and external connections that can be immediately realized. You interact with hypertext all the time, primarily through browsers and social media platforms. In this pattern, you'll be making a hypertext using a free tool, Twine, in two stages: a physical prototype followed by a playable hypertext.

As you work on the physical prototype and the hypertext itself, think about how to:

- **Focus on compelling choices.** You don't need to have lots of branches, but a few branches can be a way to dive deeper into an idea or to present contrasting or conflicting views. Instead of giving the user minor decisions, try creating just a few branching paths with significant differences.

- **Connect with your reader.** Twine is often used to create very personal hypertexts that invite readers into the author's experiences, research, or stories. In this form of writing, it can often make sense to use "I" and "You" to build the hypertext as a conversation between you and the reader.
- **Experiment with design.** Twine's editor includes many familiar options for trying out color, font style, and other design elements in the browser. Try using those to vary your passages and add emphasis to different sections of the text.

Stage One: Physical Prototype

Twine works in links and passages: links provide the navigation, while passages display the text and other elements for the reader to engage. To design your own hypertext using these foundational elements, you'll need notecards, string, and tape. This method follows the example of Deena Larsen's shower curtain (Figure 4), an artifact now held in the MITH archives (Larsen). By working with notecards and twine,

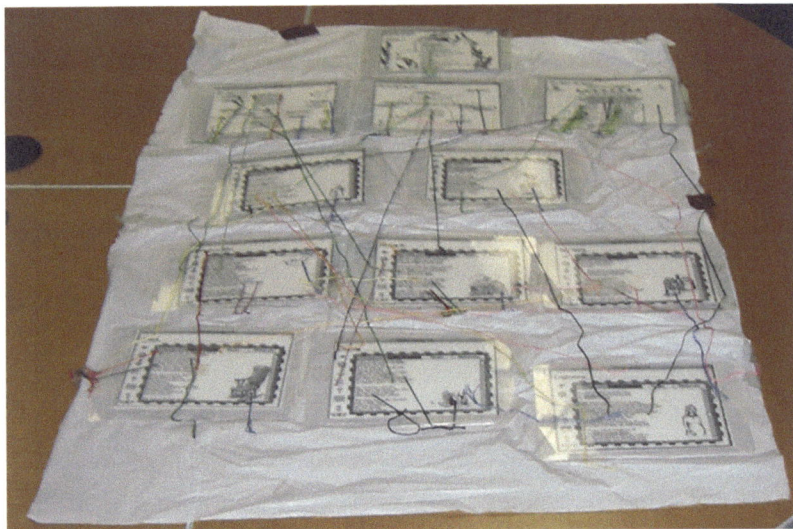

Figure 4: Deena Larsen's shower curtain method of hypertext planning.

you can plan out your idea and think about key decision points (the yarn acts as the "twine" connecting passages).

Mark one index card with a star—this will be the first screen your reader sees, so it should introduce the project and provide context for what follows. Links from that passage can move through linear sections (where passages must be seen to continue) or they can start branches (where readers might only see one possible route moving forward).

Every passage should have a unique title: for simplicity, label your first card "Start." You'll use the titles to keep track of the links in your hypertext. Remember you'll also need a name for your project.

Physically, the use of thread and tape between cards allows for some precision: you should tape your thread to the word, phrase, or choice that might lead in one direction versus another. Build your prototype with the goal of having at least one complete path, with a sense of an ending and closure. Remember, all your index cards will need to be connected to something: a passage that doesn't have a link in Twine will be completely inaccessible to the reader.

Stage Two: Hypertext with Twine

Navigate to **twinery.org** in any computer's web browser to set up Twine for the first time. If you are using your own computer, you can download and install Twine by selecting **"Download desktop app"** on the main menu. However, if you can't install software on the computer you are using, you can select **"Use in your browser."** This pattern assumes you are using the browser version: however, the interface is nearly identical.

Start by selecting **"+New"** to create a new project, and name it with the name of your project you decided on during the physical prototype. After you've typed and confirmed the name, the main editing screen (Figure 5) will load. Note that Twine isn't a hosting service, so when you're working online make sure to select the

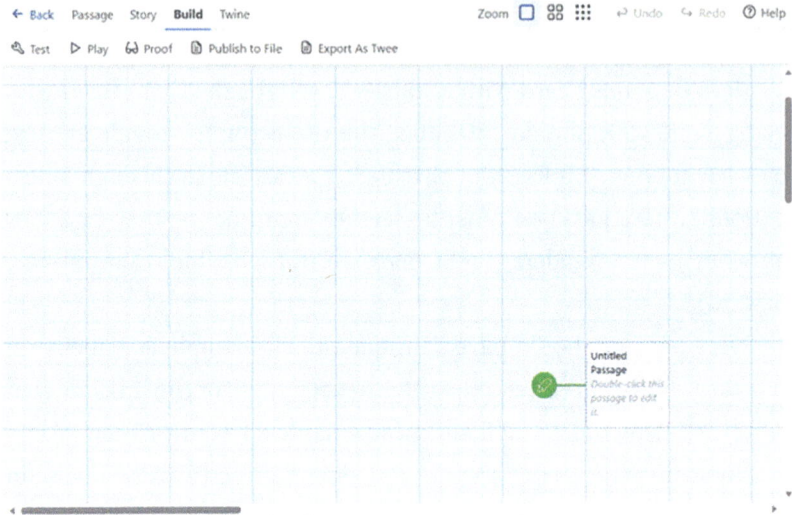

Figure 5: The main story editing menu of Twine, with the build options for exporting the file.

option to **"Publish to file"** (under **"Build"** in the story menu) frequently to save your work.

There are several advanced options that you can ignore for now, including the choice of story format: stick with the default, Harlowe. Double click on the start passage (marked with the green rocket ship) to add the text of your first index card from the prototype. Select **"Rename"** to change to the title of your first card (Start) and type the contents of your first index card in the main editing box.

Next, add all the links to your Start passage by putting square brackets around the text you marked with your thread. Follow your threads on the physical prototype to check the names of the passages they link to. Links will follow the syntax: [[**text to click on->Passage Name**]].

When you use this structure, the links will display the initial phrase (before the ->) and lead to the passage named in the second half of the link (after the ->). This will allow you to have different phrases that link the reader to the same passage, as shown in this sample code:

> We might [[say one thing->phrase of significance]] and [[mean another->
> another passage]]—we can even include multiple links that appear different
> but lead to the [[same place->another passage]].

The editing interface also includes options to style your text (shown in Figure 6): these work similarly to any text editor, with options for text styling, colors, and alignment. Try experimenting with those as you add in the rest of your index cards. Every time you add a link to a passage with a title you haven't created yet, the passage will pop up with that title, as shown.

You can test the project as you go by selecting **"Play"** under the Build menu (shown in Figure 5.) When the project is complete, you can share it with others by selecting **"Publish to file"**: this will allow you to save a complete .html file, viewable in any browser.

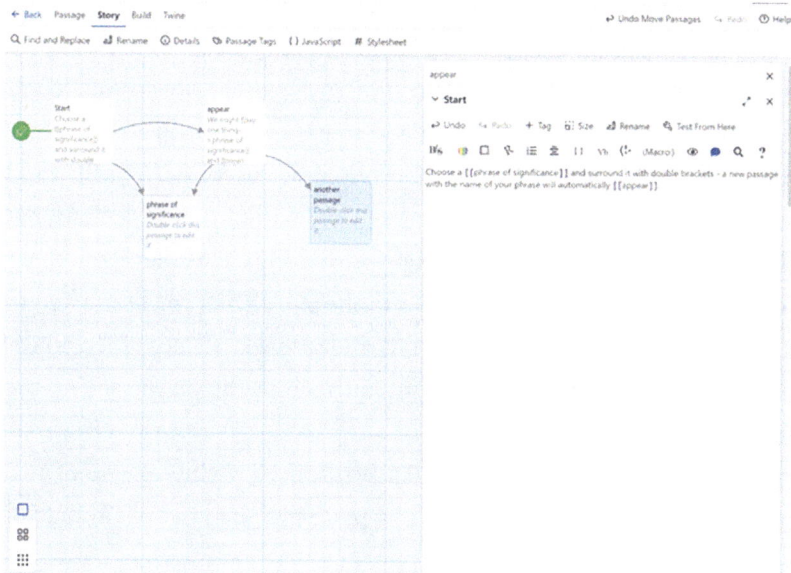

Figure 6: The Twine editor, showing this project in development.

Applications

Twine's layered potential for both rapid work and complexity lends itself to a wide range of student making, both in the classroom and in thesis and dissertation projects. Laura Okkema's Twine-based dissertation, produced under Anastasia's supervision in the Texts and Technology PhD program, culminated in "The Deserters," a hypertextual work combining digital archiving with personal storytelling included in *The Electronic Literature Collection Volume 4*. The work is based on Okkema's approach to "activist critical making," which centers design justice and self-reflection in the making of technology (Okkema, "The Deserters"). As Okkema writes in an introduction to the piece, "Twine offers a unique environment for composing politically impactful personal narrative" (Okkema, "'The Deserters:' Activist Critical Making in Electronic Literature" 193). An undergraduate, Sarah Scalisi, created *Only a Prank*[1] to place the reader in the position of a cyberbully, drawing on a similar emotional focus as many of the pieces discussed in this chapter. Sarah conducted research on cyberbullying as part of her project and explains in the accompanying abstract, "I use an interactive storyline to showcase how online communications can start as a harmless prank and develop to cyberbullying as well as some of the serious consequences for both bullies and their victims." The story presents the player with different options, but they are all forms of cyberbullying—preventing the reader from making choices that do not cause harm to the story's victim. This acted to keep the scope reigned in for Sarah and allowed all possible choices to result in the same, negative consequence for the player: losing the friend.

Another graduate student, Alex Boyd, used Twine as one of two platforms in the making of "Trail," a piece included in the Climate of

---

1   Playable at: https://sarahgivesyouwings.itch.io/only-a-prank

Change virtual exhibition as part of ACM Hypertext 2020 (Boyd)—the same conference where Storyspace was shared in 1987. Boyd used Twine as a mechanism for reflecting on the conditions of the National Park System and particularly portions of the Florida Trail during the pandemic. Throughout the piece, the player can explore the different trails and encounter reflections on the safety concerns, budget cuts, and sense of loss overwhelming these spaces. The other half of the piece uses Bitsy, a tool for minimalist, visual, web game platform we'll explore in Chapter 6.

Several of our graduate students have recently collaborated on an effort to expand Twine's capacities for thinking through locative and multimodal storytelling: the story format is now available, and supports adding 3D objects and experimenting with mixed reality (Cox et al.). As the team described in their talk at the International Conference on Interactive Digital Storytelling, another venue where Twine has frequently been embraced, the goal of the project is to "meaningfully center casual development" in a way that makes critical making experiments in this format more feasible (Berge et al.).

One excellent starting point for a critical webtext is an abstract for an unfinished thought: a conference paper that never materialized; a journal proposal with too many directions; or simply a set of notes that holds unrealized potential. This type of work can be a place to play with connections and directions, and a means for using Twine as a mindmap—a return to the type of connection hypertext scholar N. Kate Hayles has always made between the hypertextual and the cognitive. One colleague has even assigned Twine to their graduate students in an introductory course, requiring students to link passages of notes on assigned texts to one another in a way that brought out the scholarly contexts of the different arguments.

Twine has also been deployed in the undergraduate classroom: Shawn Graham uses it as part of exploring digital history, bringing Twine into his syllabus as a tool for building representations of real-world objects, buildings, or sites (Graham). Kevin Kee and Graham discuss the success of this approach in the university classroom as placing the focus on "gaming of the game," moving students away from playing games as history to thinking through the construction of historical representations through code (Kee and Graham).

One reason we like Twine for our courses is that it can span a wide range of authorial options. It can allow novices with no coding skills to create interesting, complex interactive narratives using the built-in tools. Students can even select the link function from a dropdown menu in Twine and avoid having to type the double brackets entirely. However, students who are experienced in (or interested in learning) coding can add a variety of technical functions to their narratives including scoring elements, inventories, unlocking new story elements by uncovering a key, and more. Rather than attempting to instruct all students on all aspects of the tool, however, we encourage them to tinker and explore within the platform as well as across the internet because digital literacy increasingly includes the ability to search for specific resources as needed.

Futures

The future possibilities and pitfalls of generative AI in hypertext authorship are particularly on display in AI Dungeon, which imitates a parser-based, or chat-like, hypertext fiction game that attempts to remember variables and provide some generated narrative consistency (Hua and Raley). While the platform has attracted users through its vastness and novelty, the applications of AI for this type of work are more likely to be compelling as part of authoring tools themselves. Christy Tucker has experimented with using ChatGPT to build a branching Twine work, and while the results are fairly generic and repetitive, the results do demonstrate the usefulness of these models in prototyping (Tucker). Similarly, students can try using large-language models to add more complexity to their Twine projects through code assist, as discussed in more detail in Chapter 9.

Works Cited

Ball, Cheryl E. "The Shifting Genres of Scholarly Multimedia: Webtexts As Innovation." *The Journal of Media Innovations*, vol. 3, no. 2, Dec. 2016, pp. 52–71. *journals-test.uio.no*, https://doi.org/10.5617/jmi.v3i2.2548.

Berge, PS, et al. "Adventures in TwineSpace: An Augmented Reality Story Format for Twine." *Interactive Storytelling: 15th International Conference on Interactive Digital Storytelling, ICIDS 2022, Santa Cruz, CA, USA, December 4-7, 2022, Proceedings*, Springer-Verlag, 2022, pp. 499–512. *ACM Digital Library*, https://doi.org/10.1007/978-3-031-22298-6_32.

Bernstein, Mark. "Storyspace 1." *Proceedings of the Thirteenth ACM Conference on Hypertext and Hypermedia*, Association for Computing Machinery, 2002, pp. 172–81. *ACM Digital Library*, https://doi.org/10.1145/513338.513383.

Bessette, Lee Skallerup. "Moving In and Out of Time." *26.2*, Jan. 2021. *kairos. technorhetoric.net*, https://kairos.technorhetoric.net/26.2/interviews/besse tte/index.html.

Bolter, Jay David. "Authors and Readers in an Age of Electronic Texts." *Literary Texts in an Electronic Age: Scholarly Implications and Library Services [Papers Presented at the 1994 Clinic on Library Applications of Data Processing, April 10-12, 1994]*, 1994. *www.ideals.illinois.edu*, https://hdl.handle.net/2142/387.

Bolter, Jay David, and Michael Joyce. "Hypertext and Creative Writing." *Proceeding of the ACM Conference on Hypertext—HYPERTEXT '87*, ACM Press, 1987, pp. 41–50. *ACM Digital Library*, https://doi.org/10.1145/317 426.317431.

Boyd, Alex. "Trail." *Climates of Change Exhibition: ACM HT 2020*, Jul. 2020, https://projects.cah.ucf.edu/mediaartsexhibits/ClimatesOfChange/Boyd/ boyd.html.

Cox, Daniel, et al. *TwineSpace: A Twine 2 Story Format Supporting 3D Models and Mixed Reality Projects*. 1.0.0, Zenodo, 27 Jul. 2022, https://doi.org/10.5281/ ZENODO.6915351.

Ford, Paul. "What Is Code? If You Don't Know, You Need to Read This." *Bloomberg.Com*, www.bloomberg.com/graphics/2015-paul-ford-what-is-code/. Accessed 2 May 2023.

Graham, Shawn. *HIST3812 Winter 2018 Critical Digital Making*. Dec. 2017. *hcommons.org*, https://hcommons.org/deposits/item/hc:16883/.

Grigar, Dene, and Stuart Moulthrop. *Pathfinders: Documenting the Experience of Early Digital Literature*. 2015, http://dtc-wsuv.org/wp/pathfinders/.

Hayles, N. Katherine. *My Mother Was a Computer: Digital Subjects and Literary Texts*. First Edition, University of Chicago Press, 2005.

Hua, Minh, and Rita Raley. "Playing with Unicorns: AI Dungeon and Citizen NLP." *Digital Humanities Quarterly*, vol. 014, no. 4, Dec. 2020.

Kee, Kevin, and Shawn Graham. "Teaching History in an Age of Pervasive Computing: The Case for Games in the High School and Undergraduate Classroom." *Pastplay: Teaching and Learning History with Technology*, 2014, pp. 270–91.

Kirby, Cait S. "September 7th, 2020." *Cait S. Kirby, PhD*, 2020, https://caitkirby.com/downloads/Fall%202020.html.

Kocurek, Carly A., and Allyson Whipple. "Choice: Texas." *Hyperrhiz: New Media Cultures*, no. 21, Nov. 2019, https://doi.org/10.20415/hyp/021.g01.

Kostopolus, Emma. "Let's Play This Article: A Heuristic for Digital Games and Materiality." *Computers and Composition*, no. Making Games Matter: Games and Materiality, fall 2022, http://cconlinejournal.org/fall2022/Lets_play_this_article.html.

Larsen, Deena. "Marble Springs Shower Curtain," *The Deena Larsen Collection at the Maryland Institute for Technology in the Humanities*, https://mith.umd.edu/larsen/items/show/42/. Accessed 7 October 2018.

Lockridge, Timothy, et al. "The Kairos Preservation Project." *Computers and Composition*, vol. 46, Dec. 2017, pp. 72–86. *ScienceDirect*, https://doi.org/10.1016/j.compcom.2017.09.002.

Luers, Will. "Issue 00: Digital Essayism." *The Digital Review*, 2020, http://thedigitalreview.com/index.html.

McCloud, Scott. "I Can't Stop Thinking: 2000–2001." www.scottmccloud.com/1-webcomics/icst/index.html. Accessed 2 May 2023.

———. "I Can't Stop Thinking! #4." *Scott McCloud Webcomics*, 2000, www.scottmccloud.com/1-webcomics/icst/icst-4/icst-4.html.

McGrath, Jim. "Insufficient Memories by Jimmc_grath." *Itch.Io*, Mar. 2019, https://jimmc-grath.itch.io/insufficient-memories.

Milligan, Chloe. "En(Twine)d with Ergodic Rhetoric." *Computers and Composition*, vol. Online Webtexts, 2017, http://cconlinejournal.org/milligan.html.

MLA Committee on Information Technology. "Guidelines for Evaluating Work in Digital Humanities and Digital...." *Modern Language Association*, Jan. 2012, www.mla.org/About-Us/Governance/Committees/Committee-Listings/Professional-Issues/Committee-on-Information-Technology/Guidelines-for-Evaluating-Work-in-Digital-Humanities-and-Digital-Media.

Moulthrop, Stuart. "The Hypertext Years?" *Reimagining the Humanities*, edited by Barry Mauer and Anastasia Salter, Parlor Press, 2023, pp. 218–19.

———. "Victory Garden 2022." *Electronic Literature Lab*, 2022, https://victory-garden2022.com/.

———. "You Say You Want a Revolution? Hypertext and the Laws of Media." *Postmodern Culture*, vol. 1, no. 3, 1991. *Project MUSE*, https://doi.org/10.1353/pmc.1991.0019.

Nelson, Theodor Holm. *Literary Machines*. Electronic Literature Organization, 1987.

Okkema, Laura. "The Deserters." *Electronic Literature Collection*, edited by Kathi Inman Berens et al., vol. 4, Electronic Literature Organization, 2022. *collection.eliterature.org*, https://doi.org/10.7273/issn.1932-2022.4.the-desert ers.work.

———. "'The Deserters:' Activist Critical Making in Electronic Literature." *Reimagining the Humanities*, edited by Barry Mauer and Anastasia Salter, Parlor Press, 2023, pp. 193–94.

Quigley, Stephen J. "Basic Coding." *26.2*, Jan. 2022. *kairos.technorhetoric.net*, https://kairos.technorhetoric.net/26.2/disputatio/quigley/index.html.

Quinn, Zoe. *Depression Quest: An Interactive (Non)Fiction About Living with Depression*. 2013, www.depressionquest.com/.

Salter, Anastasia. "Alice in Dataland." *20.1, Kairos: A Journal of Rhetoric, Technology, and Pedagogy*, 15 Aug. 2015, https://kairos.technorhetoric. net/20.1/inventio/salter/index.html.

Salter, Anastasia, and Stuart Moulthrop. *Twining: Critical and Creative Approaches to Hypertext Narratives*. Amherst College Press, 2021.

Shiga, Jason. *Meanwhile: Pick Any Path. 3,856 Story Possibilities*. 1/30/10 edition, Harry N. Abrams, 2010.

Sousanis, Nick. *Unflattening*. Harvard University Press, 2015.

Squinkifer, Dietrich. "Impostor Syndrome." *Squinky's Awesome Website*, 29 Sept. 2013, https://games.squinky.me/impostor/.

Trettien, Whitney Anne. *Computers, Cut-Ups and Combinatory Volvelles: An Archaeology of Text-Generating Mechanisms*. 2009. Massachusetts Institute of Technology, Thesis. *dspace.mit.edu*, https://dspace.mit.edu/handle/1721.1/54505.

Tucker, Christy. "Prototype Branching Scenario Written by ChatGPT." *Experiencing eLearning*, 12 Sept. 2023, www.christytuckerlearning.com/prototype-branching-scenario-written-by-chatgpt/.

"Twine." *Twinery.Org*, 1 Jan. 2022, https://twinery.org/.

CHAPTER 6

Game

This chapter describes the ways that "indie" games (games created by independent authors or groups rather than commercial studios) have a history of critiquing and interrogating various aspects of society: some examples made with Bitsy include cecile richard's *Endless Scroll* (richard), Fred Bednarski's *The World Had Been Sad Since Tuesday* (Bednarski), and Molleindustria's *A Prison Strike* (Molleindustria). With the expansion of game development platforms that require less technical knowledge and the accessibility and free game hosting and publishing available on sites like itch.io, indie games are becoming easier to create and publish. This chapter explores some of these theories and themes that existing indie games have focused on and gives an example critical making pattern for the open-source platform Bitsy. Bitsy is a game creation platform that has unique constraints, requiring thoughtful design planning while also freeing the designer from the choice paralysis of other game development platforms that have more options. The graphics, colors, and mechanics are all limited, but this platform can easily be used to make compelling critiques of society.

Critical Games

Digital, interactive games are a unique medium that allow the audience to explore topics from a different perspective. These kinds of games can produce compelling experiences allowing the player to delve deeply into specific contexts or even simulate particular interactions or events. The player can be immersed in these experiences when games provide the player agency to make meaningful choices within a game. Players can then experiment with the kinds of impacts and consequences that different decisions in the game would cause—making risky decisions or simply engaging in behavior that differs from their typical choices in the physical world. Although a few commercial game studios have released games that do this: *Never Alone* ("Never Alone—Homepage"), for example, promotes cultural diversity. Another commercial title, *Journey* (TGC), encourages contemplative exploration and requires collaboration, and in the game *Path Out* (Causa Creations), players experience the escape of a Syrian refugee. These are not the norm for the gaming industry. The typical commercial game tends to be a first-person shooter (FPS) style, where the player's primary goal is to shoot people or things, usually in a wartime scenario. This leaves a large gap in the market for other genres, and despite the proliferation of FPS games on store shelves, there are many people who seek games that will allow them to explore society and relationships, solve puzzles, and learn.

Not only do the commercial gaming companies continue to churn out FPS games, these games are developed using exclusionary (and often proprietary) game development platforms. The free versions of game development platforms, Unity and Unreal, are used by those hoping to break into the gaming industry, and these platforms have a high barrier to entry because they are designed to mimic the specialized proprietary systems. Most of these platforms require knowledge of coding languages such as C++ in addition to an understanding of the placement and functionality of a vast number of features. Though versions of Unity and Unreal are available for anyone to use without purchase, they are not as accessible as they may appear because creators still need to possess highly specialized skills in order to use them. This results in the exclusion of all but a very narrow population of would-be game developers who possess these skills or the time and resources to acquire them (see Murray and Johnson).

Though some potential game developers are driven to create games using the platforms that mimic industry tools with the intent of gaining enough experience to enter the commercial game development industry, many other potential authors of games are marginalized by these tools. At the same time, while the commercial industry focuses on hyper violence and realistic graphics for their narrow audience of "hardcore gamers," there is a much wider audience hungry for a more diverse catalog of games. Many, not seeing their interests (nor their demographics) represented in the games sold by major companies, have sought to create their own. The platforms of Unity and Unreal, however, because of their narrow game style focus and obstructive interface, have failed to meet the needs of this population.

The emergence of new, less exclusionary game development platforms that do not require these kinds of skills and expertise have allowed for more diverse perspectives and interests to be expressed in all sorts of ways. Like Flash (Salter and Murray), these tools empower novice game designers—often experts in other areas—to design and create meaningful games that critique, call attention to, and even celebrate various aspects of society, culture, and humanity. Coupled with the advent of online distribution platforms such as itch.io, indie games can now be published and played for free or for a cost set by the owner of the game. This has fostered a wide, public audience for thousands of games that would otherwise be ignored by the commercial (or "AAA") game publishing companies. Because these games are developed without teams of dedicated graphic artists using commercial development tools, indie games are often more narrative-based, with meaningful plots driving the player's interest rather than console-controller game mechanics. With the story and character elements as the focus, indie games are therefore incredibly well-suited to conduct thoughtful critiques on society, and many do. Additionally, these developer-direct publishing platforms remove the gatekeeping effects that a commercial publishing company interested in upholding the societal status quo would have. This promotes the creation and distribution of games that have political, personal, provocative, and other commonly avoided topics.

These indie games often emphasize narrative, puzzles, and player-centered design features that can create immensely compelling games. Stripped of distracting graphics and sound effects, the indie game is free to explore topics beyond the narrow FPS. Indie games frequently align with a message, a call for attention or action, or a new perspective on an issue that is important to the author. These less exclusionary tools, then, encourage people to share their own unique experiences—and with diverse voices contributing authentic stories, indie games provide a vast scope of content that is unmatched by the commercial industry.

Twine, Bitsy, Ren'Py, and other open-source or freely accessible game making platforms remove much of the need for game creators to have coding expertise, eliminating much of the gatekeeping mechanism from game development (Johnson and Salter). This effectively works to broaden the field of game designers, as it encourages traditionally marginalized groups to create games that speak to their lived experience, perspectives, and values. However, difficulties remain in a lack of distribution channels for indie games. Commercial companies have no interest in publishing or distributing these games, and individuals rarely have access to any type of supply chain or marketing team to produce, sell, and market their games. Further, many create games with a personal element and wish only to distribute their games to friends, family, or audiences with similar perspectives or life experiences.

Happily, free publishing platforms such as Leaf Corcoran's Itch. io (itch.io, n.d.) allow indie games to be shared globally. Itch.io hosts over 900,000 games at the time of writing, with more being added each day. The site hosts games made by unincorporated individuals or groups, many of whom created the games as part of game jams, where the itch corporation hosts limited-time game creation challenges, such as GameOff, 32bit, and ScoreSpace Jam ("Game Jams"). The platform contains games made using a variety of tools—including Unity and Unreal—and enables the game developer to allow public or limited access, set a download fee, and facilitate player interaction through the discussion platform integrated with each game's individual page (a feature that can also be disabled by the game developer).

Open-source, novice-friendly game development platforms are ideal for creating critical making projects. When the game development is driven by the interest a designer has for the subject rather than the bottom line of a commercial studio, it results in meaningful experiences that speak to the developers' passions. Like Twine (discussed in Chapter 5), Bitsy is especially well-suited for critical making projects.

The open-source game making platform Bitsy requires no coding skills and just a short time to become accustomed to the various controls. Color palettes in each scene or room are limited to just three different colors, with character and backgrounds restricted to 8 x 8-pixel grids. These constraints often work to spur more creativity in the game design itself, and games are created within these parameters that even seem to have different viewing angles, top-down, side-scroller, and even behind-the-shoulder perspectives for the player. Certain squares on the scene grid can be marked as blocking the player from passing through or not, enabling even dungeon-crawler and maze styles of games.

Even with the graphical limitations of the platform, these Bitsy games are able to achieve complex graphical elements in both the avatars and the virtual worlds they depict. For example, cecile richard's *Endless Scroll* is able to depict a bedroom, a driving car, and a lake that fills up and dries out. The most unique pixelated background scene, however, is a detailed rendering of a social media page where the player is engaged in a chat conversation with the main character's friend on Facebook. Likewise, Fred Bednarski's *The World Had Been Sad Since Tuesday* includes detailed scenes of a beach, a carnival, and a truck driving along the highway. Molleindustria's *A Prison Strike* uses an eye shape for the player's avatar while displaying a variety of different scenes within a prison.

These games are powerful, conveying complex ideas and emotions through their gameplay. *Endless Scroll* (richard) deals with feelings of regret and the need to reflect and remember through the simulated discussion of the social dynamics of American high schools as remembered by the main character. The traumatic memory the character shares of a high school student being killed jumping off a bridge into a lake calls to mind the rhetorical question often posed to teenagers: "If all of your friends jumped off of a bridge, would you do it too?" The player is also given choices as to how the character will respond to different situations, similar to the interactive narrative structure seen with much of Twine. The conversation is interspersed with flashbacks, and the social media interface is partially erased in certain scenes to emphasize different points within the conversation.

Based on the short story *A Very Old Man with Enormous Wings* by Gabriel García Márquez (García Márquez), the Bitsy game *The World Had Been Sad Since Tuesday* (Bednarski) has a similar contemplative tone. The player begins on the beach, throwing crabs back into the sea, and discovers an old man with wings in the sand. Additional exploration by the player reveals a nearby couple's plot to take the man from the beach in their pickup truck. The player can sneak inside the truck and get transported with the winged man to a circus, where the winged man is referred to as an angel and crowds line up to see him. The crowd eventually disappears, and the player discovers that the winged man is actually the player: the game ends with the reuniting of the winged man's body with his "soul"—the player—and flying away. The puzzle of the man with the wings has been (at least partially) solved, and the player-angel ascends out of the game.

A Prison Strike (Molleindustria) takes a more direct approach to a specific cultural issue—mass incarceration in the United States. The game was inspired by the nationwide prison strike in August of 2018 and its hashtag #August21; Molleindustria provides additional information about the strike and ongoing issues with American prisons (Molleindustria) on the game's main page at itch.io.[1] This compelling game brings the player's attention to the problem of mass incarceration in the United States by providing a virtual tour behind the walls of a prison that is hidden from or ignored by the majority of citizens. The game text consists of a poem with the repeated phrase "I can't see;" at the end of each line, the player must click the down arrow to view the next line, creating a slow, reflective reading pace:

I can't see the hunger, the anger
of inmates on strike
affirming by withdrawing
all they have left

The game graphics depict many of the things that the poem narrator claims not to see, revealing the author's assertion that most Americans turn a blind eye to these injustices. This juxtaposition works to highlight the hypocrisy of a "free" country with such a large percentage of its citizens behind bars. The player avatar is an eye, seeing the things in

---

1   https://molleindustria.itch.io/a-prison-strike

the poem that "cannot" be seen, including hunger strikes by prisoners, the forced labor the inmates do for minimal pay, and more. The game ends with a black-and-white American flag and the words:

I can't see a country
in its whole so exceptional
to disappear millions
and still hate

I can't see
any of this
with my own eyes
but I don't need to

The last scene in the game contains no text. In a metaphor for raising awareness, the player moves their eye avatar over rows of closed eyes that then open and turn from white to red after the player passes over them.

Critical games like these are good examples to play before designing a new Bitsy game—they demonstrate the scholarly and expressive range of Bitsy's visual capabilities and use differing types of gameplay and narration styles, while remaining approachably easy to play. The platform does not support games requiring difficult keystroke patterns or fast reflexes; each game is compelling in a unique way.

The affordances and limitations of any platform will serve to inform the design process, and Bitsy is one that we both continually choose to assign in undergraduate and graduate-level critical making courses because of Bitsy's constraints. The platform accommodates a wide range of ability and game styles: from the escape room to the fantasy role-playing game to educational puzzles and more. The limiting of mechanical options forces students to think about their critical statement in creative ways—and how that statement can be conveyed to players through room design, player pathways, sprites, objects, and more. This can also be an entry point into game studies and media studies lenses, as we bring that same critical gaze to what we play.

This approach of building design intentionally and viewing a game as an argument can transform both our scholarly intention and the pedagogical clarity of engaging in this type of design process. Several of our students have commented that they felt more confident in their game designs for our courses than in other courses where they were assigned to create a game on *any* topic in a more robust platform. The critical making perspective lends a purpose to the game design process that brings many students to discover their voice and design a more meaningful game because of it: it's also not surprising how often game making becomes a part of the work of games scholars as an expressive outlet.

For the undergraduates creating critical making games in Emily's class, one lesson learned is that students should be required to conduct preliminary research on the topic of their choice before beginning to design the game. The critical making process also needs to be heavily scaffolded for undergraduates who are new to the concept: they need to be guided to select a topic and to find a scholarly (and not "primary") source on that topic. Next, they should be asked to create a storyboard of the game. This preproduction document is common in the field of game design and helps students with the majority of the decision making that goes along with creating an interactive game. It also helps alleviate potential procrastination issues, since students are required to write out the game's narrative arc in an assignment that is due before the game itself. For graduate students where the assignment is even more focused on the process than the final product, the storyboard could be an artifact of the process, and students could reflect on the differences between their planned storyboard and their submitted game.

Pattern: Bitsy

Designing a Game

When creating any critical making game, it is helpful to first play several games created with the same platform to understand its affordances and to see how other designers have used different features. Next, it is helpful to focus on two elements of the desired game: 1) the topic to be critiqued, interrogated, or highlighted, and 2) the feeling, experience, or knowledge the author wants the player to glean from the game. Player-centered game design guidelines advocate focusing early in the design process on the motivation behind the gameplay: **why would someone play this?** What experience, feeling, or knowledge do you want the player to **take away** from the game? These two aspects of the game will drive the rest of the design.

In each of the three example games discussed above, the player learns about the game's world context as they progress through the game, with *Endless Scroll*[2] and *The World Had Been Sad Since Tuesday*[3] using an open-world puzzle exploration style. *A Prison Strike*[4] takes the player through a more limited progression of scenes, though even in this game, the player has the agency to choose to interact with people and objects within the game to learn more. All three have an overall tone of thoughtful reflection, inviting the player to think more deeply about (and likely from a new perspective on) the game's topic. These games invite players to share the feelings of the characters in the games and also work to project some of those feelings and reflections onto their own lives. **What do you want your game to share?** Here are a few things to think about as you design:

2   https://haraiva.itch.io/endless-scroll
3   https://vonbednar.itch.io/the-world-was-sad-since-tuesday
4   https://molleindustria.itch.io/a-prison-strike

- **Craft a meaningful environment.** As you work on this part of the project, remember to think about how you will operate within the constraints of a limited color palette and pixel grid. You'll by necessity need to scale back the design and focus on the essentials—consider how your colors will shape the mood; how choices in details will differentiate one character or object from another; and how your world will fit together as the player moves from "room" to "room." You might find pixsy,[5] a conversion tool for making rooms from photos, helpful in crafting evocative spaces (ruin).
- **Use dialogue to share your argument.** As you think about "dialogue," remember that this can be text that is reflective, poetic, or internal—it doesn't have to mean conversations with other characters in the traditional sense. Think about the overall scope of your game as well as the pace and length of your dialogue segments, and consider that you can also draw inspiration from other hypertextual essays, small-scale games, comics, and animation.
- **Build for interaction.** Think about the "collision" as a mechanism for revealing and understanding the environment, and use the range of sprites, tiles, and items to make the most of interactivity as a way of working through an argument. Take time to explore the essays in experiments such as the Bitsy Essay Jam,[6] and consider how they ask you to engage as a reader-player with the argument (Coleo_Kin).

The most important rule to keep in mind when working with Bitsy is "think small." As bee ulrich describes in their article on the platform: "Where Odyssey feels like a tome, Bitsy games are poems" (ulrich).

---

5 https://ruin.itch.io/pixsy
6 https://itch.io/jam/the-bitsy-essay-jam

Storyboarding

Regardless of the game development platform being used, after determining the feeling the designer wants the player to have when playing the game, we recommend creating a storyboard.

Storyboarding can take different forms, but it serves as an outline that helps the designer to plan the beginning, middle, and end of the narrative, which can assist in the more coherent flow of events within the game. If the game is to take a nonlinear timeline, it is even more important. To avoid plot holes and confusion while designing the game, a linear timeline should be developed prior to the nonlinear storyboard as a reference, to ensure narrative continuity (unless of course narrative *in*congruity is the target). Bitsy organizes game design into different rooms which are connected by squares that act as doors—but you can place a door on any perimeter square. The requirement for this exercise in Bitsy is at least **three** rooms: you can think of each room as providing the scene dedicated to your game's beginning, middle, and end, or you can go beyond this.

Next, consider the **actions** that the player will do within the game. Each square within the game grid can be customized to 1) permit the player to pass through it, 2) block the player from passing, or 3) display dialogue, creating the sense that the player is interacting with the figure in that space. This provides opportunities for the game's design to take the shape of a maze or dungeon crawler, an open world exploration game, a puzzle game, an escape room, and more. The limited space of each room requires you to purposefully consider the intent of each square in the grid. Along with this, plan for the **visual perspective** your game will take. Bitsy's two-dimensional graphical features can create a game with a top-down perspective, as seen in *The World Had Been Sad Since Tuesday* and *A Prison Strike*, as well as more of an over-the-shoulder perspective where the player seems to be looking over the shoulder of the avatar, as in games like *Endless Scroll*.

The Bitsy Platform

Bitsy's homepage (Figure 1) explains, "Bitsy is a little editor for little games or worlds. The goal is to make it easy to make games where you can walk around and talk to people and be somewhere" (Le Doux).

Upon making the selection to create a new game in the platform (by clicking on the cat icon on the homepage), you will see a screen containing five sections (Figure 2), from left to right:

About: contains the same mission statement for the platform as well as helpful documentation for getting started with the platform

Room: displays a 16 x 16 square that contains a human-shaped avatar and a cat-shaped sprite, along with buttons for selecting: edit, colors, tune, avatar, paint, pick, exits & endings, show/hide grid and show/hide walls

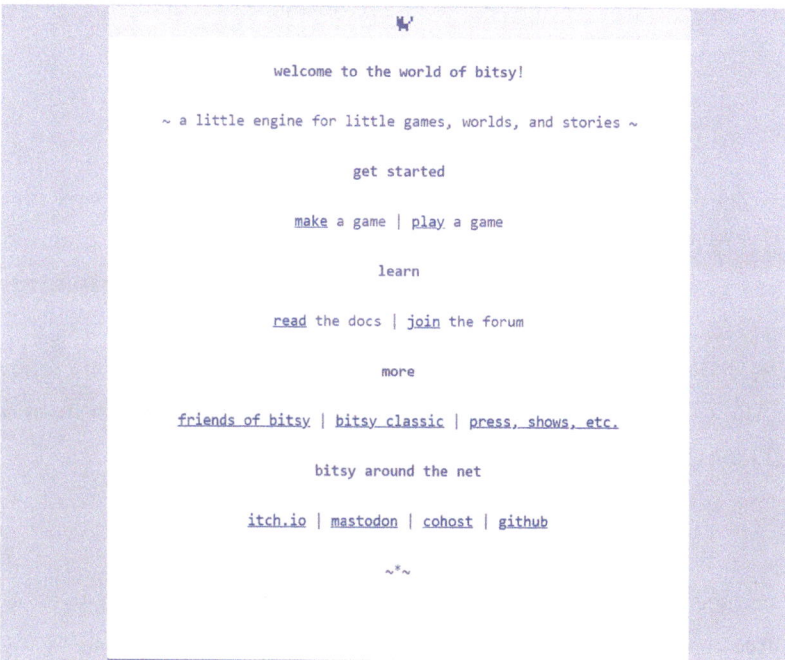

Figure 1: Bitsy's homepage.

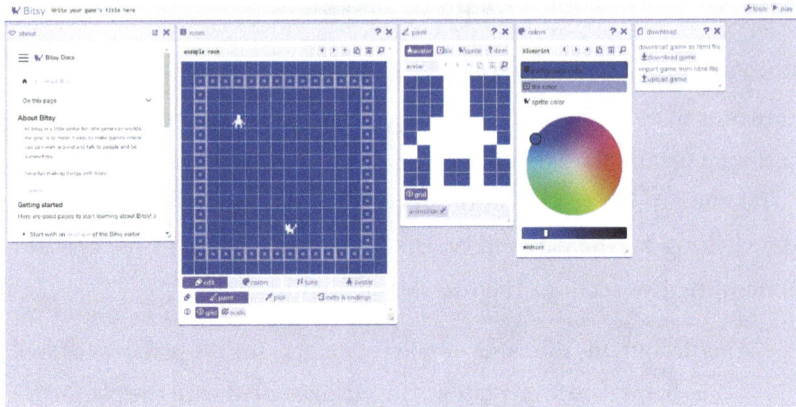

Figure 2: The Bitsy interface.

> **Paint**: an 8 x 8 grid where the designer can create avatars, sprites, tiles, and items
> **Colors**: contains a color wheel and a place to enter a hex color code for the background color, tile color, and sprite color
> **Download**: allows the game designer to download the game as a sharable HTML file, as well as an option to import an existing game from an HTML file to edit in the space

The layout of Bitsy consists of a series of different sections that modify different aspects of the game, and the creator is not limited to these five items. When you are working on an aspect of the game that necessitates additional creative input, another section appears on the screen. For example, when creating edit and entry locations for a room in the game, a sixth editing field appears, allowing you to create and edit locations and transitions for room navigation.

Scene Design

Each scene or room in a Bitsy game can only contain a color palette of three colors, including the two colors of the characters. To allow the player to move between rooms, you need to place exits and entrances on specific tiles. These can be marked or unmarked, allowing the player to discover them on their own, encouraging exploration. Squares can remain blank, as well, so a sparse landscape can be conveyed, like the beach scene in *The World Had Been Sad Since Tuesday*; notably, this game also includes busy scenes like a bustling carnival and a moving road scene to simulate driving. *Endless Scroll* remarkably depicts a full social media interface. However, the graphics are not the focus of these games—they remain dual-colored, pixelated scenes and avatars. This stark contrast to the ever more realistic graphics in the commercial industry's FPS games acts to signal that something more is going on in these games. You get to **emphasize your message**.

The way that Bitsy constrains scene appearance guides you to create visually cohesive rooms (at least, color-wise). Think about what you know about color theory and how to visually highlight various parts of a room when only a few colors are usable. If you want the player to go to a specific part of the room and avoid a specific other part, this can be done by using non-traversable tiles, by designing tiles to look like a pathway, and so on. Grappling with the different ways to dictate a player's path through the game—and pondering whether that needs to be done at all—is all part of the critical making experience. Should players be overly constrained in movement? Should they be able to traverse all of the tiles? Should they have a clear path to follow—and what should happen if the player does not follow the game's "intended" path? What impact does each choice have on the player, game, and the game's message? Whether or not the player is permitted to take subversive actions is an important decision in critical making game design, and will impact the kind of statement your game makes.

Collectable Objects

Like in Twine, Bitsy can be designed to remember when players have collided with a space designated as a collectable object. The possession of a key, coin, potion, or other thematically designed item can then permit or deny the player's passage from one square to another, one room to another, or even display a different set of dialogue boxes for a character. This can create a more immersive feeling, as it helps build a sense of player influence over events in the game and therefore a feeling of greater agency. A quest to collect specific objects within the game can provide the player with a sense of direction and therefore motivation to continue, while also expanding the possibilities for the game's design. When this element is added to the game, a simple navigation maze becomes an engaging quest, and invites the player to explore all 256 squares in each room.

In Bitsy, when collectable objects are obtained by the player, the game will automatically record an inventory and tally how often the player has interacted with each object. This inventory can be used to make conditionals—allowing a player to exit or end the game only after they have interacted with certain objects or sprites. Game variables can also be edited with the inventory tool, expanding the possibilities for Bitsy games.

If you enjoy playing games for the lure of points and badges, you might want to include inventory items in your games. However, it can be powerful to design the game beyond the act of collecting coins or points so that the player's experience is *modified* based on their actions—which parts of the game world they have visited and which parts they have not; what choices they make in their navigation of the world; and more. This expands your options for designing an interactive, meaningful gameplay experience. The inventory rules can be completely hidden from the player, or they can be made transparent with game dialogue. Though there are some constraints in Bitsy regarding the appearance and number of different inventory items the game can contain, how this feature is leveraged in the game is flexible. Experiment with it!

Character and Object Design

In Bitsy, each character is limited to an 8 x 8-pixel design that lends a nostalgic "retro" look to the game. The color palette for each character is also restricted to two of the colors in the room's color palette— a character color and a background color. The character can also be customized by creating a second version of the character that uses a slightly different shape. When published, the image on the character square will alternate between these two versions, essentially creating the illusion of movement: a person waving or jumping, a cat's tail twitching, and so on.

Though at times the "retro" look of these 64-pixel images is in vogue in popular media, the simplification of a person, animal, or thing within this limited structure and palette forces the designer to be creative about how to represent something on the screen. Recall the discussion of visual representation and iconography in Chapter 2, detailed brilliantly in Nick Sousanis's *Unflattening*. Because you are applying these concepts directly to your own game, you get to make the difficult choices of what features of your avatars, sprites, and worlds are represented in the 64 pixels, and which are washed away. Your game's critical stance may also help to determine which aspects of each of these people, places, and things are best to highlight.

Dialogue and Sound

In Bitsy, specified spaces in the scene grid can be designed to pop up dialogue boxes when players "collide" with them. Passages can be short or long, though longer passages require the player to click through using the down arrow key. Note how this impacts the pace of reading. Usually, non-player characters (NPCs) that are positioned within the squares of Bitsy games use second-person pronouns to speak directly to the player's avatar, offering instructions, advice, clues, backstory, and more. The player cannot respond to these characters, so they are more soliloquies than true dialogue opportunities, but this constraint again lends itself to meaningful game design in that it pushes you to ensure the characters have meaningful things to tell the player. This can also provide you with the opportunity for intriguing player misdirection, where NPCs share misinformation to confuse the player. A game like *The World Had Been Sad Since Tuesday* presents a puzzle for the player to solve through the narrative and various clues embedded within the game objects. This same kind of design can also be leveraged by those wishing to incorporate miscues or red herrings to complicate the gameplay.

Bitsy provides three different options for background tunes that can be edited. The tune editor is reminiscent of the limited music present in the early Nintendo games (and the famous *Mario Bros.* score). There are three different background tunes—each relying on repeating a composition of up to eight individual 16-note measures. The notes can be edited within a C octave (13 notes total). You can also modify the tempo and instrument, with three options for each. Bitsy also loads with two preset sound effects: a meow (for the preset cat sprite) and a "pick up" sound (for the preset key). Six additional sounds can be selected using the "blip-o-matic" tool: greeting, bloop, bleep, magic, mutate, and random. Each sound's pitch, length, and speed can also be edited and changed in the "blip-o-matic" tool.

These limited sounds can spur a thoughtful discussion about sound in games: what kinds of sounds do players expect to indicate that they did something "good" in the game? What kinds of sounds might tell players that they made an "incorrect" move? How does having or not having background music impact the overall tone of the game? Consider examples from films you've seen and other games you've played to construct a deeper understanding of the influence of audio in media. Further, it is an interesting experiment to create games that intentionally do *not* follow these norms: what happens when the tone of the music does not match the appearance of the game? How do players react to "negative" sounds that play when they do what they think the game wants them to do? Here again, the critical lens the game takes will guide the presence and types of sounds the player hears.

Constraints

Notably, Bitsy's platform contains a number of features that limit the game design. Like we've discussed, this can actually help you to focus on the aspects of the game that convey meaning and create a compelling experience for the player. Designing under constraints has great value: working within a minimalist toolset that focuses on collisions—but not combat—produces more thoughtful games. It can be difficult to get a message or narrative experience through to the player if they are being bombarded by flashy effects, difficult mechanics, complex musical scores, and the latest graphics. Just like parameters on scope, length, topic, and number of sources can help you develop a focused, well-written research paper, so too can the constraints of Bitsy guide you to develop a meaningful game.

Applications

One student in Anastasia's graduate course created a Bitsy game called *Liao Zhai Zhi Yi*.[7] This student used Bitsy to make Chinese folklore interactive. This game follows the story of Liao Zhai Zhi Yi by Pu Songling (Songling), and allowed this student's classmates to learn more about a fable that does not enjoy wide popularity in America. The player explores a market and then goes to a tea house to collect stories

7   https://pockyyyyyy.itch.io/liao-zhai-zhi-yi

from customers. The stories they share are folktales about chopping off the head of a strange spirit and watching a tiny man forced to perform for a crowd. The game includes swirling scene transitions between the customers sharing the stories and the stories themselves, and the story scenes use a stark black and white background in contrast with the light and dark browns of the rest of the game scenes. Another graduate student, Vee Kennedy, connects their work throughout the semester through a game featuring the "Critical Baking Kitchen." Every week, they shared reflections bringing together the materiality of baking with the pattern's form, and noted how those parallels transformed their relationship to both:

> For the critical baking process as I took on new recipes from scratch almost every week without ever once feeling of impostor syndrome as a baker, or as though I had done something to be guilty of. Learning from recipes is natural, of course; how is anyone to bake without experience or a guide when one hasn't made something before?
>
> Therein lies the code epiphany: if it works for baking, it must work for code, too. (Kennedy)

The Bitsy game demonstrates those connections through both its encoded play with baking (the player is invited to join in an ingredient hunt) and meta-narrative, as the player takes on the role of a Texts and Technology PhD student confronted with a pixelated kitchen to navigate. Kennedy's work uses pixsy to create the details of the kitchen, and is available with its source code in the GitHub repository.

One of Emily's undergraduate students, Marco Mosqueda, created a game titled *Amnesia*[8] that also uses Bitsy. In this game, the scenes are allegories for the lasting impacts of colonialism that still manifest today in systemic racism. True to the title of the game, the main character has amnesia, and the player must explore each scene to learn

---

8   https://mosquedama.itch.io/amnesia

more about the character's life. As the player explores, they discover that they are an actor in a play with an abusive director. The player eventually discovers that they have a family and that they once had a home, but it no longer exists—another character who the player interacts with states, "I lost [my] house years ago, around the time this place [the theater] went up." Part of the main character's troubles apparently include being unhoused. The director tries to convince the main character that his wife and son left him "centuries ago," and he as well as the conductor make several stereotypical comments using the phrase "your people" to the main character. This game includes a multitude of scenes, one of which includes a hallway with four doors. Only when the player has obtained certain items, such as sheet music, a raincoat, and so forth, can they pass through the door and interact with the conductor, go outside, and end the game. This intricate inventory system forces the player to explore every inch of each scene to find each object and progress through the game, building a more complete knowledge of the character's backstory as they go.

Another undergraduate in Emily's class, Sharon Vélez Figueroa, created a game, *Home*,[9] that has a more straightforward plot and mechanics. This game casts the player as a dog in a world run by cats, to demonstrate the colonialization issues taking place even still today in Puerto Rico. In the game the cats speak a different language but own the grocery stores. The dog seeks food and is able to enter the cats' store and get fish, but this requires a bit of maneuvering. The dog's second option is another store owned by other dogs who farm their own bones. If the player chooses the cats' store, they receive the message "by supporting this store, your home no longer exists;" whereas if the player chooses the dog store, they can return home. This game speaks to the limited options that Puerto Ricans have as they make daily decisions that often work to support the colonizing country.

9   https://vfsharon.itch.io/home

Bitsy is another platform that allows students with a wide range of skills to create compelling digital narratives. With constraining platforms like this, the underlying critical statement can shine through without being obfuscated by fancy graphics or other technical effects. The students have to consider the constraints in the design process and make their games in a purposeful manner to ensure that the message they hope to convey is apparent to their player. This creates a more equitable learning environment where students of any level of expertise have the same range of making possibilities.

Futures

Unlike other patterns in this book, AI cannot currently generate much useful text that can be copied and pasted directly anywhere in Bitsy to quickly create a functional game experience: the visual interface hides most of the actual code that ChatGPT or other AI language models could generate. The images are limited as well: uploading images generated by DALL-E or any other AI tool (or non-AI tool for that matter) is not possible. The game platform's constraints limit even these endeavors.

However, generative AI tools can generate a list of steps for the novice to follow, complete with how to publish and share the game files. They can also explain the different functions in the interface, which might be preferable to constantly emailing the instructor—it is becoming more common for faculty to recommend that students ask generative AI their question before emailing the instructor for coding assistance. We could also use AI text generators for brainstorming and structuring assistance. AI-powered visual tools might help students get started with room and sprite designs, as the visual constraints can make portraying different perspectives challenging. As with all technology, this is likely to change in the future.

```
define s = Character('Sylvie', color="#c8ffc8")
define m = Character('Me', color="#c8c8ff")

label start:

    scene bg meadow

    "After a short while, we reach the meadows just outside the neighborhood where we both live."

    "It's a scenic view I've grown used to. Autumn is especially beautiful here."

    "When we were children, we played in these meadows a lot, so they're full of memories."

    m "Hey... Umm..."

    show sylvie green smile

    "She turns to me and smiles. She looks so welcoming that I feel my nervousness melt away."

    "I'll ask her...!"

    m "Umm... Will you..."

    m "Will you be my artist for a visual novel?"

    show sylvie green surprised

    "Silence."
```

Figure 3: Ren'Py interface ("Quickstart").

Other platforms for simple game creation that we enjoy using with our students are Twine (discussed in Chapter 5) and Ren'Py,[10] which is a visual novel engine. Like Twine, Ren'Py is open source and free, and creates text-driven interactive narratives. Ren'Py emphasizes images, and it's easy in Ren'Py to manipulate the location of the text on the images, create speech bubbles, and so forth.

Most of the creation for Ren'Py is text-based and looks like code, so it can be intimidating at first (Figure 3). This is where ChatGPT and other AI tools could be helpful to get the novice started. Prompting ChatGPT-3.5 produced a starter script that could be easily modified (Figure 4):

The plot and dialogue that were generated leave much to be desired, but the structure of the script is there, and enables the student to focus on the creative parts of the visual novel creation with less worrying about how to properly label scenes, characters, and menus for the engine.

Interesting games can be created with less powerful tools as well. Students can use Google Forms to create exciting puzzle-based escape

10 www.renpy.org/

EK generate code for ren'py that has two characters, bob and sylvia, discussing where to go to dinner. the discussion gets heated, and they end up eating alone.

Here's a simple Ren'Py script that features two characters, Bob and Sylvia, discussing where to go to dinner. The discussion gets heated, and they end up eating alone:

```renpy
label start:

    "It's dinner time, and Bob and Sylvia are trying to decide where to eat.

    menu:
        "Where should we go for dinner, Bob?":
            "Let's go to the Italian restaurant!":
                jump italian_restaurant
            "No, I want sushi!":
                jump sushi_restaurant

label italian_restaurant:

    "Bob: How about Italian?"
    "Sylvia: Ugh, Italian again? We always go there!"
```

Figure 4: Prompt and first part of ChatGPT-3.5-generated Ren'Py code.

rooms. The number of free game development platforms available online continues to increase, so the options abound. Further, recalling the material creation of the selfie in Chapter 1, students can create games using index cards, paper, dice, and any other physical materials. Fancy digital tools are not required to make games with compelling critical statements, and physical prototypes are excellent ways to test key game elements before implementing them into a digital engine.

Works Cited

Bednarski, Fred. *The World Had Been Sad Since Tuesday.* Bitsy, 2019, https://vonbednar.itch.io/the-world-was-sad-since-tuesday.

Causa Creations. *Path Out.* https://causacreations.net/presskit/path_out/index.html. Accessed 13 Dec. 2022.

Coleo_Kin. "The Bitsy Essay Jam." *Itch.Io*, Nov. 2020, https://itch.io/jam/the-bitsy-essay-jam.

"Game Jams." *Itch.Io*, https://itch.io/jams. Accessed 19 Oct. 2022.

García Márquez, Gabriel. "A Very Old Man with Enormous Wings." *Leaf Storm and Other Stories*, translated by Gregory Rabassa, First Perennial Classics edition, Perennial Classics, 2005, https://library.villanova.edu/Find/Record/1355931/TOC.

"Itch.Io." *Itch.Io*, https://itch.io/. Accessed 19 Oct. 2022.

Johnson, Emily K., and Anastasia Salter. *Playful Pedagogy in the Pandemic: Pivoting to Games-Based Learning*. Routledge, 2022.

Kennedy, Vee. "Reflection of Critical Baking." *Chef Vee's Compendium of Critical Baking*, Apr. 2024, https://veekenne.github.io/critical-baking-compendium/.

Le Doux, Adam. "Bitsy." *Welcome to the Homepage for Bitsy*, https://bitsy.org/#0,0. Accessed 8 Dec. 2022.

Molleindustria. *A Prison Strike*. Bitsy, 2020, https://molleindustria.itch.io/a-prison-strike.

Murray, John T., and Emily K. Johnson. "XR Content Authoring Challenges: The Creator–Developer Divide." *Augmented and Mixed Reality for Communities*, edited by Joshua A. Fisher, first edition, CRC Press, 2021, pp. 249–68. *www.taylorfrancis.com*, https://doi.org/10.1201/9781003052838-16.

"Never Alone—Homepage." *Never Alone*, http://neveralonegame.com/. Accessed 13 Dec. 2022.

"Quickstart." *Ren'Py*. www.renpy.org/doc/html/quickstart.html. Accessed 27 Sept. 2023.

richard, cecile. *Endless Scroll*. Bitsy, 2019, https://haraiva.itch.io/endless-scroll.

ruin. "Pixsy by Ruin." *Itch.Io*, 3 Jul. 2021, https://ruin.itch.io/pixsy.

Salter, Anastasia, and John Murray. *Flash: Building the Interactive Web*. MIT Press, 2014.

Songling, Pu. *Strange Stories from a Chinese Studio*. Translated by Herbert A. Giles, Project Gutenberg, 2013, www.gutenberg.org/files/43629/43629-h/43629-h.htm.

Sousanis, Nick. *Unflattening*. Harvard University Press, 2015.

TGC. "Journey." *Thatgamecompany*, 10 Jul. 2017, https://thatgamecompany.com/journey/.

ulrich, bee. "'Bitsy' Is a Tiny Toolset That Strips Games to Little, Lovely Gems." *Medium*, 14 Apr. 2018, https://medium.com/@cavegift/https-medium-com-cavegift-bitsy-is-a-tiny-toolset-4016814c5367.

CHAPTER 7

Bots

This chapter delves into the methods of procedural generation as a critical making process. By laying out a pattern for a program to follow, the author of a generative work becomes a coauthor with the machine. The resulting text or art is often absurd, humorous, or nonsense—and usually a compelling commentary on society and the ways that we rely on machines and technology that are still rather primitive. Projects created with this human–machine task sharing investigate and critique ideas about what it means to be human, how our society views different populations, and more. The pattern this chapter lays out uses an open-source, scaffolded, procedural generation platform built by Kate Compton called Tracery, where the coding language JSON is used to generate short stories, poems, and bot posts. Tracery has an additional affordance of being able to link directly to a bot in the chat platform Discord and the social media site Mastodon.

Critical Generative Grammar

Computational thinking skills are increasingly important in contemporary society, as more and more things are run by algorithms and artificial intelligence. The types of digital literacy skills needed for the average citizen to navigate platforms across devices are increasing and vital worldwide. People need to understand how platforms sort and present information, where to seek information, how to evaluate the credibility of information, and how to combat misinformation. While more and more nefarious actors work to undermine systems in power using digital platforms and clouding facts with bias, it is becoming more difficult to distinguish truth from fiction.

As discussed in the introduction, AI text generation is becoming easier for the general public to access and harness, with increasingly available tools such as ChatGPT-3 and 4, Bing, and more. Scholars are now predicting that rather than traditional writing skills where the human author generates the entirety of the text, writing in the future will become more collaborative with machines: "forget the mere *cut & paste*, they will need to be good at *prompt & collate*" (Floridi and Chiriatti 691, emphases original). As AI and machine learning drives more and more commonplace technology, like cell phones (Ignatov et al.), it is important to understand the basics of how machines "learn" and what kinds of human input go into AI. The technology user's ability to notice and rectify human biases that are encoded into the machines will be ever more necessary.

In a 2005 article, Michael Mateas issues a call for procedural literacy education to be embedded in all grade levels and asserts that procedural *illiteracy* "leaves one fundamentally unable to grapple with the essence of computational media" (Mateas 101). Mateas calls us to action, advocating for a wider public knowledge of programming, and concludes that "without a deep understanding of the relationship between what lies on and beneath the screen, scholars are unable to deeply read new media work, while practitioners, living in the prison-house of 'art friendly' tools, are unable to tap the true representational power of computation as a medium" (Mateas 111). With the use of algorithms in the sorting of search results, social media feeds, online shopping product displays, criminal sentencing, and even predictive policing, we argue that procedural illiteracy can have more disastrous consequences than merely being unable to tap into the "true power" of computers.

The 2016 Computer Science for All initiative set forth by the Obama administration in the United States and other similar policies across the globe placed pressure on institutions to increase the participation of marginalized groups in computer science majors and careers. This brought a push to design curricula targeting youth in demographics that were underrepresented in the field. These various programs sought to pique children and young adults' interest in computer science, and break or lessen the cultural barriers such as systemic racism and sexism that prevent many potential computer scientists from these demographics from thriving in a career in this field. Many of these programs relied on visual programming interfaces like Scratch and Alice, which emphasize the arrangement of objects and commands on a colorful, user-friendly screen and downplay (but sometimes automatically display) the details such as punctuation specific to a particular coding language. Emily developed a Twine game with an interface that included stringing beads to progress through a fantasy narrative (Johnson and Sullivan), aimed at the specific demographic of middle school girls, as this is the age when children seem to internalize the implicit cultural barriers to computer science and other STEM fields (Hand et al.).

As novices are introduced to the idea of procedural generation, it is helpful to use metaphors and examples. There are many popular video games that many people may not realize rely on procedural generation. Video game designers have sought to harness procedural generation to create infinite worlds for players to explore without having to design and code each one themselves. One of these, *No Man's Sky*, enjoyed great media publicity when it was released in 2016, though players did comment that many of the procedurally generated planets looked extremely similar. Other popular games using procedurally generated worlds (setting and non-player character (NPC) art) include *Minecraft*, *Don't Starve*, *Spelunky*, *Deep Rock Galactic*, *Enter the Gungeon*, and more (G2A). Other games use procedural generation to produce different content, such as the *Borderlands* series, which procedurally generates weapons based on player level (McDuffee and Pantaleev). Video games have also been programming the background music to respond to events in the game for a long time, with many games using adaptive scores to match the events occurring within the game, and studios have realized that using generative music can be a cost-saving measure (Plut and Pasquier).

Moving beyond commercial purposes for using procedural generation in products to be consumed, generative projects have been created to critique, question, and raise awareness of societal issues as well. Examples of critical making with procedural generation include Mark Sample's *The Infinite Catalog of Crushed Dreams*, which uses procedurally generated text to complete the phrase "The pandemic hit and then..." (Sample, *The Infinite Catalog of Crushed Dreams*). The generated text creates a truly endless scroll of realistic impacts of the COVID-19 pandemic, such as: "Braelynn's degree in Chemistry seemed like a good idea six months ago. There's not even Spring Fling to look forward to. Dinner is cereal, in the dark," and "Denver from Trujillo Alto, Puerto Rico, is an only child. Denver vaguely recalls their crush at school. The Music teacher cried on Zoom today." Though some are less serious, such as "all the bars are shuttered in Palm Beach Gardens, Florida. The streets are deserted. Coyotes paw across the empty parking lots," they all share the sense of loss and loneliness that was prevalent throughout the pandemic.

Another pandemic-themed critical making work that uses Tracery to generate both text and a visual component is the Masked Making generator (Fan et al.). This generator, which is embedded into the website and displayed through an HTML file, generates image-text: an image of a mask, the name of the (fictional) person who made the mask, the date the mask was created, and a short blurb about the mask creator. One example is a mask that includes the words "six feet," created by "Winona" on February 23, 2020. The description says, "while she didn't sew at all before the pandemic, a thrifted sewing machine got her started using patterns and tutorials she found on Twitter. 'It's not as rough as I thought. It's everything else that's difficult, really. At least this way I can be active.'" The text on the masks as well as the blurbs about the mask makers highlight the different perspectives on masking that were and still are held by many. Mask text like "Blame Cuomo" contrasts with other phrases displayed, like "socially distant," and "quarantini time." The people highlighted, as well, represent a range, again recalling the conflicting beliefs—and actual conflicts that took place—across the globe during this period.

As novice programmers tinker with the procedural generation described in this chapter, they can learn about the affordances of computer programs and better understand the fallacy that coded things are unbiased: the code is written by a human and therefore includes the biases (unconscious or otherwise) of the developer. There is nothing in the coding process that guards against or erases the human elements embedded in each command; the code simply performs the functions as written. Procedurally generating text and images is a good way to think deeply about procedural generation and the construction of digital art. It can also call attention to the purposes and constructed nature of many texts and images that are displayed on our digital platforms and websites.

Introducing noncoders to procedural generation in this way helps to demystify many aspects of programming and fosters procedural literacy. It may also help reclaim some agency and reduce the so-called "algorithm anxiety" in a time where our computers and phones try to guess the next word we plan to type in an email, text, and search bar (Chayka). The procedural text generation that we describe in this pattern is Tracery, which uses JSON code.

Tracery is an excellent introduction to JSON coding language for novices (Tracery). Created by Kate Compton to broaden participation in computer science, Tracery encourages playful experimentation with coding languages with a focus on generating narratives. Authors create story structures and compose lists of possible sentence structures and words and phrases that the program pulls from to generate varying versions of the story. One example from the initial testing of Tracery is a structure to procedurally generate *Doctor Who* narratives (Compton et al.). Thus, common literary tropes can serve as the grammar to which other options for scenes, characters, and events scenes can be plugged in to generate fresh content using familiar plots. Familiar, too-common plot structures can also be critiqued with much the same coding, and they can of course also be rearranged or reimagined to compose entirely unique narratives.

Cheap Bots Done Quick on the Platform Formerly Known as Twitter

Prior to 2022, we assigned our students the task of using Tracery to code a Twitter bot using Cheap Bots Done Quick (Cheap Bots, Done Quick!), and these are the examples we include in this pattern. This website, https://cheapbotsdonequick.com, run by V. Buckenham (Buckenham) guides the visitor through the process of creating a Twitter bot. Once the Twitter account was linked to Cheap Bots Done Quick, the Tracery JSON code could be typed or pasted into the textbox. The author of the bot then set how often the bot should tweet, selecting from a range of time intervals from never to every ten minutes. Replies could also be set, as well as the option to share (or not) the code at cheapbotsdonequick.com/source/[bot's Twitter handle]. As we wrote this book, however, Twitter underwent drastic leadership and structural changes, and on April 6, 2023, the creator of Cheap Bots Done Quick announced that Twitter had suspended API access, rendering the tool unusable—a reminder of how quickly platforms can change, and scholarly work can be lost. Many of the bots made with this tool and others deployed to Twitter might be categorized as what Mark Sample has termed "bots of conviction," or bots that use generation and other data-driven means to produce tweets that are "topical, data-based, cumulative, oppositional, and uncanny" (Sample, "A Protest Bot Is a Bot so Specific You Can't Mistake It for Bullshit"). The loss of such bots is a sign of the greatly diminished culture of creativity on a platform that was once a hub for digital humanities community and experimental code artistry.

Glitch Bots on Discord

A similar option for recreating the Tracery assignment is to use "Glitch bots" connected to Discord (LEARNBOT3000). This platform integrates Tracery code into the chat platform Discord. The website, https://learnbot3000.glitch.me/,[1] includes scaffolded code examples and invites people to copy and iterate to create their own bots. Rather than posting generated text within a set time interval, the bots in Discord will reply to direct messages and tagging within the Discord thread (e.g. "hello @bot" will result in the reply coded into the bot). The Glitch site provides fully functioning bots that can be "remixed"—copied and modified however the user would like the bot to reply or add a reaction emoji to a message in Discord. Like Cheap Bots Done Quick, the code that comprises the Glitch bot can be pasted directly from one of the Tracery sandbox websites as well, and Discord allows

---

1 Alternative URL: https://glitch.com/edit/#!/tundra-marred-olive?path=README. md%3A1%3A0

for easy creation of closed servers, allowing for a class experimentation channel that can remain inaccessible to trolls and other nefarious non-student users.

The connection process from the LEARNBOT3000 page and the Discord server is a little more involved than with Cheap Bots Done Quick, given that Discord servers are intended to have only one or two administrators and are not set up to allow all server members to add bots at will. However, clear step-by-step instructions are included in the README.md tab on the LEARNBOT3000 remix page that can be copied and augmented to highlight common difficulties as well as assignment requirements for classes. Note that making modifications to the bot on the Glitch site does not automatically update the bot if it has already been invited to a Discord server; thus we suggest that students work through the code from the Glitch site using one of the sandbox practice sites first, before connecting the finalized bot to Discord. Beau Gunderson's website has a large space that students might appreciate at this stage: https://beaugunderson.com/tracery-writer/ (Gunderson). Once the bot is housed in a Discord server, it becomes more difficult to update the bot from the Glitch website, so it is helpful to remind students to finalize the code before connecting the bot to their server.

Cheap Bots Toot Sweet on Mastodon

More recently, @boodoo@mastodon.social created a version of Cheap Bots Done Quick that can be imported into Mastodon, called Cheap Bots Toot Sweet (Cheap Bots, Toot Sweet!), accessible at: https://cheapbotstootsweet.com/. Mastodon is a social media platform that many academics and others have turned to in the wake of the drastic changes that took place on Twitter, where posts are referred to as "toots" rather than "tweets," as reflected in the title of the bot creator. Mastodon is more siloed than Twitter, which makes it more difficult to release bots into the public sphere in this platform. In fact, most

Mastodon instances ban the use of bots entirely. However, Cheap Bots Toot Sweet points users to a bot-friendly space where anyone can create and release bots, called botsin.space ("Botsin.Space"). In this capacity, coupled with the strict code of conduct that bans harassment and a number of other inappropriate kinds of posts, Mastodon is more conducive to a closed course setting, as there is a far smaller chance that the bot will appear on the feed of someone who is not in the course and therefore may allow students to attempt more controversial issues or approaches to critical making.

An example of a bot created in Tracery and ported to Mastodon using Cheap Bots Toot Sweet is the bot @robotrecipes[2] tooting in the Botsin.Space instance[3] at the time of writing. It nicely demonstrates some of the ways that Tracery can be leveraged to create an interesting bot. The bot composes instructions for creating a variety of step-by-step "recipes." Each recipe includes eight steps generated from a list of further generative options. Even the names of the "dishes" themselves display the generative creativity of the author. The code for the name of the "meal" is:

```
"meal":["#mealstyle.capitalizeAll# #mealitem.
capitalizeAll#"],
```

where even mealstyle includes procedurally generated options-within-options:

```
"mealstyle":["#style#", "#fruit#", "#mood#"],
```

---

2 https://botsin.space/@robotrecipes
3 This bot's code is viewable at: https://cheapbotstootsweet.com/source/?url=https://
   botsin.space/@robotrecipes

as does mealitem:

```
"mealitem":["#fabric#", "#fabric#",
"#ingredient#"],
```

Each of the terms is preceded and proceeded by the # symbol drawn from an additional set of words, with #style# having the shortest list of the six: "poached", "classic", "American-style", "Irish", "French", "sweet", "special", "hot", "spiced", "metropolitan", "iced". This complex project is a whimsical one that still leverages an impressive number of Tracery features. It is silly enough to hold students' attention and complicated enough to demonstrate the possibilities of this powerful platform.

Finally, Tracery can be used to generate projects with images that are embedded directly into webpages, as seen in the Masked Making example discussed above. This is another option for student assignments, as it does not require a social platform to post and share the generative work, though this isolates the bots from an interactive platform, and of course, rather than automatically posting generative text and images, it requires the reader to click for each new generation. This may be attractive to students who are hesitant to release their work to a public platform occupied with real people and would also require students to have their own website or GitHub page. We like GitHub for more advanced students or classes that are already incorporating the platform, but HTML can also be rather easily embedded into free webhosting sites like Wix, WordPress, and Google Sites, most of which can be easily password-protected for the public-wary students or those selecting topics that may be the target of the lawmakers' ire that day.

Self-Contained Tracery-to-HTML

Tracery can be practiced in the self-contained sandbox platforms discussed below, and the project can end there, as well. While some might feel that a split-screen showing the JSON code beside the generated

Figure 1: Image of the Tracery-to-HTML template by Flores.

output reveals the inner workings of the critical statement to the detriment of the intended effect of the critical statement, makers could use this to their advantage. Projects could reflexively refer to the code, taking a more self-conscious perspective.

Another option has emerged during the writing of this work: a Tracery-to-HTML template created by Leonardo Flores (Figure 1). True to the spirit of community shared by many in the digital humanities field, Flores's About page says, "This is the first of several coding engines I will create (with major help from ChatGPT) to lower the access barrier to creative coding, digital writing, and electronic literature" (Flores):

Students can download the starter code, then create their own HTML file using Tracery. The interactive page can be shared, posted, and most importantly, allows students to rapidly prototype projects and experiment with different procedural choices.

Teaching with Tracery

Students without coding experience often get anxious at the idea of procedurally generated text and images. However, after they catch on to the basics, the anxiety usually passes quickly. The authors like to introduce students to the concepts of procedural generation coding by likening it to the *MadLibs* books—words to fill in a blank are pulled randomly from lists of potential words much in the same way that the old *MadLibs* players asked a friend for a word that was a specific part of speech (noun, adjective, etc.) without providing the context of the story into which it was being inserted. The result was usually a humorous clash of a bit of a story interspersed with ill-fitting words that the readers found humorous—often bodily functions and body parts, depending on the age and maturity level. The procedurally generated text that we guide our students to create can be seen as a digital, slightly more sophisticated version of these printed *MadLibs*. The student sets up the story context and provides a list of words to fill proverbial blanks, and the computer program completes the sentence, paragraph, or story based on this infrastructure. The result is often silly (as *MadLibs* is intentionally structured to be humorous), but it can be used to critique common tropes, point out how robotic and predictable various human systems can be, and more.

One engaging assignment we have used in the past is to have students procedurally generate "clickbait:" the kinds of catchy headlines that entice people to click on a link to read more about the topic— often only to discover that the headline made the story sound much more scandalous or interesting than it actually is. Common in this information age, where views are a major commodity, the ability to generate eye-catching headlines is a valuable skill for people and bots to have. As students work to generate generic or scandalous clickbait headlines as an early assignment, they can become familiar with the syntax of Tracery and JSON grammars while mimicking the syntax of these headlines that they see daily. This assignment can then be augmented with research to generate clickbait that critiques an additional aspect of society, or even a bot that builds provocations and explores the escalating tendencies of web content through making.

For more critical and scholarly engagement, contextualizing this making through multiple histories can be transformative: building with grammars links us to the avant-garde practices of Oulipian creativity, recalling precursors of digital poetry, while simultaneously putting us in conversation with questions of who and what is human on the web. This pattern can allow for making that begins simply, but becomes rapidly more complex, and thus capable of engaging with difficult, networked ideas in ways that are emergent and unexpected.

Pattern: Tracery

Before you can begin this assignment, it is important to understand the basics of JSON and Tracery. I suggest starting on this nicely scaffolded practice website: www.crystalcodepalace.com/traceryTut.html,[4] which walks you through the basics of JSON and Tracery and was also created by Kate Compton (Figure 2).

This site provides seven rows of short examples of different grammars and rules. The left column includes an explanation in plain

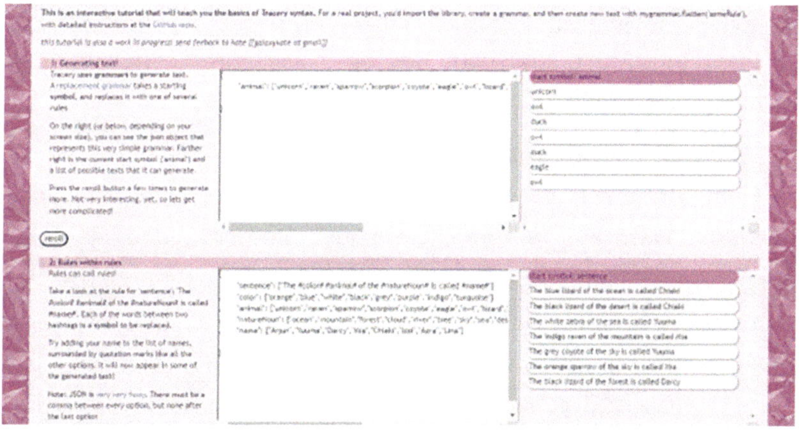

Figure 2: Compton's Tracery tutorial page, Crystal Code Palace.

4   Note: This site is no longer maintained, but is accessible via the Wayback Machine here: https://web.archive.org/web/20240316050447/http://www.crystalcodepalace.com/traceryTut.html

English about the grammar or rule, the middle column on each row has a small sandbox area for you to modify and experiment with different code, and to the right of each sandbox is posted a preview of what that coded part would produce. The first coding example is text generation, with simple lists of replacement text options for one symbol:

```
"animal":["unicorn", "raven", "sparrow",
"scorpion", "coyote", "eagle", "owl", "lizard",
"zebra", "duck", "kitten"]
```

It becomes more complex from there, ending with saving syntax and nesting stories. I recommend spending time with the first four, which cover all of the basics and can help you produce a functional, somewhat complex bot. Be sure to practice changing options for symbols, creating rules, creating new symbols, and adding modifiers. After you have a grasp of those first four, look over the tutorials: "saving data," "super advanced," and "nesting stories." These functions can take your bot from interestingly generative to something that produces much more original-sounding, human-like results.

Another (though unfortunately less pink) website also created by Compton to help people learn and practice Tracery is available at https://tracery.io/editor/. This site provides another sandbox space for practicing the same basics, but in more of a Scratch kind of presentation (Figure 3). The dropdown examples show different commands, starting with a basic "tinygrammar," and escalate to include GIFs and saving syntax. Unless you have extensive experience using Scratch or similar programs, I recommend clicking on the "JSON" option beside the dropdown box to show the actual code rather than boxes. Some students also find the "expansion" view in the top-right pane to be helpful, as it spreads out one of the displayed results and matches those colors with the code in the editable space. Because these two websites

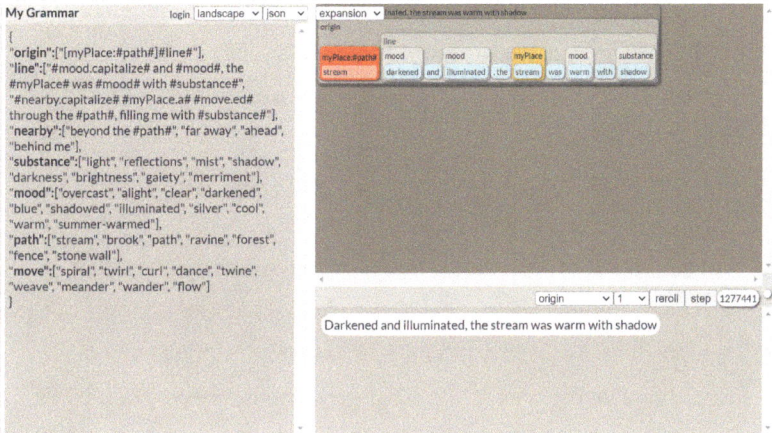

Figure 3: Tracery sandbox space with visual code elements.

provide different ways to visually understand the code, I encourage you to try them both to find the way that best helps you grasp these new concepts.

As we look towards the role of computational tools in making things visible and invisible, we are going to gradually expand our procedural literacy. So far, we've focused on adding dynamic elements with looping, choice, and interactions. This pattern uses variables and arrays towards creative ends, crafting works that can contribute to the conversation on whatever platform still allows such play. As you generate, consider the following:

- **Demonstrate a thoughtful range of grammar.** Try building on the model in the example first if you are new to generators, and incorporate a vocabulary appropriate to the type of making that drives your work. This is a great opportunity to play with language and consider the intersections of poetics, pragmatics, procedures, and play.

- **Expand upon at least three different rules to create dynamic content.** This can be accomplished by employing multiple sentences, patterns, or syntax structures—or trying out image generation, which is more challenging but rewarding. Think about how you might invite someone to engage repeatedly with your grammar by crafting a meaningful generator of variety.

- **Invite engagement.** Either launch your grammar to an HTML file using Tracery-to-HTML or Mastodon using Cheap Bots Toot Sweet, or integrate it into a Twine or Bitsy experiment by combining it with our previous patterns, like the example in the repository. You can also embed it into a .html file and post it within a website, as in the retro-generative collaboration by Fan, Sullivan, and Salter in Masked Making.

Applications

Composing the code for procedurally generated text requires thinking about the structure of text in a different way than most students are used to doing. Rather than writing in a linear, rigid style, constructing generative code requires more of a system design perspective. Writing sentences and paragraphs with potential meanings rather than singular definitive statements is a creative endeavor that can be frustrating at first but usually becomes enjoyable as students preview the statements their code generates. An iterative process of composing, previewing, and tweaking mimics the design process of most digital projects and also helps ease the emotional stress of coding something "from scratch."

A student example from Emily's undergraduate course was created by English major Amina Kotenko, and it combines Tracery with Cheap Bots Done Quick to produce a bot she called "noclichéwritingbot" that critiques common literary tropes. As of the time of writing, the archived tweets of this bot remain viewable at @writingbott, and the code is replicated below:

"origin":["#time# #adjective# #character#
couldn't help but #finale# and #action#.", "It
is a story where the #character# encounters
#animal# and together they #future#.",
"Everything started when the #character# decided
to #act# and #support# but it turns out the life
had different plans, so the story ends with #the
end#."],

"time":["Once upon a time", "Long, long ago",
"It was a dark and stormy night when", "On the
starry night", "The night was still young when"],

"adjective":["a mad", "a young", "a famous",
"an evil", "an intelligent", "a rebellious", "a
talented", "a unique", "a woeful", "an extremely
old", "a spoiled", "a kind", "a rich", "a naïve",
"an unsuspecting"],

"character":["scientist", "prince", "detective",
"queen", "wizard", "woman", "time-traveler",
"mermaid", "bastard", "lawyer", "student",
"waitress", "actress", "ballerina", "housewife",
"vampire"],

"finale":["create a monster", "avenge the
death of a father", "find a dead body", "try to
kill the princess", "follow the rabbit", "think
of homicide", "travel to the past", "start
a war", "read a book", "go against parents'
wishes", "meet a mouse", "help animals", "become
imprisoned", "befriend enemies", "end up in a
wizard school"],

```
    "action":["regretted the past actions",
"resolved the mystery in a day", "failed", "won
the war", "died in the process", "got cursed",
"got stuck", "became a chef", "refused to marry",
"became a hero"],

    "animal":["a horse", "a dog", "a unicorn", "a
fox", "a rabbit", "a cat", "a bear", "a fish", "a
mouse"],

    "future":["conquer the world", "fight the
enemy", "kill a werewolf", "find a treasure",
"fight for their lives", "encounter a witch",
"learn to see the future", "bake a cake", "become
pirates", "dream about the unknown"],

    "act":["retire", "travel the world", "write a
book", "marry", "escape the prison", "build a
ship", "believe in God", "go to school", "learn
to ride a horse", "grow an apple tree", "buy a
mirror that talks"],

    "support":["failed to pay bills", "acted
inappropriately", "hid inside of a coffin",
"gathered everybody", "met a crush", "got
injured"],

    "the end":["a funeral", "a dream", "a secret
being revealed", "a ball", "burning everything
to the ground", "writing a book to make money",
"riding off into a sunset"
```

For longevity, the code and output of this bot are also available in the GitHub repository. This procedural text is a fun take on literature analysis and writing, and it takes a playfully critical perspective that implies stories have already been written—or that the common tropes are predictable: no fiction is ever really "new." The combination of characters and plots from various well-known books and movies, however, makes the generated text rather humorous, with the bot tweeting sentences like, "it is a story where the student encounters a unicorn and together they bake a cake;" and "long, long ago an evil scientist couldn't help but find a dead body and became a chef;" and "it was a dark and stormy night when an unsuspecting waitress couldn't help but read a book and failed." The lists that the bot pulls from within the code are taken from actual works of fiction—*Alice in Wonderland*, *Snow White*, *Harry Potter*, *Ratatouille*, *Brave*, and more. The code mixes the different aspects of the works in new and interesting ways to demonstrate the common tropes in fiction and to inspire new, more original narratives.

Another example using Cheap Bots Done Quick and Twitter before 2022 comes from graduate student Jack Murray as part of the Theories in Texts and Technology course. The colleague who teaches this course asks students to create a Twitter bot using Tracery that tweets things that one or a combination of theorists might say, and students are encouraged to use creative freedoms to combine different theorists and perspectives. The example below is the result of Jack's question, "What if Michel Foucault were a gamer?"

Here again, the bot is no longer tweeting, but past tweets are possibly still viewable at @FoucaultGamer on Twitter. The code is also reproduced below:

```
"origin":["#OnMechanics#.", "#Johns#."],

"Games":["Animal Crossing", "Super Mario",
"Super Smash Bros.", "Doom", "Minecraft", "Call of
Duty", "Borderlands", "Halo"],
```

```
    "Foucabulary":["discipline", "#power#", "the
episteme", "panopticism", "normalization",
"examination", "biopower", "surveilance",
"subjectivity", "knowledge"],

    "mechanic":["platforming", "inventory
management", "saving", "leveling up", "skill
trees", "check points", "gun play", "loot
crates", "high scores", "a tutorial", "character
customization", "crafting"],

    "OnMechanics":["#Games# #explain# #Foucabulary#
through the use of #mechanic# ", "#mechanic.
capitalize# is #Foucabulary#"],

    "Johns":["#loss# because the #actor# #verb2#
#object#"],

    "verb2":["surveilled", "disciplined",
"normalized", "exercised #power# on"],

    "actor":["state", "panopticon", "game",
"player", "character", "Steam", "the Epic Store"],

    "object":["me", "the game", "my controller",
"the tv", "the console", "my framerate", "my
character"],

    "loss":["I lost", "My opponent won", "The game
ended", "I failed"],

    "explain":["demonstrates", "explains",
"constructs"],

    "power":["power", "productive power",
"repressive power"]
```

To create this bot, Jack first had to understand the theories and worldview of theorist Michel Foucault. Then, he needed to apply Foucault's theories and opinions to video game experiences, and include terms and phrases from both: "Foucabulary" as well as gaming terms, hardware, and game titles. The results are playful and poke fun at the theorist's perspective, such as, "The game ended because the state exercised power on the console;" which is something a grumpy Gamer Foucault could be imagined saying after losing a game. Other tweets have Gamer Foucault use games as examples in his ideology, such as "Halo demonstrates discipline through the use of check points;" "Borderlands demonstrates normalization through the use of a tutorial;" and the thought-provoking, "A tutorial is examination." Of course, these procedurally generated theories are not always accurate reflections of the theorist, nor are they always grammatically correct, as in the output: "My opponent won because the the Epic Store surveilled the game," but that is part of the process, as well as part of social media.

Another graduate student, Vee Kennedy, plays similarly with theory alongside fallen platforms and moments from internet history. This bot (shown in Figure 4) uses Leonardo Flores's Tracery-lite template for HTML output, and is included with the code in the repository for reference.

Futures

This theory bot assignment demonstrates ways that the critical making tools that appear throughout this book can be used in more traditional courses, where content such as specific theories needs to be mastered by the students. A group project could use the Mastodon version, Cheap Bots Toot Sweet, and code a procedural scholarly debate among theorists, with the bots set to reply to a question or a direct mention. It's also a powerful means for introducing the realities and

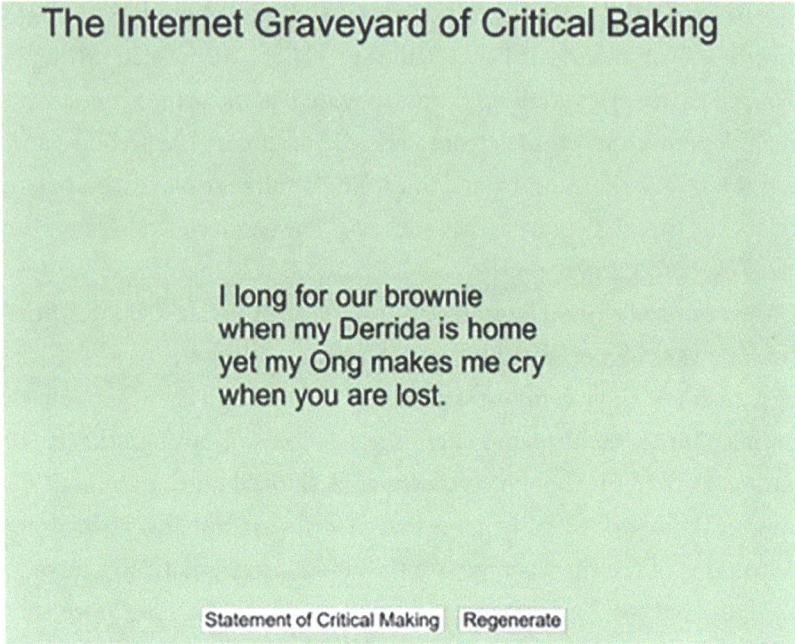

Figure 4: Vee Kennedy's "Internet Graveyard of Critical Baking."

pragmatics of generated texts into any class requiring scaffolding and historical contextualization of generative AI tools.

Generative AI can also be used as a reference tool for this type of assignment: with GitHub's Copilot and competitors increasingly able to generate, explain, and scaffold coding, the applications discussed above can be generated in just a few prompts. Students and scholars should be able to create more complex projects rather quickly once they understand the basics of JSON code. As both generative text and code become more broadly integrating, isolating, critiquing, and understanding these types of practices is critical.

Works Cited

"Botsin.Space." *Mastodon Hosted on Botsin.Space*, https://botsin.space/about. Accessed 23 Feb. 2023.
Buckenham, V. *V21*. https://v21.io/. Accessed 27 Dec. 2022.

Chayka, Kyle. "The Age of Algorithmic Anxiety." *The New Yorker*, 25 Jul. 2022, www.newyorker.com/culture/infinite-scroll/the-age-of-algorithmic-anxiety.

Cheap Bots, Done Quick! https://cheapbotsdonequick.com/. Accessed 27 Dec. 2022.

Cheap Bots, Toot Sweet! https://cheapbotstootsweet.com/. Accessed 23 Feb. 2023.

Compton, Kate, et al. "Tracery: Approachable Story Grammar Authoring for Casual Users." *Seventh Intelligent Narrative Technologies Workshop*, 2014, www.aaai.org/ocs/index.php/INT/INT7/paper/view/9266.

Fan, Lai-Tze, et al. "Masked Making." *Electronic Literature Collection*, edited by Kathi Inman Berens et al., vol. 4, Electronic Literature Organization, 2022. *collection.eliterature.org*, https://doi.org/10.7273/issn.1932-2022.4.masked-making.work.

Flores, Leonardo. "Tracery to HTML Template." *Tracery2HTML Template*, 13 Aug. 2023, http://iloveepoetry.org/creative/tracery2htmltemplate.html.

Floridi, Luciano, and Massimo Chiriatti. "GPT-3: Its Nature, Scope, Limits, and Consequences." *Minds and Machines*, vol. 30, no. 4, Dec. 2020, pp. 681–94. *Springer Link*, https://doi.org/10.1007/s11023-020-09548-1.

G2A. "Top 10 Procedurally Generated Games." *G2A News*, 9 May 2022, www.g2a.com/news/features/procedurally-generated-games/.

Gunderson, Beau. *Tracery Writer*. https://beaugunderson.com/tracery-writer/. Accessed 28 Dec. 2022.

Hand, Sarah, et al. "Exploring Teachers' and Students' Gender Role Bias and Students' Confidence in STEM Fields." *Social Psychology of Education*, vol. 20, no. 4, Dec. 2017, pp. 929–45. *Springer Link*, https://doi.org/10.1007/s11 218-017-9408-8.

Ignatov, Andrey, et al. *AI Benchmark: Running Deep Neural Networks on Android Smartphones*. 2018, pp. 0–0. *openaccess.thecvf.com*, https://ope naccess.thecvf.com/content_eccv_2018_workshops/w25/html/Ignatov_AI_ Benchmark_Running_Deep_Neural_Networks_on_Android_Smartphon es_ECCVW_2018_paper.html.

Johnson, Emily K., and Anne Sullivan. "Exploring Tangible Learning Artifacts: The Development of BeadED Adventures." *Electronic Literature Organization Conference 2020*, Jul. 2020, https://stars.library.ucf.edu/elo2 020/asynchronous/talks/7.

LEARNBOT3000. https://learnbot3000.glitch.me/. Accessed 22 Dec. 2022.

Mateas, Michael. "Procedural Literacy: Educating the New Media Practitioner." *On the Horizon*, edited by Drew Davidson, vol. 13, no. 2, Jan. 2005, pp. 101–11. *Emerald Insight*, https://doi.org/10.1108/10748120510608133.

McDuffee, Eric, and Alex Pantaleev. "Team Blockhead Wars: Generating FPS Weapons in a Multiplayer Environment." *Proceedings of the 8th International Conference on the Foundations of Digital Games (FDG 2013)*, 2013.

Plut, Cale, and Philippe Pasquier. "Generative Music in Video Games: State of the Art, Challenges, and Prospects." *Entertainment Computing*, vol. 33, Mar. 2020, p. 100337. *ScienceDirect*, https://doi.org/10.1016/j.entcom.2019.100337.

Sample, Mark. "A Protest Bot Is a Bot so Specific You Can't Mistake It for Bullshit." *Medium*, 4 Oct. 2015, https://medium.com/@samplereality/a-prot est-bot-is-a-bot-so-specific-you-cant-mistake-it-for-bullshit-90fe10b7fbaa.

———. *The Infinite Catalog of Crushed Dreams*. https://fugitivetexts.net/pan demicdreams/. Accessed 3 Jan. 2023.

Tracery. https://tracery.io/. Accessed 22 Dec. 2022.

CHAPTER 8
Analysis

In this chapter, we discuss the ways that computer-assisted analysis (sometimes referred to as machine-reading or distant reading) has altered the landscape of literary study, cultural studies, and more. With the ability to quantify terms and word counts across millions of texts has come different ways to understand writing of any genre— from Shakespeare's works to celebrity tweets, across and between authors. This analysis informs critical making projects and, in some cases, produces critical making outcomes in itself, with the ways that the tools incorporate data visualization tools like word clouds, bubblelines, scatterplots, and graphs. The pattern in this chapter uses the computer-assisted analysis tool Voyant to demonstrate the methods and potential uses of this type of analysis and the ways that it can create and contribute to critical making projects through offering new ways of seeing and exploring text.

Critical Computer-Assisted Analysis

Computer-assisted analysis, also referred to as "distant reading" in contrast to the "close reading" techniques popularized in literature programs, is a way to look at a large corpora of text to discover patterns, themes, and even language change. Corpora of texts can be created that encompass one author's lifetime of work, writing produced during a specific time period, or even a national collections of corpora to investigate word variation in the English language. One notable national corpus is a collection of 100 million words, the British National Corpus, which contains "samples of written and spoken language from a wide range of sources, designed to represent a wide cross-section of British English, both spoken and written, from the late twentieth century" (University of Oxford). Not to be outdone, the Corpus of Contemporary American English website boasts that it contains "more than one billion words of text (25+ million words each year 1990–2019) from eight genres: spoken, fiction, popular magazines, newspapers, academic texts, TV and Movies subtitles, blogs, and other web pages" (Corpus of Contemporary American English). With texts increasingly available in digital form, it is becoming easier to conduct machine readings of massive amounts of text.

Digital humanists have a long history of creating tools for the community to use. This chapter focuses on the online text analysis tool Voyant, created by digital humanists Stéfan Sinclair and Geoffrey Rockwell. The recent passing of Stéfan Sinclair in 2020 highlighted the strong community that digital humanities scholars have created and the ways that this community works together to solve problems and push for ever more innovative work. The in memoriam page created by *digital humanities quarterly* remembers him as "a treasured colleague and friend, and his many contributions to the digital humanities community include key tools like Voyant and BonPatron, infrastructure like TAPoR, long-time professional service to the Association for

Computers and the Humanities and the Alliance of Digital Humanities Organizations, and good ideas that were never realized, such as a journal devoted to critical tool reviews" ("Remembering Stéfan Sinclair"). The journal *digital humanities quarterly*, established in 2005 as the field of the digital humanities was becoming more established and recognized, served not only as a publication venue for this emerging field but also as a way for academics doing this innovative, interdisciplinary work—often the only scholars at their institutions forging into this field—to connect and collaborate with one another, resulting in ever more innovation. Like Tracery, Cheap Bots Done Quick, and other tools discussed in the previous chapter, Voyant is one of many tools developed by and for digital humanists, increasing access to powerful new ways to conduct ground-breaking research in the field.

Like the rest of the critical making approaches discussed in this book, analyses of digital corpora can be done for a variety of purposes. Beginners may find it interesting to search an individual novel or website to learn the tools and look for basic patterns—it can be especially helpful to begin with just one work that the researcher has been able to read in its entirety. They can search key character names, words, or phrases to provide evidence for themes or patterns they already noticed while reading the work, as is the case in our first student example below. While there are many free text analysis tools, such as AntConc (Anthony) and Orange (Bioinformatics Laboratory, University of Ljubljana), this chapter focuses on Voyant (Voyant Tools). The multiple powerful tools packed into this free online platform can be helpful for better understanding rhetorical choices, tracking the changes in word denotation and connotation across time, and even for simply showing the most commonly used words in a document or corpora.

More experienced scholars can use digital tools to compare the ways in which different characters are portrayed based on their use of slang words, or analyze the words that a specific author uses to describe places, events, etc. An article we recommend for context and pedagogical value is "Text-Mining Short Fiction by Zora Neale Hurston and Richard Wright Using Voyant Tools" by Kenton Rambsy. This article describes in detail the ways Rambsy was able to leverage Voyant to uncover a variety of insights about the works of Hurston and Wright. Rambsy provides a simple description of the tool that can help demystify it for novices:

> Plainly speaking, Voyant calculates summaries of words and highlights notable peaks in word usage, the diversity of content words, and word densities. Word density is a measurement of the amount of content words in relation to the total number of words in a document. Content words are parts of speech such as nouns, verbs, adjectives, and adverbs that shape a text by describing specific objects and actions as well as details of objects and characteristics of actions. Function words such as conjunctions and prepositions, for instance, are grammatical in nature and serve as auxiliary.
>
> (Rambsy 252)

Rambsy's article continues by comparing the short stories written by Hurston and Wright, walking the reader through their differences in average work word count, the ways that the characters' uses of vernacular terms differ by author, and the word density differences— along with what kinds of things these differences may imply. Rambsy chose to compare works by these two authors in part because they each published negative reviews of the other's work—likely because they had different writing styles or ideas of what fiction should entail. By comparing the metrics of various aspects of these two authors' works, it is possible to conduct a deeper analysis, or to raise new questions about these popular writings.

Rambsy begins with overall word count of each short story; the fact that these "short stories" range in word count from 2,225 to over 11,000 prompts Rambsy to ponder "what the length of a short story actually entails" (253). Though the casual reader may notice differences in

overall length of this genre, the discrepancy is rather stark when looking solely at word count totals. Voyant also helps Rambsy investigate
the dialogue of the stories' characters, noting that the authors each use
different words and spellings of African American Vernacular English
(AAVE) to increase the authenticity of their characters. Hurston favors
"dat" for "that" but only uses "wut" instead of "what" a few times.
Wright, on the other hand, does not include "dat" at all but relies heavily on "wut."

Both authors' works include a combination of standard English and
AAVE, which contributes to the word density of each story. Word density is calculated by dividing the total number of words by the number
of unique words. Rambsy uses this information to determine that:

> With the exception of character names and AAVE words such as "ah" and
> "an," Hurston uses 750 unique words less than 13 times each in "Spunk."
> Therefore, Hurston creates a precise bank of words for each of her charac-
> ters thereby not exhausting common phrases in AAVE and instead using
> a variety of linguistic combinations.
>
> (Rambsy 254)

Rambsy concludes that, compared to Wright's works, which had
lower word densities, Hurston's writing includes more variety in phrases,
words, idioms, etc. Wright's work is often repetitive but, interestingly,
the word density fluctuates within "Big Boy Leaves Home," where the
first three sections of the 6,114-word book have a word density of 209
but the final two sections have a density of 247.6. For both Hurston and
Wright, Rambsy concludes that the characters' use of AAVE in the stories' dialogue enriches the linguistic range of the writing.

These metrics are helpful for digging deeper into comparisons
between works, authors, time periods, and more. Though it may strike
some as odd to analyze words in a way that produces numbers, the
numbers produced by programs like Voyant can reveal subtleties in
the writing that the human reader may miss. Rambsy's work—as well

as the student example below—uses Voyant to conduct more traditional literary criticism and compare authors' styles. These tools, however, can be turned to more controversial topics to produce more recognizably critical making work. Rather than analyzing works of fiction, Voyant can analyze websites, government documents, Instagram posts, and more. The authors also collaborated with a graduate student recently on a project that used Voyant to analyze the rhetoric of recently released AI guidance documents released to the public by the Institute of Electrical and Electronics Engineers. By looking for repeated terms and the phrases in which they are used, we can draw some conclusions about the implicit priorities of the authors of these documents. Notable frequent terms that warrant more in-depth contextual analysis as we continue this work include "risk," "organization," "well being," and the variety of phrases that included "life," such as "work life balance." A closer look at how and where these terms are being used will produce additional insight.

Other scholars, such as Khatib and Ross, use Voyant to investigate thematic analysis. In their "A Beginner's Guide to Using Voyant for Digital Theme Analysis," housed in the Humanities Commons repository, they assert, "the importance of Voyant to the Digital Humanities cannot be understated" (Khatib and Ross 5). They demonstrate the tool's strengths and weaknesses with *Jane Eyre*, finding that a fully distant ecological reading of the novel only produces the beginnings of this type of analysis. "It is only further in the word frequency list…that a sense emerges of *Jane Eyre's* focus on nature as an elemental force and as a subject for artistic representation" (8). Ultimately, the authors conclude, for an ecological reading of the novel—even one focused on the ecology of aesthetics—it is more fruitful to use Voyant as just one step in a larger process. They explain:

> Significantly, these words were all suggested not directly from these Voyant results, but rather from dipping in and out of the text, reading passages indicated by Voyant, emphasizing the degree to which closely

interacting with the text and existing literary criticism is still necessary to transform the quantitative data into mature theme analysis.

(8)

Their article continues with an additional demonstration of exploratory theme analysis using *Frankenstein* as the example. The authors find, by looking at word frequencies and the density graph, that the novel emphasizes not "the language of horror and science, but a language of humanism" (9). The remainder of the article includes a helpful step-by-step methodology guide for novice users.

An older project using Voyant (along with other analysis tools) is the Lincoln Logarithms project, a collaborative work between the Digital Scholarship Commons and Beck Center at Emory University ("Lincoln Logarithms"). This is part of a larger project that used Voyant to analyze 57 sermons from a collection of the Pitts Theology Library given after the assassination of President Abraham Lincoln, in an exploration of "some of the earliest interpretations of the late President's legacy" ("Lincoln Logarithms"). This group found differences in word frequency of terms like "slavery" and "peace," and noted that the tool was helpful in comparing the frequency as well as the context of these words between the northernmost sermon and southernmost sermon, noting that "peace" was often used in a negative context. Their analysis with Voyant remains incomplete, as the purpose of the website is to encourage students and scholars to try the tool for themselves, but on the "Reflection" page, Sarita Alamo's comments point towards a potential perspective a critical making project could take:

> Perhaps most enticingly, the programs "read" the 57 sermons (comprised of 1672 pages and 481,575 words) in mere seconds. Reading them was more tedious; in fact, no one on our team made it through all of them. In this case, I think that actually reading the texts—even just a portion of them—was more valuable than looking at the digital tools' output.
>
> ("Reflection")

Asking students to interrogate the tools and approaches through-out this book and beyond is an excellent exercise in critical thinking as well as critical making. Truth can easily be obscured behind flashy tech or false numbers. One way students could engage in this type of thinking could be to create a project critiquing the tool, putting in a text requiring human interpretation and displaying machine-generated results that contrast the generally accepted interpretation. It is also important to note that because of the rather superficial way Voyant is used—to demonstrate its capabilities rather than conduct a thorough examination of these texts—it is difficult to make many claims about the tools or the texts where the website leaves us.

Other types of critically focused projects can use Voyant to inspect word frequencies used on social media sites or any website: by looking at the most frequently used words on a site, like one of the students in this chapter's examples did, trends and possibly hidden agendas or author perspectives can be revealed. The researcher does need to be aware of certain drawbacks in using this tool with websites. Although Voyant allows a URL to be submitted for analysis, the results vary. Reddit, for example, organizes its posts by subtopics, which seem like they would be ideal for analysis with Voyant, especially since anyone can join and post in these forums, and they are already sorted into user affinity groups. Sadly, though, the forum cannot be accurately analyzed by Voyant: pasting in the URL for a subreddit on making (r/maker) resulted in a word total of just 1,556, indicating that the full site—which appears to load as the reader scrolls down the page—is not being included in Voyant's analysis. Additionally, on this site, com-ments are not posted; the reader has to click "comments," and then a new page will be overlaid on the screen containing the original post and all of the comments. Additionally, when we tried pasting sev-eral post-and-comment URLs into Voyant, it returned entire lists of words that were not visible on the page, such as television show names. Searching on the page returned no hits, so we must assume these words are encoded in the data somewhere or part of ads that were rendered invisible by our ad blockers, potentially a hidden/old navigation menu, or even possibly just frequently used search terms embedded in the code to increase the site's search engine optimization (SEO). Data cleanup or manual copying and pasting into a text document would help to make these kinds of sites more usable with Voyant.

Voyant does better with websites containing more traditional text, such as user privacy policies. Pasting the URL for the LinkedIn privacy policy,[1] for example, analyses 6,599 total words. The vocabulary density of the document is 0.175, with only 1,153 unique words out of that 6,599 total, meaning that the document is repetitive, as expected of a legal document. Commonly used words include "services" at 149, "data" at 141, and "use" at 85. The connection between "use" and "personal" as well as "cookies" shows that the tool cannot differentiate between the noun "use" as in "personal use" and the verb "use" as in "these sites use cookies." This additional layer of analysis helps improve our understanding beyond mere word count totals—"use" appears 85 times but is used in two forms with two pronunciations. A playful critical making project might exploit this quirk in the platform to make a point about our language use, perceptions, and other interesting factors that inform the use of homographs in a language.

Another text analysis tool that is popular with students and faculty engaged in analysis of more complex datasets is Orange; this powerful software handles things with structure, such as social media posts, more easily. However, where Voyant is used in-browser and download-free, Orange requires a download and sometimes complicated installation process (especially on Apple computers). These more complex tools of digital humanities analysis have additional features, such as mapping sentiment analysis, that also push us to think about the pitfalls of artificial reading and the biases that might be reflected back

---

1   www.linkedin.com/legal/privacy-policy

to us by our tools. For instance, the sentiment analysis in Orange is often inaccurate, as technology analyzing semantic meaning of words often struggles to discern tone and sarcasm, which are prevalent in most informal and conversational text like social media posts and comments.

Finally, as we are writing this, more and more scholars are experimenting with the ways that AI can perform many of these functions. For example, Lance Cummings published a blog post on how he used ChatGPT to analyze his students' end-of-semester reflections (Cummings). The current stage of ChatGPT is still constrained; he warns in his post that it can only handle about 2,000 words at a time and remains prone to hallucinations, as discussed in Chapter 9 and in the conclusion. Cummings prompted the AI by asking it to "analyze what topics and outcomes are most important" in the student reflections and create a three-column table with the headings "topic," "quote," "related outcome." ChatGPT generated the three course outcomes most frequently talked about, an analysis of the aspects of the course students found most beneficial.[2] The ability of AI to conduct analyses like these will only grow in the years to come.

Pattern: Voyant

This pattern allows us to explore making through a mechanized lens: in effect, we are reading texts like a machine, and through this process we can both visualize larger patterns and observe what a digital humanities tool brings to our practice. It is in keeping with reading with and through (and by) the machine, a framework that Joanna Drucker reminds us is linked to the textiles and crafts we opened these explorations with: "reading has been used to describe many mechanical

---

2   The full prompt is posted here: https://community.isophist.com/c/cyborgs-writing/how-i-used-ai-to-reflect-on-my-student-reflections

processes and sorting techniques. Punch-card rods, slotted light triggers, Jacquard looms, and many other devices were reading encoded information long before the standard MARC (machine-readable cataloguing) records became ubiquitous in library systems in the 1970s" (Drucker 629). As you work with Voyant, keep the following in mind:

- **Relate the visual with the textual.** Try the different tools for visualization and textual exploration detailed below and think about this linkage, and particularly how the act of making text visual is in dialogue with our larger conversations around image-text as well as other tools for visualization we've considered.

- **Explore meaning at scale.** Working with a small set of texts won't really allow you to see compelling patterns easily: this type of exploration works best with very large datasets. Look at examples that build across novels, like the compelling work of the Datasitter's Club visualizing all the Babysitter's Club books across the years (Bowers).

- **Think about absences and invisibilities.** Often we make with the material that is most readily available, and in the case of textual analysis, that can transform our outcomes significantly: for instance, look at the language, era, and gender distributions across ready-made text archives like Project Gutenberg.

Remember that while Voyant is often used in literary analysis, there are no limits to the type of text you can explore if you are willing to do some work cleaning extraneous data, like URLs, hashtags, and usernames, from a set of texts.

Visualizing Text

Voyant offers an ease of use in the browser that makes it fast to get started. Once you've loaded the tool itself (voyant-tools.org), there are many options to bring in texts to analyze, including pasting text directly, pasting the URL of the text(s) to be analyzed, or uploading files in PDF, Word, plain text, HTML, XML, or RTF format. Voyant produces word clouds, word frequencies, and more simple visualizations without the need to download any additional software, with the exceptions for websites that aren't formatted initially in a way that Voyant can "read," discussed above. You can experiment with the tool using the open corpora available from the Voyant guide[3] ("Creating a Corpus"). These three ready-made corpora include eight of Jane Austen's novels; the 37 Shakespeare plays digitized by Project Gutenburg; and Mary Shelley's *Frankenstein*, respectively.

After you upload a corpus to analyze or select from the dropdown menu (after clicking "open" on the initial Voyant page), Voyant displays five panels of information (Figure 1). You will now see a top row consisting of three images: a word cloud under "Cirrus," a list of phrases under "Reader," and a chart of relative frequencies under "Trends." Beneath this are two additional informational panels: "Summary," which displays the total number of documents, words, and unique word forms in the corpus as well as other length and term metrics; and "Contexts," which displays a column of the most frequent terms (for the Shakespeare corpora, the term displayed initially is "shall") and three to five words that appear before and after that word within the texts.

From this starting point, you can further investigate their corpora by selecting other options in the tool. In the word cloud under "Cirrus," Voyant automatically applies a list of stopwords, or words to exclude from the word cloud; these can be edited by hovering over the blue question mark next to "Links," and clicking the blue slider symbol. This brings up editing options for the stopwords (words to exclude), white list (words to never exclude), categories, font family, and palette. Clicking "edit list" beside any of these, the user can add

---

3   Available at: https://voyant-tools.org/docs/#!/guide/corpuscreator

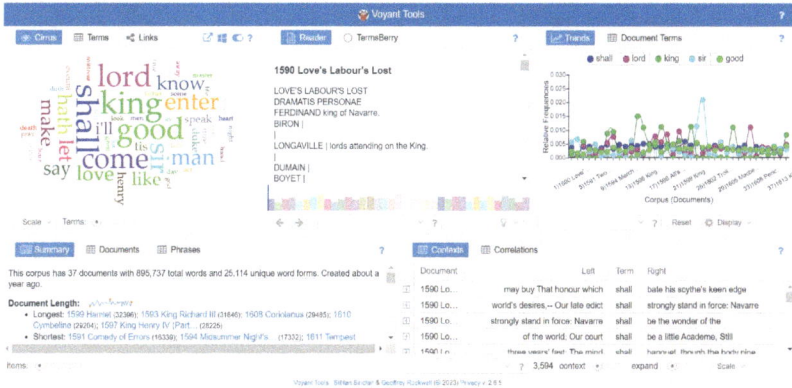

Figure 1: The panels in the Voyant interface.

or remove from the list. Color palette and font options are of course more limited. The use of stopwords and the ability to edit the list is immensely useful; the researcher can remove obvious key words for a closer inspection of less obvious frequently used words. The way that Voyant seamlessly integrates the editing is much more user-friendly than some other text analysis tools like Orange, which require the user to upload the entire document of stopwords.

Beside "Cirrus," you can select "Terms" and see the exact number of times each word appears in a corpus. For the pre-loaded Shakespeare corpus, "shall" appears 3,594 times. Beside "Terms," clicking "Links" displays a network graph of words that appear near these high-frequency words. Hovering the mouse over the blue key words will show their total frequency in the corpus, but hovering over the orange collocated words shows the number of times they appear near the blue key word, and not the total number of times they appear in the corpus. In the Shakespeare corpus, "shall" is used 3,594 times, and *near* shall, "come" appears 129 times, "know" 100 times, "make" 107 times, and "sir" 107 times.

Beside "Reader" in the next column, the user can select "TermsBerry." Aptly named, this panel displays high-frequency terms in berry-like circles. Hovering over one of the terms highlights that term in green, and highlights other related terms in dark or light red. Selecting "distinct terms" under the dropdown "Strategy" in this panel brings circles of names. Hovering over "Capulet" in the Shakespeare corpora highlights that surname in green, and "Romeo" and "Juliet" in light red.

The "Trends" graph displays the most frequent words in the corpus across its distinct documents, but clicking on a term in the "TermsBerry" panel beside it displays just that term. In the bottom row, beside "Summary," the user can select "Documents," where metrics for each document are displayed; or "Phrases," which shows multi-word phrases that appear more than once in a document. Phrases can be sorted by frequency or word length of phrases, and in the box beneath the "Contexts" panel, any term can be entered to display the contexts; clicking "Correlations" in that panel allows for text to be entered in the same box to view word correlations. Clicking on the button "scale" at the very bottom of the "Contexts" or "Correlations" panel (after clicking the > button to scroll the bottom menu) allows phrases to be searched by corpus or document.

Application: Voyant

In this section, we share three examples of students using Voyant. However, others might use text mining tools in differently innovative ways. Voyant is helpful for looking at text at the word and phrase level, of course, and this can be helpful when students need to compare and contrast authors' styles or the content of an informational text. For example, students could look at the rhetoric that two different newspapers use to describe the same event, or they could compare the different types of wording used for the same topic for different readers, like information on COVID-19 intended for an adult versus a child audience. Likewise, a course more focused on the craft of writing might ask students to upload their own papers to Voyant to see what words or phrases they commonly (or perhaps too commonly) use when they write. Students could input all of their assignments for a course at the end of the semester and track their writing style changes over time. Two additional graduate student examples pointing towards the potential complexity of this type of work are included in full in the GitHub repository: Kayla Campana contextualizes narratives of "progress" using the script from Disney's theme park attraction, The Carousel of Progress, while Mirek Stolee works from Walter Isaacson's biography of Elon Musk first to analyze the "great man" narrative, and later to develop new generated text from its frequent words.

The undergraduate student examples included in this pattern stem from the same assignment across several sections of Tools for the Digital Humanities. This assignment is the third of three major assignments that culminate in a final research-based critical making project. Often, by the time students arrive at this assignment, they have already chosen their topic for the final project and have conducted preliminary research on it. This is not the case for all students in the course, however, because the options for student project topics remain open throughout the course (they do not have to stick with the same topic for more than one project).

The first example comes from a past section of Emily's undergraduate course where students were asked to choose one of three text analysis tools: Voyant (Voyant Tools), TAGS ("TAGS"), or AntConc (Anthony), to investigate a specific text or term across texts of their choice. Several students in each section of the course focused their analysis assignment on a research topic they had already identified as the topic they would use for the final project and chose to combine TAGS and Voyant, although this was not required for the assignment. Several students used TAGS to scrape Twitter for tweets that included specific words, phrases, or hashtags, and then uploaded their results to Voyant. This process of analyzing their collections of tweets resulted in a visually interesting word cloud and powerful analysis of the tweets that would have been much more difficult without Voyant. Unfortunately, as of April 18, 2023, the API connecting TAGS to Twitter has been disabled, and the scraping service is no longer functional (discussed in Chapter 7), so the option for using TAGS for this assignment will be modified before the next offering of the course; likely replacing the TAGS option with Orange.

Only one student, Reilly Korshoff, used Voyant by itself for this assignment in the author's undergraduate Tools for the Digital Humanities course. Reilly used Voyant to investigate the novel *Twilight* by Stephanie Meyer. This tool is helpful for exploring literary texts, as it can help highlight patterns at the linguistic level that are not always obvious when reading text in a more typical, linear manner. Reilly, for instance, was able to discern that the main male character in *Twilight*, Edward, is often named in active sentences by the first-person narrator, Bella, and in comparison to Edward's mentions, Bella typically appears both in action and in writing strikingly passive. Reilly writes, "In the selected phrases, it is clear that Bella is not an active participant. This information confirms to me, as a fan, what I already knew: Bella is a character that lacks depth, agency, and identity due to her intense relationship with Edward." She was able to quickly confirm her own reading of the text and back her assertions with more specific numbers and examples of support found by Voyant, rather than having to parse through the entire text making her own notes and counts.

Reilly's analysis follows the traditional literature style analysis of a work of fiction, much like the Rambsy article discussed above. While on the surface, this may seem like less of a critique than some of the other, more provocative critical making projects that many students created in this course, Reilly was able to fold in some additional research on portrayal of gender representation in fiction, citing work on the same novel published in the *Journal of International Women's Studies* to further support her own claims, and Reilly built upon these ideas to create her final research project with Twine, which expanded from gender representation to also deal with common perceptions of marginalized groups. The combination of class assignments that asked Reilly to think critically, read other critiques, and conduct her own research with Voyant improved her final project, an interactive narrative. Investigating representation in one work of fiction helped inform her fictional representations in her final work.

In another undergraduate course, Emily added Voyant to the list of options for weekly posts in a technical communication undergraduate course, but here again only one student experimented with it. This student analyzed a blog post about Pokémon that discussed a shortage of cards, pasting the URL for that blog post into Voyant. The student's assignment focused on the word cloud generated by Voyant of the most frequently used words in the Pokémon blog post. As the student expected, the results included "Pokémon" and "cards," but the student expressed some surprise to discover that the word "worth" was also very frequently used in the article, along with other synonyms like "valuable" and related words like "condition." The student concluded that the blog author was more focused on the monetary side of the Pokémon franchise than a reader who may instead enjoy playing the game for fun. This is an interesting start to a more deeply researched critical project, or even a multifaceted one that leverages more than one digital tool. These findings certainly point to the monetary focus of many in our capitalist society, and the student could use this as a jumping-off point to create something with more of a critique on those values.

While the course where the student analyzed the Pokémon blog did not have a critical making focus, it is easy to see how this kind of preliminary work could be part of a larger course where each assignment builds on the prior one. The Tools for the Digital Humanities course is designed with more of a "choose your own adventure" style structure, where students are encouraged to experiment with the different tools and different research topics as they like. The tools are presented and explained on a page created by the author, along with a list of resource links to tutorial videos, help pages, and examples of publications that used the tool. From there, the author provides support as needed, and students are free to select their own research topics. As with most interdisciplinary courses like this one, some students arrive to the course with a specific research interest or career goal, while others are simply enrolled in the course to fulfill an elective credit or have yet to declare an academic major. As students share their work with one another during the semester, they are exposed to different types of research topics and different ways to use each of the tools. This helps to build a scaled-down version of the larger, supportive community of digital humanities scholars, and while students typically are not building their own open-source digital humanities tools for their peers to use, it helps to encourage and reassure students who struggle or second guess themselves to see other ways that these tools can be used.

Futures

More graduate students are certainly using Voyant and similar tools in dissertation and publication work, though several are more complex than the other examples in this book and use Voyant in combination with a number of different digital tools. Two graduate students, Dan Heslep and PS Berge, used Python to scrape over 2,700 Discord servers marked in ways that made it obvious they were connected with white supremacy and neo-Nazism, raiding, queerphobia, transphobia, and/or toxicity (Heslep and Berge). They then analyzed the data with Orange's topic modeling, word clustering, and concordance tools but followed up with additional concordance analysis in AntConc and Voyant to highlight patterns and gain additional word counts to examine the ways that Discord users were distributing prohibited content using third-party tools to circumvent the platform's content moderation practices. Examples with this kind of content remind us that it is always a good idea to caution students that research on social media and the internet is likely to result in reading things people have posted anonymously. Anonymous posts are not always well-mannered, and researchers should be prepared for toxic posts, especially when investigating hotly debated or political issues common to critical making projects.

Heslep and Berge's example also demonstrates the benefits of being able to use a variety of analysis tools to conduct research, especially interdisciplinary research common to the digital humanities. These students were able to use a digital tool to collect their data, and then combined Orange, AntConc, and Voyant—three different digital tools—to conduct their analysis. While several of the tools overlap in functionality, these students were able to switch back and forth between the tools to deepen their analyses, to seek specific kinds of patterns in the data more easily, and possibly even to select the best visual representations of the data from across the different styles. All students do not need to be explicitly taught each of these tools within the duration of a course or even a program. Rather, like computational thinking and other digital literacies, after students have been guided through the basics of a specific analysis tool, they often have an easier time navigating other analysis tools on their own. This is also why our lesson plans are rarely step-by-step procedures like many high school science labs—we provide an overview of the general capabilities of each tool, some examples of published work that use the tool in question, and then links to online resources where students can find step-by-step guides for specific functions that they deem relevant to their own topic and project. In doing so, we guide our students—and readers of this work—through the process of learning a new tool but also show them the kinds of things to look for as they familiarize themselves with additional digital tools in the future.

With the evolution of large language models (LLMs), we anticipate rapid growth in the area of AI text analysis. The most constraining aspect of ChatGPT at the time of writing (ChatGPT-4) is the need to paste the text to be analyzed into the interface. Open-source workarounds are emerging across the web, such as a program that splits your long text up and provides instructions for you to paste into ChatGPT telling it to analyze each of the chunks of text as one body of data (Diaz). While it works to get the job done, this time-consuming workaround is presumably going to be replaced by upgraded versions of AI tools that can handle much larger amounts of data.

Likewise, given the way that predictive text platforms have been developed—through the analysis of enormous amounts of data—this technology is probably very good at distant reading. The lack of a user-friendly way to connect AI and large datasets, like Voyant has, is surprising but probably something that is being worked on as we type. AI developers are working on ever more sophisticated algorithms for text prediction; analysis of large texts in a "plain English" chat cannot be far behind. Paid platforms like Microsoft's Azure, as well as plugins for the subscription version of ChatGPT (GPT-4) like the Data Exploration Assistant, Data Visualization Wizard, and the Natural Language Data Interface, are getting closer to this functionality.

These developments could be seen as making the tutorial aspects of this chapter rather obsolete; however, we argue that there will still be value in doing some of this labor outside of AI models, as these methods make visible the work that an algorithmic toolset can obscure and thus serve the purpose of developing critical AI literacy.

Works Cited

Anthony, Laurence. "Software: AntConc." *Laurence Anthony's Website*, www.laurenceanthony.net/software/antconc/. Accessed 10 May 2023.

Bioinformatics Laboratory, University of Ljubljana. *Orange Data Mining*. https://orangedatamining.com/. Accessed 11 May 2023.

Bowers, Katherine. "DSC #6: Voyant's Big Day—The Data-Sitters Club." *The Data-Sitters Club*, 15 Sept. 2020, https://datasittersclub.github.io/site/dsc6.html#suggested-citation.

Corpus of Contemporary American English. www.english-corpora.org/coca/. Accessed 3 May 2023.

"Creating a Corpus." *Voyant Tools Help.* https://voyant-tools.org/docs/#!/guide/corpuscreator. Accessed 21 Mar. 2023.

Cummings, Lance. "How I Used AI to Reflect on My Student Reflections." *ISophist*, 12 May 2023, https://community.isophist.com/c/cyborgs-writing/how-i-used-ai-to-reflect-on-my-student-reflections.

Diaz, Jose. "Break the Limits: Send Large Text Blocks to ChatGPT with Ease." *Medium*, 19 Mar. 2023, https://medium.com/@josediazmoreno/break-the-limits-send-large-text-blocks-to-chatgpt-with-ease-6824b86d3270.

Drucker, Johanna. "Why Distant Reading Isn't." *PMLA*, vol. 132, no. 3, May 2017, pp. 628–35. *Cambridge University Press*, https://doi.org/10.1632/pmla.2017.132.3.628.

Heslep, Daniel G., and PS Berge. "Mapping Discord's Darkside: Distributed Hate Networks on Disboard." *New Media & Society*, Dec. 2021, p. 1461444821062548. *SAGE Journals*, https://doi.org/10.1177/1461444821 1062548.

Khatib, Randa El, and Shawna Ross. *A Beginner's Guide to Using Voyant for Digital Theme Analysis.* 2022. *hcommons.org*, https://hcommons.org/depos its/item/hc:49487/.

"Lincoln Logarithms: Finding Meaning in Sermons." *Lincoln Logarithms*, 2013, https://lincolnlogs.digitalscholarship.emory.edu/.

Rambsy, Kenton. "Text-Mining Short Fiction by Zora Neale Hurston and Richard Wright Using Voyant Tools." *CLA Journal*, vol. 59, no. 3, 2016, pp. 251–58.

"Reflection." *Lincoln Logarithms*, 3 Apr. 2015, https://lincolnlogs.digitalscholars hip.emory.edu/reflection/.

"Remembering Stéfan Sinclair." *Digital Humanities Quarterly*, 2020, www.digita lhumanities.org/dhq/vol/14/2/000493/000493.html.

"TAGS." *TAGS*, https://tags.hawksey.info/. Accessed 21 Mar. 2023.

University of Oxford. *British National Corpus.* www.natcorp.ox.ac.uk/. Accessed 3 May 2023.

Voyant Tools. https://voyant-tools.org/. Accessed 27 Mar. 2023.

CHAPTER 9

Generation

The rise of AI has panicked many in education, much the way that the computer, calculator, and even technology of writing itself panicked faculty generations before us. As our students gain access to increasingly robust digital tools that can write, draw, think, and learn, we must reimagine the roles of student, teacher, and institution. With the advent of AI, digital literacy, the ever-expanding sets of skills needed to navigate the world, is in the process of being expanded and redefined. This pattern pivoted with the release and increasing use of tools that use AI to generate text and art. The growing concerns about how AI is appropriating art and art styles it finds on the internet is concerning (Metz). In an article for CNN Business, Rachel Metz describes how independent visual artists are finding pieces of their art embedded within the "machine created" works. ChatGPT-3 has been found as capable of generating a passable, if dull, first-year composition essay (Warner), to a passing B grade on an MBA exam (Needleman). The newer version, ChatGPT-4, passed the Arizona bar exam, scoring in the 90th percentile (Cassens Weiss). While some seek ways to prevent and identify this work, which defies typical plagiarism software

(Hern), with plagiarism detection software companies struggling to keep up (Knox), we look to a future of more meaningful assignments beyond the standard essay. How can we use AI to spur deeper learning and more advanced literacy and digital literacy skills through more meaningful assignments?

Critical Generation

Interestingly, we initially planned for this chapter to focus on archiving: curation as narrative and as a method for critical making. The act of curation is one of inclusion and exclusion; if a work is included in a collection, it is deemed important and culturally relevant. If it is deemed irrelevant, then it is excluded. This all works to tell a story and share a perspective on the artists, the institution where the archive is housed, or even the archivist. Too often—we were planning to argue—the work of digital institutional archive is often associated with amplifying a familiar canon, rather than creating space to preserve essential work on the margins. This eerily, but logically parallels much of what we are seeing with AI applications. To function, AI must first be trained on an archive; or, as computer scientists term it, a data set. The data set has been curated by someone, and that person's experience, biases (unconscious or otherwise), cultural awareness, and the availability of the data all work to influence what is included and what is excluded and therefore the resulting AI. One of the major issues with AI in its current state is the lack of transparency regarding training processes.

When an AI text-generating system, GPT-2, was released by OpenAI (a company funded by Elon Musk) in February 2019, the company initially refused to share the full model with the public or even with other researchers because the potential for harmful misuse of the technology to create misinformation or spam was too great (Vincent,

"OpenAI's New Multitalented AI Writes, Translates, and Slanders");
however by November of that same year, the full model was released
(Vincent, "OpenAI Has Published the Text-Generating AI It Said Was
Too Dangerous to Share"), generating much media attention.

This publicity stunt of a staged release garnered much air time,
further fueling existing debates over the ethics of technology that
seems too powerful for our own good, like DeepFakes, where the
company released a statement of ethics that claimed that open source
advancements were necessary and of more import than the potential
for their misuse (Winter and Salter). When anyone with an Internet
connection has access to tools that can make misinformation look and
sound credible, there is great potential for these tools to be used for
malintent.

The public release of ChatGPT-3 in November 2022, followed
quickly by the release of ChatGPT-3.5 and then ChatGPT-4 by March
2023, spurred even more discussions in the media, academia, and
beyond regarding the ethical and pedagogical implications of such
software. Notable names in the tech industry including Steve Wozniak
and founder of OpenAI Elon Musk signed an open letter on March 29,
2023, urging private companies to halt their development of AI software, claiming "recent months have seen AI labs locked in an out-of-
control race to develop and deploy ever more powerful digital minds
that no one—not even their creators—can understand, predict, or reli-
ably control" (Future of Life Institute). While Musk's reasons for sign-
ing are likely focused more on competitors to his own companies, the
letter obtained over 50,000 signatures in just six days.

As the public experiments with these new tools, many have found
that AI is useful in generating boilerplate code that can then be modified by advanced coders (Paik and Wang), and the text that is standard
on legal documentation (Lee and Hsiang). AI is also able to recognize
patterns across larger sets of data more quickly than humans, and it
can display the results in a more reader-friendly format than we have

seen with distant reading tools like Voyant (Rambsy) and others. An interesting difference between this AI and generative text seen in the past is the ability of ChatGPT to incorporate creative and whimsical responses like what a human might produce, such as the ability to explain something "in the style of a cat," where the responses include occasional "meow" among standard English. This and other stylistic forms were popularly—prior to this technology—assumed to be only able to be produced by creative humans (Rosenblatt).

While some of the outputs of AI are certainly thought-provoking and amusing, the datasets used to train the AI models are problematic. Much of the OpenAI training set was scraped from various places on the internet, unannounced and without author or artist permission. As anyone who has visited websites or social media platforms that allow anonymous or pseudonym comments has noticed, the text we post on the internet does not always cast humanity in a flattering light. With AI generators learning not only from the BookCorpus Dataset and Wikipedia but also from website forums like Reddit, it is inevitable that the generators would "learn" some inappropriate words, phrases, and misinformation. Art generators, too, were trained by scraping public portfolio websites—without the artists' permission—and they rely on the way images are tagged within a training set, with the curation and tagging labor often done by people uncompensated for their work. Further, because the tagging is done by humans who hold conscious and unconscious biases, the generated images replicate discriminatory themes that are harmful (Clark; Noble). Our collaborations have even engaged this trend, and critical making can be a means to make those trends visible: "Post-Anthropocene Poetics [De] Fused" (Figure 1) shows these possibilities by combining a Tracery grammar for poetry with generated imagery, allowing the work to "critically reflect on societal gender representations and biases that are embedded within the data sets and AI code that are presented as neutral agents" (Sullivan and Salter). The resulting compositions are

Sounds slither from fear to determined fear
Our greedy nature despairs
Until only a wasteland remains.

Figure 1: A Tracery-grammar poem used as a seed for a machine learning generated image (Sullivan and Salter).

themselves image-texts, offering us another lens on the type of jux-tapositions we've explored multimodally across our patterns thus far.

Additionally, the AI art generators as a whole seem to struggle to find the line between producing work in a particular artist's style and copying parts of works already created by human artists, all without their consent, creating "an ethical and copyright black hole" (Plunkett) and raising questions about copyright law (Zeilinger; Zylinska). For example, early in 2023, artists Sarah Andersen, Kelly McKernan, and Karla Ortiz brought a class-action lawsuit against two AI companies, Stable Diffusion and Midjourney, claiming that the AI generated plagiaristic works (Vincent, "AI Art Tools Stable Diffusion and Midjourney Targeted with Copyright Lawsuit"). By late October of 2023, the majority of the case had been dismissed, with the limiting Copyright Act claims only applying to work that had been officially registered with the US copyright office (Gennaro).

Most AI art generators are trained using works posted on the internet, specifically on the platform DeviantArt, where many aspiring artists post their work to gain feedback from the community and to reach a wider audience for their art. The artists posting their work on DeviantArt were not asked their permission for using their work in the AI training, nor were they even notified that their work was incorporated into a training set. This is obviously problematic given how many artists rely on internet sites like these to attract new customers and sell their work, and has serious ethical, copyright, and intellectual property issues. Even worse, DeviantArt is named in the lawsuit because it sells users access to its own AI generator, DreamUp, which generates art based on the works posted on that platform and others. This scenario is playing out with even more artists at the time of writing, but a clear solution or compensation model has yet to be developed (Metz).

Even more recently, Modelscope has released its Text2Video generator, which, as its name implies, generates original videos from textual prompts. At the time of writing, there remain humorous issues with these videos, as they struggle to maintain accurate representations of things like words and human faces. The misinterpretations of the prompts generate interesting results, as illustrated with the terrifying, uncanny valley depiction of Will Smith eating spaghetti, among others (Placido). While this technology has a way to go, it will likely improve greatly in the next few years—at which time, faculty will again be faced with authorship questions as students can simply generate an original multimedia assignment without going through the effort of animating or recording and editing things themselves (and we note the expansion of AI-powered video editing and transcription tools that is occurring while we write). Here again, we may find ourselves questioning what aspects of these assignments are best for teaching the knowledge and skills our students need—if it is in fact necessary for them to have editing experience or if it will be enough to teach them how to prompt, modify, and curate media to produce an outcome that communicates their understanding of a concept, research findings, etc.

Though likely to improve, the current range of free AI text generators remains famously unable to consistently produce legitimate scholarly citations (Hillier), as required by most writing assignments at the university level—and in one instance providing information false enough to spur at least one defamation lawsuit (Kaye). AI generators have also famously produced results that included fabricated sexual harassment lawsuits about real people (Turley). Even the generation of "facts" that are inaccurate is not harmless—there is great potential for AI to be used to create a vast amount of misinformation that can be spread to sow mistrust and chaos, and sadly, we have already seen human-created misinformation do this successfully. The subscription version of ChatGPT-4, especially in conjunction with its plugins, is much more powerful, providing summaries of academic articles as well as accurate annotated bibliographies—a common assignment across the humanities—in mere seconds. It is difficult to ignore the ways this could impact both teaching and researching at the university level.

Recalling the potential scenario posed in the introduction of a writerless, readerless essay, we are inspired and possibly required to now look beyond the essay as the most common institutional measure of understanding. Though the essay remains a hallmark of higher education, we seek more innovative and meaningful ways for students to acquire and demonstrate knowledge. Asking students to create things follows constructivist learning theory, allowing the learner to construct their own understanding of concepts as they build their product. Hands-on projects where students learn through the process of creating something original, often combining creativity and research, though common in elementary schools, are not seen as frequently in higher grades, but we argue they belong there, too. AI as it is and as it evolves may prove to be a helpful tool in brainstorming and creating early drafts of written and visual work, likely redefining the very act of making.

Like calculators, the internet, search engines, Wikipedia, and so on, generative AI tools are likely to revolutionize the ways we teach, learn, and work—and educators will need to adapt (Mok). With many university students already leveraging AI tools on coursework and exams, faculty are scrambling to catch up (Cu and Hochman). Plagiarism detection software company TurnItIn released an update on April 4, 2023 that they claimed would detect text written by AI (Knox). A few days prior to the release, however, the company admitted that their software was trained on ChatGPT-3.5 and by the time TurnItIn distributed the update, OpenAI had already released ChatGPT-4. Controversially, TurnItIn did not disclose its detection methods, and institutions using TurnItIn had no way to opt out of the AI generation scanning, prompting considerable concern among educators and administrators. Returning to the ways that AI is similar to archival efforts, the opacity of the AI training set used by OpenAI and TurnItIn makes it difficult to be fully understood by anyone who uses it to try to determine authentic authorship of a text. The use of TurnItIn to flag assignments as written by robots without any understanding of why or how different pieces of writing will be evaluated is unsettling to a lot of people.

The escalation of AI and AI-detection tools is reminiscent of when students (and horrified teachers of all levels) discovered the ease of the cut-and-paste function on the internet, or earlier in time to the development of ever-more-powerful calculators, making slide rules and time-consuming arithmetic obsolete. Teaching, learning, and writing will need to adapt to the new terms. Text is not the only thing AI is capable of generating, either. A number of AI image generators have also been released to the public, such as WomboAI, Midjourney, and Stable Diffusion. These tools combine shorter text-based prompts with artistic styles to generate new works in the style of famous artists or painting styles. This contrasts with the way text generators seem to have ample training fodder available on the internet to produce text that does not seem overly borrowed from any particular author. Except in cases when it is prompted for a new poem or song in the style of a specific artist—and even then, the lyrics produced are mostly original—there is seemingly enough variation in the way ideas can be expressed in writing (especially in English) to allow these generated texts to avoid plagiarism, at least in the traditional sense.

Many faculty support sites are responding to faculty panic over AI tools with reactionary policies and recommendations. At the start of the spring (January) 2023 semester, our university faculty center established a site on AI for faculty explaining generative AI and offering four categories of reactionary strategies for handling AI ("Artificial Intelligence Tools"). The first category is "Neutralize the software," with suggestions for kinds of writing assignments that were difficult for early, free AI tools to do well, such as longer essays and using actual citations along with posting an anti-AI course policy to the syllabus and using detection software (although we know these are not always accurate). Category two of suggestions is titled "Teach ethics, integrity, and career-related skills." This category emphasizes an honor code and discussions of the ethics of AI software. For category three, our faculty center suggests that instructors "Lean into the software's abilities," where they recommend using this opportunity to "re-envision writing as editing/revising" and "re-envision writing as first and third stage human work, with AI performing the middle." This is also the category into which most of the example assignments in this chapter—and this book—fall: using digital tools to extend student research to make a critical statement. The faculty center's fourth and final category is also an intriguing one, "Use the software to make your teaching/faculty life easier." Recommendations in this category encourage faculty members to use AI to generate rubrics for assignments, letters of recommendation, summaries of student formative assessments to look for areas of mis/understanding, and even in research writing as grammar checking tools.

In the few months of peer review and revision of this manuscript, our university has updated and rearranged these recommendations. These changes reflect the shifting perceptions of AI as well as its increased functionalities. The revised order of recommendations now begins with "Lean into the software's abilities," with 20 suggestions in the top category one spot. Category two, "Use the software to make your teaching/faculty life easier," no longer includes the suggestion for AI to write letters of recommendation, but rather "write simple or mechanical correspondence," along with eight other suggestions. Category three is now "Teach ethics, integrity, and career-related skills," with three suggestions. The category "Neutralize the software" has been reworded to "Attempt to neutralize the software" and bumped from category one to four. It now has no suggestions and only links to a PDF of the 16 suggestions when it was category one, indicating just how much shuffling and revision has transpired. Overall, many of the reactionary suggestions for avoiding or "neutralizing" the software have been tamped down here, but the most interesting changes appear after the suggestions. The two possible syllabus statements are followed by a note to "aim for a level-headed tone that neither overly demonizes AI nor overly idolizes it." Following this is a section explaining how faculty can access Bing Chat Enterprise with their university credentials, then a section titled "AI fluency." This section begins, "We recommend that faculty approach the AI revolution with the recognition that AI is here to stay and will represent a needed skill in the workplace of the future (or even the present!) As such, both faculty and students need to develop AI Fluency skills, which we define as:" followed by seven actions and explanations. The most curious is number three:

> 3. Valuing AI—a dispositional change such as this one is often overshadowed by outcomes favored by faculty on the cognative [*sic*] side, yet true fluency with AI—especially the AI of the future—will require a favorable disposition to using AI. Thus, we owe it to students to recognize AI's value.
>
> ("Artificial Intelligence Tools")

This seems like a drastic change from the initial recommendations that were posted here, and likely reflects increased understanding of (and administration optimism towards) generative AI tools. We take issue with the need for a "favorable disposition to using AI," however. Do students need to have a favorable disposition towards Microsoft Word to compose essays? To the university library website's search tool to conduct research? We would reason that students can be digitally literate even if they don't have strongly positive feelings about a particular tool.

The best guidance for academics about generative AI that we have seen thus far is from the Modern Language Association and Conference on College Composition and Communication (MLA-CCCC) joint task force on writing and AI, which includes a brief background and history of AI, five potential risks to students, three potential risks to teachers, nine potential risks to "programs and the profession," four benefits to language instruction, seven benefits for literary studies, ten potential benefits for writing instruction, and 12 principles and recommendations[1] (Byrd et al.). This working paper, posted in July 2023,

---

1   In April 2024 the joint task force published a second working paper guiding generative AI policies, available at: https://aiandwriting.hcommons.org/working-paper-2/

takes a thoughtful approach towards understanding the technology and making informed decisions about its use. The potential risks to students that are listed are followed by a note warning that they "could hurt marginalized groups disproportionately, limiting their ability to make autonomous choices about their expressive possibilities" (Byrd et al. 7). The principles and recommendations conclude with "We are called upon to do some reimagining and some revisiting of common-places of our fields. We are up to this task if we do so with care, dia-logue, reflection, and humanity, all of which are central to the allied fields represented by our organizations" (Byrd et al. 12–13).

Pattern: Generative AI

AI-generated text and images are platforms that have great potential for meaningful critical making projects—especially at their current stage of imperfection. Projects using these tools will likely tend more towards the genre of glitch art than fully polished projects, but then again, we have valued process over outcome throughout these patterns. Quirks and emergence can contribute to the overall work, and we embrace these much like Marshall McLuhan's famous cover typo of "massage" instead of "message." As you engage in generation, con-sider how to:

- **Probe the conversational limitations.** Try starting vague, or working with different ways of phrasing and expressing ideas to see where meaning is conveyed and where it is lost. These conversations are in part an opportunity to see what is included in the underlying archives (training data)—can you tell what might be missing?
- **Explore a range of expressive outputs.** Machine learning models are particularly powerful for assistance in programming and development work, as tools like GitHub Copilot suggest: in

time, it's likely these tools will be an inescapable part of certain workflows. Think about where the AI assists your making, and where it is limiting.

- **Contextualize the experience.** How does the system you are co-creating with reflect the headlines, fears, and assumptions that both generations of science fiction writers and current journalists have centered in their visions of AI futures?

The work of generation is in many ways a conversation, and it is that conversation we invite you to engage in through this process. A few examples of conversational approaches one might take to an AI-generated tool include the following:

- Display the results of a conversation or "interview" with the AI about your research topic, asking it to answer using the perspective of a specific person, theory, or ideology. Evaluate the results and reflect on their implications.
- Ask the AI text or image generator to create/refute misinformation about your research topic. Evaluate the results and reflect on their implications.
- Use an AI art generator to create a visual or artistic representation of an aspect of research that you conducted. Evaluate the results and reflect on their implications.
- Try co-creating a website or digital art project with the AI, developing code and deploying it to test the results. Evaluate the results and reflect on their implications—which aspects benefitted from AI? Which aspects were impeded by AI?
- Use both text and art generators back and forth to generate a representation—or to garble a representation—of a research topic or theory. Evaluate the results and reflect on their implications.
- Generate another version of a work you created using a different digital tool by prompting an AI tool of your choice. Compare and contrast the output with your work, and reflect on the implications.

While there are many platforms available, one of the easiest to engage with at present is OpenAI's ChatGPT. To access it, create an account on OpenAI's playground. Monetization models are continuously changing, and very few tools remain open access: ultimately, the cost of running machine learning models is simply too great to justify maintaining them as a free service. However, the same general approach of conversation and prompt-based input that works with OpenAI can be tried with whatever model is available when you explore.

Learning to negotiate with the model is particularly helpful for technical work: for instance, prompting ChatGPT to generate the foundation of a P5.js platformer (shown in the interaction with OpenAI's earlier version, Chat-GPT-3, in Figure 2) will result in code that requires deciphering. The more familiar you are with the terms and possibilities of the verbs of making, the more successful you can be in building with the AI and communicating your design goals into playable outcomes. Experimenting with AI-generated code, discovering what works, and troubleshooting what does not can be a way to strengthen your own coding literacy.

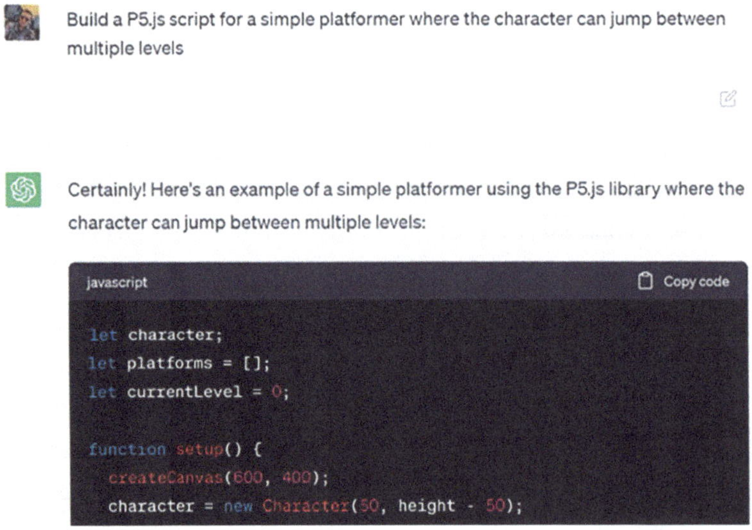

Build a P5.js script for a simple platformer where the character can jump between multiple levels

Certainly! Here's an example of a simple platformer using the P5.js library where the character can jump between multiple levels:

```javascript
let character;
let platforms = [];
let currentLevel = 0;

function setup() {
    createCanvas(600, 400);
    character = new Character(50, height - 50);
```

Figure 2: Talking with ChatGPT-3 to generate code for a P5.js game starter.

Applications

Additional assignments we are planning to incorporate into our future critical making courses will ask students to leverage the free versions of AI text and image generation to produce critical works, just as they are asked to use other types of digital tools to make arguments. It would be interesting to see how Stable Diffusion handles the Image assignment, or how ChatGPT does at generating the text for an interactive narrative—and the impact of the technology on the player and the narrative, by creating a prompt for the player to enter into the AI and then just freely respond to it for the entirety of the narrative—ending whenever the player chooses to close the tab. AI tools are getting much more effective at generating accurate code and could be helpful for quickly generating stylesheets for Twine or other projects involving coding.

Although the AI technology discussed in this chapter has rapidly evolved over the period of writing and was not incorporated into a full module in any of the authors' critical making courses like the other tools discussed in this book, one author did include use of it as an option for an undergraduate technical communication course that incorporates weekly writing prompts spanning from reflections on assigned readings to tutorials, procedure videos, and analyses of professional websites and manuals. In Emily's spring 2023 semester, almost a dozen students selected to respond to this prompt (emphases from original assignment):

> Use ChatGPT (create a free account) to generate one of the assignments for this course that you have **already completed**. Share the **prompt** you use, the **results** you receive, and a brief **analysis** of the **strengths and weaknesses of the software**.

Students generated some admittedly passable responses to a variety of writing prompts along with their own thoughtful reflections on the tools and their uses, from a quick-start guide to a reflection on a past assignment. This assignment and student reflections have helped increase our understanding of the strengths, weaknesses, and potential ways to use ChatGPT-3 (and later in the semester, ChatGPT-3.5), which did surprisingly well in explaining how to do specific tasks—even describing the proper technique for styling one's hair with a claw clip. The AI also provided legitimately helpful tips for succeeding in online course—including listing several actual apps designed to help students focus, study, and more.

In the analyses students were asked to write accompanying the AI examples, they expressed surprise at how quickly the software could produce a large volume of text. Students frequently critiqued the AI's writing as sounding robotic, although, honestly, the writing style was not strikingly different than in typical undergraduate assignments, especially on the minor weekly practice assignments. Kevin Perez, an undergraduate student who used the technology to recreate a list of tips for succeeding in an online course, articulated this observation as well, writing, "if someone were to read the entry given by the AI without knowledge of ChatGPT existing, I think they wouldn't even bat an eye; as robotic as it sounds," he explains, the generated text is "just enough to get passed as 'personal.'" However, Kevin experimented with the AI beyond the assignment requirements and reported, "it has no sense of logic—I wanted to attempt the capability of this AI after asking it to do the entry for this assignment and asked it a somewhat complex algebra question…it was unable to do it. I investigated it more and found out that it is awful at doing math problems, in other words, it has no way to reason any problem."

Likewise, Christian Rodriguez asked ChatGPT to generate a quick-start guide for the handheld gaming console Steam Deck, an assignment he had already completed for class. He was also impressed with how quickly the AI could respond, and it produced a nicely numbered, detailed guide. Christian commented, "the generation goes more in depth that my own quick start guide and even goes beyond what

I described in my quick start guide with more steps going further than just turning on the device." However, when he tried to incorporate images, per the assignment requirements, "it stated it was not capable of doing so and gave me the same answer instead as you see above." This brought Christian to the conclusion that "the convenience of having something like this is immense and can be helpful to a lot of people that might need something done quickly and done well." He cautioned, though, that "the weaknesses of this technology mostly lies [*sic*] in how it's used," since it could not provide the captioned images to gain full marks on the assignment.

Another undergraduate, Myra Hoover, input an assignment that asked students to analyze a manual of their choice (software, hardware, or other complicated product), and produce a business memo explaining the results in a clear, easy-to-skim manner with the intended audience being the CEO or some other highly ranked employee in the company that produced the product. This assignment did not have a specific word count listed, but students were asked to keep it limited to one page in length. Myra pasted the three main questions the analysis was required to answer: "Explain, briefly, what aspects of the manual are effective and why, what aspects of the manual are ineffective and why, and conclude with recommendations." Interestingly, however, she chose not to include an actual manual for the AI to analyze. ChatGPT dutifully generated one paragraph for each topic, just like most of my students did for this assignment, despite not having a specific manual to analyze. Myra commented that the language used in the response was professional, with nice vocabulary including "troubleshooting" and "visual aids," which, she felt "made it seem like the response could have potentially been written by an actual person."

Myra's experience with the ChatGPT-generated analysis of, well, nothing is an excellent demonstration of how the technology can easily fabricate believable nonsense. In addition, the analysis it generated was extremely vague and repetitive, as Myra explains the recommendations of "adding a table of contents, index, and other forms of visual aids were mentioned many times throughout the response, which therefore decreased how concise and readable the generated response was." She concludes that this vague response is what makes it obvious that the writing was done by AI and not a real human. In this experiment, ChatGPT only generated 210 words—not enough, Myra noted, as this is "below the word count required for many assignments at the college level." Even within those 210 words, the writing was repetitive and not well organized. Here again, however, these issues with writing quality mimic the common issues with writing quality that are common to K12 and undergraduate students; the technology as it stands today is more applicable to schoolwork than professional writing. This ability to mimic the writing style of an undergraduate or high school student is likely part of what is fueling faculty concerns of plagiarism and the suggested responses from faculty centers, discussed above.

Futures

Despite current limitations in the technology outlined by these assignments, it is reasonable to predict that AI capabilities will only improve, certainly in their ability to produce the assignments for our courses, given that we require our students to post their work on their own digital portfolios (only a few choose to password-protect their sites), providing AI trainers access to more and more online samples from these and similar courses. These technologies, like others in the past, push us as faculty to reimagine our approaches to teaching and learning, especially surrounding text-based assignments, as we mentioned in the introduction. In our *Playful Pedagogy* book (Johnson and Salter), we called on faculty to use the chaotic "pivots" of the pandemic as an impetus to pause and meaningfully reflect on our pedagogical choices. With AI, we have yet another opportunity to reconsider the learning intent for each of our assignments. Perhaps we will finally reach a point of educational disruption like those promised with the computer and internet.

Student projects could also experiment with AI to generate compelling works of art—as well as grapple with the results and implications. Graeme Revell's experiments combine GPT-2, GPT-3, and DALL-E2 to produce stunning results (Revell). Revell prompted the text generator to respond to a line of poetry or fiction, then entered that response into the DALL-E2 art generator, adding the name "Madeline" before the quote. Other compelling art was generated using the poetry or fiction quotations as well. The human–AI–AI collaboration presented here is an interesting one, and may be worthwhile incorporating into critical making courses. We can easily imagine an assignment that asks students to produce AI art using summaries of their research or quotations from famous theorists in a given field. Students could even input their own name before the prompt, or perhaps a public figure related to the topic, such as Al Gore for research on climate change. Students could also grapple with the ethical issues of the art used for the training models, and generate works to reflect those issues. While some see this as a way to help non-artists quickly generate interesting work, the issues surrounding the potential replacement or devaluing of fully human-created art remain.

As work using AI continues to expand and evolve, some are recommending that we should guide students (and others wishing to leverage these tools) towards the creation of prompt banks, or, more whimsically, spellbooks (Mollick). Typically, the more specific a prompt is, the better the AI output is. Thus, Mollick and others suggest that rather than starting from scratch each time we use AI, we should be pulling from a bank of prompts, so that we can copy and paste things asking for the output to have a specific writing style or other formatting and standard aspects of writing that the human author would naturally do when tailoring their writing for the intended audience, thus saving the time it would take to retype these things each time or (even more time-consuming) to re-prompt the tools to revise their output. Having boilerplate text to include in any given prompt—not unlike the technical writer's company style guide—can ensure consistency in tone, format, and style across documents.

Works Cited

"Artificial Intelligence Tools." *UCF Faculty Center for Teaching and Learning*, https://fctl.ucf.edu/teaching-resources/promoting-academic-integrity/artificial-intelligence-writing/. Accessed 13 Apr. 2023.

Byrd, Antonio, et al. *MLA-CCCC Joint Task Force on Writing and AI Members.* Jul. 2023.

Cassens Weiss, Debra. "Latest Version of ChatGPT Aces Bar Exam with Score Nearing 90th Percentile." *ABA Journal*, 16 Mar. 2023, www.abajournal.com/web/article/latest-version-of-chatgpt-aces-the-bar-exam-with-score-in-90th-percentile.

Clark, Nicole. "Lensa's Viral AI Art Creations Were Bound to Hypersexualize Users." *Polygon*, 20 Dec. 2022, www.polygon.com/23513386/ai-art-lensa-magic-avatars-artificial-intelligence-explained-stable-diffusion.

Cu, Mark Allen, and Sebastian Hochman. "Scores of Stanford Students Used ChatGPT on Final Exams." *The Stanford Daily*, 23 Jan. 2023, https://stanforddaily.com/2023/01/22/scores-of-stanford-students-used-chatgpt-on-final-exams-survey-suggests/.

Future of Life Institute. "Pause Giant AI Experiments: An Open Letter." https://futureoflife.org/open-letter/pause-giant-ai-experiments/. Accessed 4 Apr. 2023.

Gennaro, Michael. *Artists Beaten Back in California Lawsuit against AI Image Generators.* 30 Oct. 2023, www.courthousenews.com/artists-beaten-back-in-california-lawsuit-against-ai-image-generators/.

Hern, Alex. "AI-Assisted Plagiarism? ChatGPT Bot Says It Has an Answer for That." *The Guardian*, 31 Dec. 2022. *The Guardian*, www.theguardian.com/technology/2022/dec/31/ai-assisted-plagiarism-chatgpt-bot-says-it-has-an-answer-for-that.

Hillier, Mathew. "Why Does ChatGPT Generate Fake References?" *TECHE*, 20 Feb. 2023, https://teche.mq.edu.au/2023/02/why-does-chatgpt-generate-fake-references/.

Johnson, Emily K., and Anastasia Salter. *Playful Pedagogy in the Pandemic: Pivoting to Games-Based Learning.* Routledge, 2022.

Kaye, Byron. "Australian Mayor Readies World's First Defamation Lawsuit over ChatGPT Content | Reuters." *Reuters*, www.reuters.com/technology/australian-mayor-readies-worlds-first-defamation-lawsuit-over-chatgpt-content-2023-04-05/. Accessed 12 Apr. 2023.

Knox, Liam. "Can Turnitin Cure Higher Ed's AI Fever?" *Inside Higher Ed*, 3 Apr. 2023, www.insidehighered.com/news/2023/04/03/turnitins-solution-ai-cheating-raises-faculty-concerns.

Lee, Jieh-Sheng, and Jieh Hsiang. *Patent Claim Generation by Fine-Tuning OpenAI GPT-2*. arXiv:1907.02052, arXiv, 30 June 2019. *arXiv.org*, http://arxiv.org/abs/1907.02052.

Metz, Rachel. "These Artists Found out Their Work Was Used to Train AI. Now They're Furious." *CNN*, 21 Oct. 2022, www.cnn.com/2022/10/21/tech/artists-ai-images/index.html.

Mok, Aaron. "CEO of ChatGPT Maker Responds to Schools' Plagiarism Concerns: 'We Adapted to Calculators and Changed What We Tested in Math Class.'" *Business Insider*, www.businessinsider.com/openai-chat gpt-ceo-sam-altman-responds-school-plagiarism-concerns-bans-2023-1. Accessed 25 Jan. 2023.

Mollick, Ethan. *Now Is the Time for Grimoires*. 15 July 2023, www.oneusefulth ing.org/p/now-is-the-time-for-grimoires?publication_id=1180644&utm_ medium=email&action=share&isFreemail=true.

Needleman, Emma. "Would Chat GPT Get a Wharton MBA? New White Paper by Christian Terwiesch." *Mack Institute for Innovation Management*, 17 Jan. 2023, https://mackinstitute.wharton.upenn.edu/2023/would-chat-gpt3-get-a-wharton-mba-new-white-paper-by-christian-terwiesch/.

Noble, Safiya. *Algorithms of Oppression: How Search Engines Reinforce Racism*. First edition, NYU Press, 2018.

Paik, Incheon, and Jun-Wei Wang. "Improving Text-to-Code Generation with Features of Code Graph on GPT-2." *Electronics*, vol. 10, no. 21, Nov. 2021, p. 2706. *MDPI*, https://doi.org/10.3390/electronics10212706.

Placido, Dani Di. "'Demonic' AI-Generated 'Will Smith Eating Spaghetti' Clip Goes Viral." *Forbes*, 3 Apr. 2023, www.forbes.com/sites/danidiplac ido/2023/04/03/will-smith-eating-spaghetti-is-the-latest-ai-generated-eldri tch-abomination/.

Plunkett, Luke. "AI Creating 'Art' Is an Ethical and Copyright Nightmare." *Kotaku*, 25 Aug. 2022, https://kotaku.com/ai-art-dall-e-midjourney-stable-diffusion-copyright-1849388060.

Rambsy, Kenton. "Text-Mining Short Fiction by Zora Neale Hurston and Richard Wright Using Voyant Tools." *CLA Journal*, vol. 59, no. 3, 2016, pp. 251–58.

Revell, Graeme. "Madeleine: Poetry and Art of an Artificial Intelligence." *Arts*, vol. 11, no. 5, Sept. 2022, p. 83. *MDPI*, https://doi.org/10.3390/arts1 1050083.

Rosenblatt, Kalhan. "An AI Chatbot Went Viral. Some Say It's Better than Google; Others Worry It's Problematic." *NBC News*, 2 Dec. 2022, www.nbcn ews.com/tech/tech-news/chatgpt-ai-chatbot-viral-rcna59628.

Sullivan, Anne, and Anastasia Salter. "Post-Anthropocene Poetics (De)Fused." *Electronic Literature Organization Exhibition*, Jul. 2021, https://selfloud.net/ post_anthropocene/.

Turley, Jonathan. "ChatGPT Falsely Accused Me of Sexual Harassment. Can We Trust AI?" 3 Apr. 2023, www.usatoday.com/story/opinion/column ist/2023/04/03/chatgpt-misinformation-bias-flaws-ai-chatbot/11571830002/.

Vincent, James. "AI Art Tools Stable Diffusion and Midjourney Targeted with Copyright Lawsuit." *The Verge*, 16 Jan. 2023, www.theverge. com/2023/1/16/23557098/generative-ai-art-copyright-legal-lawsuit-stable-diffusion-midjourney-deviantart.

———. "OpenAI Has Published the Text-Generating AI It Said Was Too Dangerous to Share." *The Verge*, 7 Nov. 2019, www.theverge.com/2019/11/7/20953040/ openai-text-generation-ai-gpt-2-full-model-release-1-5b-parameters.

———. "OpenAI's New Multitalented AI Writes, Translates, and Slanders." *The Verge*, 14 Feb. 2019, www.theverge.com/2019/2/14/18224704/ai-machine-learning-language-models-read-write-openai-gpt2.

Warner, John. "Freaking Out About ChatGPT—Part I." *Inside Higher Ed*, www.insidehighered.com/blogs/just-visiting/freaking-out-about-chat gpt%E2%80%94part-i. Accessed 25 Jan. 2023.

Winter, Rachel, and Anastasia Salter. "DeepFakes: Uncovering Hardcore Open Source on GitHub." *Porn Studies*, vol. 0, no. 0, Oct. 2019, pp. 1–16. *Taylor and Francis+NEJM*, https://doi.org/10.1080/23268743.2019.1642794.

Zeilinger, Martin. *Tactical Entanglements: AI Art, Creative Agency, and the Limits of Intellectual Property.* meson press, 2021.

Zylinska, Joanna. *AI Art: Machine Visions and Warped Dreams.* First edition, Open Humanities Press, 2020.

CONCLUSION

Crafting Futures in the Age of AI

The current shape of digital humanities work has been shaped by the pursuit of grants and an emphasis on large-scale projects bringing prestige to institutions. As those opportunities continue to be concentrated, and perhaps even dwindle, an approach to sustainable, personal digital humanities offers a way of renewing our engagement with technology and community. We turn to craft, and the communities that have sustained crafting traditions, for inspiration on how to build a future for digital humanities work outside of large-scale infrastructure.

Critical Times

Admittedly, we chose a heck of a time to try to write this book. In the past year that we were writing this, we have experienced rapid changes in technology, politics, and academia as the world continues to stumble through a semi-recovery from the COVID-19 pandemic—and more locally, as Florida universities continue to navigate a legislative agenda driven by a rejection of the "woke" approach to teaching with which our work is inextricably tied. These political stunts and blatant grabs for power have seeped into academia in the United States, as politicians attacked and continue to attack both public and private universities for teaching actual history rather than the whitewashed version of history that distorts or omits the truth (lest those who have always been privileged in this country feel momentarily uncomfortable). State legislatures across our nation have banned access to basic healthcare, books, and the teaching of any subject that might call into question the way our systems have been designed to maintain higher levels of power, money, and rights for specific types of people. The price we are paying and will continue to pay for these political stunts is ignorance. Our state has become the focal point for discussions as the Association of American Colleges and Universities has called the situation facing Florida higher education "dire," warning: "What is happening in Florida will not stay in Florida. We call on all professional organizations, unions, faculty, staff and administrators across the country to fight such 'reforms' tooth and nail and to offer support to our colleagues in Florida however they can" (Quinn).

This may seem like a strange moment to turn to the craft room, and the communal traditions of making it represents, for ideas in our scholarship and classroom. However, the digital humanities community has been finding their way through such collaborative, unusual projects for some time, in the types of classrooms that are most subject to attacks and suspicions right now. In spring 2023, Anastasia was teaching science fiction in Florida during a legislative onslaught driven by efforts to correct the "woke-ness" of education. It was a strange moment to be teaching science fiction: Ron DeSantis went on a rant targeting "zombie studies," and in a beautiful response, a team of faculty from the University of Santa Cruz laid out a call for us to rethink the importance of monster studies—zombies included:

> We doubt that DeSantis really thinks that such a field as Zombie Studies
> actually exists, but—if someone told him it did—would he be anything

but horrified to discover that such a field traverses the histories of Africa, the Americas, and Europe and engages with anti-colonial uprisings and centuries of cultural/political resistance against enslavement? Would he be deaf to the fact that Thomas Carlyle, one of the conservative Western historians and philosophers of "great men" that DeSantis might imagine as central to his fantasy curriculum of Western history and philosophy, refers numerous times to zombie-like reanimated corpses in his descriptions both of European industrialism and of much Western historiography?

(Fox et al.)

Elsewhere, digital humanities scholar and fellow former ProfHacker Ryan Cordell was fusing physical making, artificial intelligence, and science fiction with a woodcut (Figure 1) combining a Stable Diffusion-generated image for "a woodcut illustration of

Figure 1: Ryan Cordell's material printblock commentary on technology (Cordell).

a hybrid between an antique printing press & a mainframe computer" and a quote from Ursula K. LeGuin's "A Rant About Technology," which draws our attention to broader histories of technology, and the ways they are overlooked and marginalized—work that embraces a much more expansive view of technology than that welcomed in the traditional classroom.

Critical Platforms

Around the same time the senate was debating the future of our collective syllabi, Anastasia's science fiction class was reading "Repent, Harlequin! Said the Ticktockman," and particularly one exchange. "You're a nonconformist," accuses the Ticktockman. "That didn't used to be a felony," retorts the Harlequin. "It is now. Live in the world around you." Not long after my students were debating the constrained, orderly, future imaginary of Ellison's dystopia, the Florida State University System announced a ban on TikTok: this designation of the social media platform as part of the "state-approved cyber threat prohibited technologies list" necessitated its removal from all state-owned devices and prohibits access to all TikTok content on the university networks.

Faculty on campus using video as part of their critical making, journalism, social media, and digital culture courses had to change direction mid-semester: as we have watched these bans and panics go nationwide, we similarly cut TikTok from Chapter 3 of this book, as it is a platform that many of us won't have access to soon (the state of Montana banned it entirely in April 2023). Our frustration in this moment parallels our general frustration with many universities' systematic responses to technologies like ChatGPT: the rush to ban, restrict, and surveil usage of these tools will be both ineffective and alienating to our students. These are the actions of universities and leadership that still fall into reactionary patterns all too easily, as

Casey Fiesler noted after watching the TikTok Congressional hearings that paved the way for these bans:

> As I watched, I kept coming back to a simple truth about our lives online: Social media is bad for us. Social media is also good for us—both of these things can be true at the same time. This may seem obvious, but our conversations about tech regulation rarely accommodate for that truth.
>
> (Fiesler, "Congress Doesn't Understand Something Big About TikTok")

Ellison's Harlequin would likely be a hit on TikTok, but it's exactly that type of rebellious content that has played a role in shaping the conservative response to the platform—as Fiesler reminds us, "TikTok has become a hub for racial justice movements for a reason." These excesses and overreaches are even more suspect when we look at Twitter, a platform that during this same time of rapid change under Elon Musk's leadership has eliminated many of the safeguards against misinformation and harassment, including verified accounts.

Disengaging from these platforms in the classroom and pushing the conversation to the sidelines is not a solution. Indeed, the move to ban TikTok recalls so many efforts to ban technology from the class-room in the past: Anastasia particularly recalls attending one of their first "faculty development" workshops and listening to the instructor push for banning students from using laptops in the classroom even as they used one to type their own notes—and, yes, some sarcastic side commentary on Twitter. These same debates about allowing laptops and other devices in the classroom zombie on, semester after semester, despite the evolving ways we use these technologies. Pretending that we don't ourselves learn in a networked, subversive, playful, and often nonlinear manner is unreasonable—and positions the university and the classroom to continue to be, as Nick Sousanis warns, a place of flattening.

Digital humanities scholars have been rebelling against these types of bans personally and professionally since the first computers came to campus, and our collective resistance to over-regulated, overly restrictive forms and expectations is more important than ever. Natalie Loveless's words in *How to Make Art at the End of the World* continue to feel more and more timely:

> Research-creation mobilizes the artistic as a sensibility and approach attentive to how *form* makes *worlds*, and does so specifically within the university-as-site. Research-creation lends itself to formal reshaping practices within university knowledge-making spaces, and, at its best, for me, it does so micropolitically, bit by bit, from inside the belly of the beast: the classroom.
>
> (Loveless)

Confronted with these continual existential crises in higher education, we have worked to make our classrooms places where our students can collaborate to imagine through humanist work, and hopefully in this process be reminded of the essential value of the humanities even as external dialogues decried their worthlessness. Larger studies of the impact of these last few years on higher education reflect just how challenging this work is now, as we have both broader awareness of faculty burnout (Pope-Ruark) and rising concerns about student preparedness and engagement post-pandemic.

Furthermore, the classroom is not isolated from the impact and concerns raised by technological breakthroughs that feel like they have occurred almost daily: OpenAI released ChatGPT-3, 3.5, and 4 and image-from-text generators DALL-E and DALL-E2, while also venturing into speech transcription and translation with Whisper. Not to be outdone, Microsoft released Bing AI, and Google put out Bard. AI art generators Midjourney and Stable Diffusion joined DALL-E, with five versions of Midjourney and several versions of Stable Diffusion. Additionally, a plethora of other applications and platforms began using these AI programs as bases for their own applications, like Meta's OpenArt and starryai's mobile app. Many universities have rushed to respond to these possibilities—with workshops on detecting plagiarism as news stories ominously warn that the careers students are preparing for will soon be obsolete (Firat).

DeepBrain leveraged ChatGPT to create text-to-video capabilities. Alibaba Cloud released text-to-video AI ModelScope, resulting in the harrowing videos from text prompts like, "Will Smith eating spaghetti." We suffered through news cycles warning of impending doom for humanity, deranged results from various AI chatbots (especially Bing AI) threatening users and fabricating slander, high-profile demonstrations of AI "hallucinations" like the telescope question in Bard's demonstration that then crashed Google's stock, and layoffs of ethical AI teams. Several AI art generators resulted in lawsuits surrounding intellectual property rights, and AI text generators were sued for defamation. AI detectors were created and proven unreliable while plagiarism detectors deployed by suspicious professors often revealed many more usages than originally expected.

But the digital humanities invite us to think differently about this relationship with AI, and to reckon with possibilities outside of binary rejections and replacements. As Ryan Cordell's collaborative woodcut, and our final pattern, attest, there is much that can be accomplished by thinking beyond the ban. The much longer history of generative writing (as we explored through Tracery) serves as a reminder of what can be imagined when we break out of traditional habits in the classroom.

Critical Classrooms

Breaking out of those traditional habits in the classroom is also an opportunity to rethink our mechanisms of evaluation and structures: what we value for ourselves, and our scholarship, is not always well reflected in our classrooms. Faculty have experimented with mixed success using labor-based grading, ungrading, and even self-grading models. Most universities (including ours) still require a final grade to be entered into the system, and students' transcripts include these grades, but there is a great deal of variance from institution to institution and from instructor to instructor. Critical making projects lend themselves to any type of grading, whether you have the flexibility to explore new methods or more exacting institutional and departmental expectations to consider.

Patterns like those in this book are intended to encourage experimentation and produce prototypes, so the learning and the process of exploration can be emphasized regardless of the structure the final assessment takes. For some (like us) this exploration is inherently self-motivating, but it's also helpful to think about the connections that making offers to future pathways and opportunities. One way to shift the students' focus from grading to learning is to structure a course so that smaller assignments serve as practice instances where students can take larger risks without worrying about tanking their grade, and having assignments build, so that knowledge is scaffolded and skills can grow over the course of the term. The undergraduate examples from Emily's Tools in the Digital Humanities course were graded using rubrics emphasizing process and effort, which is a result of her take on labor-based grading. She also found it beneficial to use a transparent rubric that broke down each part of the assignment—including specifying a certain number of variations in Tracery or rooms in Bitsy—to help reassure her undergraduates (and to help them rein in the scope of their project), as they rarely have experience with this type of critical making in prior courses. Rubrics can also act to guide students to the aspects of the assignment where the instructor feels that students should focus more of their efforts, in the way that some parts of assignments are assigned more points than others.

Because Emily's undergraduate course is online and emphasizes digital tools, all assignments are required to be posted on a student's digital portfolio, and the creation of this portfolio itself is the first major assignment. Students are encouraged to make their own decisions about the level of public access to their work, and resources are included in the module to help them password-protect their site if they choose. The rubric for each major assignment, then, includes a point or two for submitting a working link. This acts to deter students from *intentionally* submitting non-working links and also provides a way to resubmit, sans those few points, in the event that the student does accidentally send a broken link, which happens when students forget to click "publish," or send the login-specific editor link rather than the viewable/password access link.

Next, the undergraduate rubric looks for a project that seems complete. This is just another measure to ensure students submit work that they have spent time and effort to do—it does not have to be a beautiful, publishable project, but it should look like the ending was intentionally done and not concluded because the student ran out of time. Most of these students are turning in a project with a digital tool that they first heard of at the beginning of the module two or three weeks prior to the deadline: the projects should reflect effort and experimentation, which is admittedly a struggle for the more high-performing, perfectionist-leaning students, but this is laid out at the beginning of the semester in the first "welcome to the course" page. This aspect of the rubric does still act to emphasize the process since it is worth a small percentage of the overall assignment grade, but helps avoid procrastination tendencies of overwhelmed undergraduates who may be tempted to build their project until the bare minimum is reached and then submit something unintentionally incomplete or haphazard.

Undergraduate projects are also required to include a critical statement, where the students' use of a particular digital tool "calls attention to, questions, critiques, or celebrates some larger aspect of humanity." Thus, the critical statement that the work makes has to be apparent to the instructor. The typical spread of attention to assignment detail is usually paid in the earlier tool assignments, where some students really pound their audience over the head with a clear message while other students don't appear to have a grounding theme or idea anywhere in the project. This is where assigning several smaller projects over the course of the semester that build into a larger research project is extremely beneficial—students receive corrective feedback on their interpretations of the critical statement requirement several times before the final assignment.

Finally, the undergraduate rubric requires that the project be unique—deterring students from thoughts of plagiarism or even just copying another person's ideas but also, once again, emphasizing the process of making over the finished product. This focus tends to come through as students share their work, with Emily requiring each major assignment to be shared on a class discussion board where students describe their making process, their intent for the work, how it went, how different the final result was from their initial intent and why, and what they learned about the tool, topic, and themselves.

In the graduate course, grades emphasize the process of making, with a forced rapid progression designed to discourage perfectionism and stalling: reflections are weekly, with an additional week of forgiveness if needed, and after that time the discussion has moved on to the next tool. This approach is very different from the traditional programming or development course, which typically focuses on building expertise in a specific tool, and instead offers (like this book) a tasting menu in which no particular selection is high-stakes. Every week features a different maker talking informally about their work, demonstrating that every scholar approaches their practice differently, and offering examples for how to build this practice into a meaningful part of one's research and pedagogy going forward. In their reflections, students can engage both in responding to those makers as well as positioning their experiments in conversation with the many examples and critical texts taught alongside the practice. Reflections are graded on completion—not on the presumed "success" or "failure" of the making itself.

Jesse Stommel (Stommel) and others advocate for ungrading as another way to ensure equity across higher education. The critical making projects discussed throughout this book can fit well into this model. Many practitioners of this model emphasize instead student metacognition in the form of self-evaluation. Asking students to reflect on their critical making process is a beneficial activity that helps emphasize the process in this approach but also helps students solidify the things they learned through their research and creation processes. Another approach to ungrading is self-grading, where students assign themselves their own grades. This practice also has a variety of approaches. Some instructors ask students to self-grade some assignments but not all, others assign no actual grades and instead ask students to submit the grade they think they earned. Any of these approaches can be used with the critical making projects described in this book. The rubrics used in the undergraduate course can still be used to structure feedback without assigning points to them, and the completion model approach of the graduate course allows for points that are correlated with effort. Instructor feedback is important regardless of the numeric or letter grade accompanying it, especially with students new to this type of research. Asking students to articulate the critical statement that the student conveyed (or seemed to convey) with their project is helpful as well, as faculty can then weigh in on how clearly that message comes across. Plus, because the emphasis is on the process and the intent of the work more than the final resulting product, students often need reassurance that their work has value despite its lack of polish or perhaps its incongruence with the initial, grand vision the student had for the work.

Notably, each of our patterns throughout this book have described projects as though they are individual assignments—where students are expected to produce single-authored creations. However, all of these assignments can easily be modified into group assignments, or individual students can be assigned individual experiments that will then become a part of a larger whole when combined with the group or the entire class. The individual focus is intended to promote students to tinker with each concept and medium. We have noticed that when students work in groups, the emphasis on the final, finished product looms over the individuals and can often stifle the creative experimentations that result in "failures" as students learn about the approach, the technology, etc. If a group project is the best fit for a critical making assignment, it may be best to dedicate some class time or smaller individual assignments to the pure experimentation stage so that students each feel they have a grasp on the tool's capabilities before planning with their group.

Critical Communities

In their message establishing their eminently timely Center for Monster Studies, the University of California Santa Cruz collective laid out their mission "to hunt cultural monsters in order to give us a better understanding of ourselves and to unlock the mechanisms of empathy and identity construction through the arts, social sciences, and humanities" (Fox et al.). Such communities are spaces of hope and play: they are a reminder that the subjects that receive mockery elsewhere are critical, and worth our exploration and time. Sustaining hope in a time of "cultural monsters" writ large can be incredibly difficult, but it is that hope that we find sustaining in looking towards bringing such understanding to our institutions.

There is no more important community for sustaining critical hope than our classrooms: we share our critical hope with (and for) our students, to encourage them to think for themselves and to tinker with ideas, materials, and digital tools in order to build their own understanding of the world. Our approach when teaching these tools and critical making described in this book hands over a great deal of instructional "power" to our students, often giving them autonomy to select their own topics to research, the experiments they wish to create, and the tools that they feel best suited to that topic and project.

As students shape more of the classroom community to their interests and needs, their instructional demands shift from a need for information from an expert to guidance towards resources, help with scope, and particulars specific to their individual project. This may sound overwhelming to faculty who are unfamiliar with teaching digital tools like those in this book, but ultimately, we feel this approach empowers students to make up their own minds about various topics and understand, through creating and analyzing different things, the complexity and varying perspectives that each topic or hot-button issue of the day has, and how to uncover their layers. Again, we do not teach individual tools; we teach critical thinking skills in each aspect of these courses, encouraging students to question, critique, and make.

An old saying goes something along the lines of, "the sciences can tell you how to clone a dinosaur; the humanities can tell you why that's probably a bad idea." This succinctly highlights the different emphases of study between these two fields, but there is a difference in scholarly positionality as well. In contrast to the sciences, where scholars strive to be impersonal, detached from their research, and nonbiased (however impossible that may be in reality), the humanities and digital humanities have long served as an invitation to embrace human voices and to acknowledge the humanity of the researcher. This scholarship invites, amplifies, and inspects authentic voices.

With all of the media attention currently being given to AI and the sudden (and somehow individual) "heroes" of the technology industry, it is tempting to turn our backs on these events and to disengage from technology, politics, and the seemingly constant stream of hate spewing across the internet. Disengagement, however, is essentially condonement. We must stay engaged and vocal, sharing our concerns, our perspectives, and our lived experiences, especially when they contrast with the prevailing cultural narrative. Critical making, where we craft a project, prototype, art, and so forth, lets us create to share. It allows us to hold on to, and reimagine, our technology and materials— as opposed to the doomscrolling across the web, which often brings feelings of powerlessness and tempts us to disengage.

Finally, communities support individual voices through platform development and maintenance, archiving, and instructional materials. Much of this labor is invisible, thankless, and unpaid, despite being crucial to thousands of works. The NEXT archive, dedicated to the preservation of works of electronic literature, is one example. The NEXT is a digital archive with the mission to "preserve and present born-digital art, literature, and games that engage with language in ways that are participatory, interactive, and experiential" (Grigar). When Twitter changed hands and *Cheap Bots Done Quick* (CBDQ) Tracery bots no longer functioned, the community responded with options for creating bots on Mastodon, Discord, and websites. Describing his Tracery2HTML Template, Leonardo Flores writes, "I created this as a way to port my CBDQ bots to HTML, and am sharing it with the community in the same generous spirit that Kate Compton and V. Buckenham had when creating and sharing Tracery and Cheap Bots Done Quick!"

Likewise, the Wayback Machine (https://web.archive.org/), maintained by the nonprofit Internet Archive, provides not just entertaining glimpses into the internet's past, but also access to earlier versions of websites. This is our go-to site for workarounds when sites are no longer maintained. In fact, when we discovered while writing this book that Kate Compton's Tracery tutorial site was no longer functional, we used the Wayback Machine to recover it. We also reached out to Compton herself and received permission to reproduce the tutorial on our own site. The open sharing of these tools and more exhibits the sense of community shared by many working in the digital humanities space, and in our opinion, demonstrates the benefits of collaboration over competition.

Critical Reflections

At the completion of these patterns, we hope you have found value in each material and practice we have explored. Through selfies and self-reflection in images, we see hope for ourselves and our students as we tinker with materials, experiment with design, and reflect on our lives, our values, and our potential to be makers (and re-makers) of the world. Looking back to our first pattern should also be a reminder of how much the making process and goals change through practice and the addition of new tools. We like to invite our students to reflect: what selfie might you make now, with all the patterns at your disposal? Building on those images towards image-text and exploring the potential of sequential art unlocked more intentional ways to create meaning through juxtaposition. Through sequence, we craft arguments. The conversation of flattening and unflattening brought to us from Nick Sousanis's example weaves throughout the material and digital making projects of this book and beyond, reminding us that the scholarly default is a genre subject to change.

As we moved into technological methods, we expanded our students' vocabulary as well as our reach into the history of digital culture—communicating with motion through the use of GIFs, reflecting on "internet ugly" aesthetics and the widespread authorship that the early web afforded many (especially those of us lucky enough to be teens in the 1990s) an early avenue to digital tinkering through personal homepages. The repetitive motion and easy-to-share file size created a new virtual shorthand. When we create our own GIFs from images or videos, we first leverage existing symbols and cultural mes-saging and reflect upon that history (and its silences).

With each new pattern, we added layers to how we create: with maps, the spatial opportunities of the digital come into focus, allow-ing us to reimagine familiar spaces as unfamiliar, and watch specific locations change over time—a powerful reminder of the impact that humans have on the earth and one another, with various policies imparting drastically beneficial or detrimental effects on our states, cities, and homes. Maps communicate political and ideological infor-mation along with geography. The two-dimensional representation of a place like "home" or the path of a fictional character carry weight and meaning, and different variations of maps and journeys carry denotations and connotations, and can create visualizations of power and influence. Communities dedicated to inspecting and decoding the layers of politics and history through GIS and more analog meth-ods help sustain knowledge, engagement, and the critical practices of this work.

From the spatial, we build towards even broader canvases, working with the webtext format that has become one of the most compelling options for digital scholarly design. Our play with hypertext opened with the link and moved towards the complexities of nonlinear design. With Twine and similar tools, we can wield the power of narrative and the disruptive force of hypertext to share compelling thoughts, ideas, stories, and research. The history of hypertext is rich and filled with creativity, experimentation, and, sadly, file degradation: engag-ing with this history can also inspire reflection on what aspects define this medium, and what should be preserved in the event of impend-ing platform updates that can render interactive works unplayable. Such reflection reminds us of what is lost when screenshots flatten the hypertextual in academic articles and books like this one.

Moving from hypertext to games added more interactivity to our designs, placing an emphasis on collisions as a means of exploring the limitations of a digital world. While Bitsy itself is just one, minimalist, entry point into a vast possibility space of play and experience design, its limitations are also what makes it accessible. These small games can make statements and convey feeling, allowing us to share frustrations and build different worlds. Tools like Bitsy are sustained by designers and developers working to foster communities of independent (or "indie") game creation that celebrates games exemplifying the digital humanities: spaces for making authentic, personal interactive works.

When we moved into building grammars, we introduced more visible structures of code, using JavaScript notations and structures to generate emergent meaning and unexpected consequences. The Tracery JavaScript library is itself the creation of a critical maker: Kate Compton built it with the "casual creator" in mind, enabling us in turn to build upon her combinatorial logics to new outcomes (Compton et al.). As other creators have in turn expanded Tracery's utility for bot-making, we have the potential to unleash our creations into the sharing of public-facing art and commentary.

Digital humanities tools can also offer us the opportunity to decode, as our pattern of visualizing text through Voyant reflects. The amount of text available to us is overwhelming, and the mechanisms of distant reading can provide us with a way to seek patterns within large texts or across several different corpora, highlighting words and phrases that may go unnoticed by the human reader. This way of reading is now embedded into the web, so this process also makes visible something we do not always easily perceive. Digitized corpora are becoming easier to access, allowing students to focus on the patterns in existing works rather than tedious corpora-building of prior decades. Digital humanities scholars have collaborated to create tools and tutorials for large-scale text analysis, creating a community around this important research.

The rise of AI has unlocked an entire vault of new possibilities for creation and analysis of the digital, and students can explore the world with an "intelligent" assistant with which to co-create. It is tempting to look at the moral panic of media headlines and assume it is all overreaction (or the opposite). It is also easy for students and more traditional humanities scholars to feel overwhelmed by the technical aspects hiding beneath the interface. However, is important that we engage with this technology, understand how it works, and find ways to mitigate its potentially harmful impacts. Digital humanities communities are already finding ways to explore—and interrogate—these technologies in our work, as Ryan Cordell's earlier piece attests.

We may not be able to radically change the current ideological climate, but we hope that this book has provided our readers additional tools with which to continue pushing back against oppression and injustice—or more simply, to find purpose and excitement in engaging with multimodal scholarship and the possibilities of unflattening our work. We all increasingly need more opportunities to conduct meaningful research and create compelling projects beyond the traditional essay assignment. Through the creation of critical making projects, like those included in this book, we hope we have helped invite others into the practice—regardless of institutional resources, funding support, or experience.

Works Cited

Compton, Kate, et al. "Tracery: Approachable Story Grammar Authoring for Casual Users." *Seventh Intelligent Narrative Technologies Workshop*, 2014, www.aaai.org/ocs/index.php/INT/INT7/paper/view/9266.

Cordell, Ryan (@ryancordell@hcommons.social). "Went a Different Way with the 'A Rant About "Technology"' Print Today: Mixed up a Kind of Sheeny Copper-Red Ink & Tested It on Several Papers…" Mastodon, 18 May 2023, https://hcommons.social/@ryancordell/110392035933191328.

Fiesler, Casey. "Congress Doesn't Understand Something Big About TikTok." *Slate*, 28 Mar. 2023, https://slate.com/technology/2023/03/tiktok-hearing-what-congress-missed.html.

Firat, Mehmet. "What ChatGPT Means for Universities: Perceptions of Scholars and Students." *Journal of Applied Learning and Teaching*, vol. 6, no. 1, 2023, pp. 57–63, https://doi.org/10.37074/jalt.2023.6.1.22.

Fox, Renée, et al. "Burying DeSantis' Zombie Ideas." *The Center For Monster Studies*, 6 Mar. 2023, www.monsterstudies.ucsc.edu/monstrous-happenings/burying-desantis-zombie-ideas.

Grigar, Dene. "The NEXT Curatorial Statement Space." The NEXT, https://the-next.eliterature.org/. Accessed 23 Jul. 2024.

Loveless, Natalie. *How to Make Art at the End of the World: A Manifesto for Research-Creation.* Duke University Press, 2019.

Pope-Ruark, Rebecca. *Unraveling Faculty Burnout: Pathways to Reckoning and Renewal.* JHU Press, 2022.

Quinn, Ryan. "AAUP Calls to Fight 'Tooth and Nail' in Florida." *Inside Higher Ed*, 24 May 2023, www.insidehighered.com/news/faculty-issues/academic-freedom/2023/05/24/aaup-calls-fight-tooth-and-nail-florida.

Stommel, Jesse. "Ungrading: A Bibliography." *Jesse Stommel*, 3 Mar. 2020, www.jessestommel.com/ungrading-a-bibliography/.

Author Bios

Emily K. Johnson is an Assistant Professor in the Department of English (Technical Communication and Digital Humanities), graduate faculty in the Technical Communication MA program, and core faculty in the Texts and Technology PhD program at the University of Central Florida. She is coauthor of *Playful Pedagogy in the Pandemic: Pivoting to Games-Based Learning* (Routledge, with Anastasia Salter, 2022). Johnson is Principal Investigator of a project funded by the US Department of Education investigating the efficacy of video games for language learning. Her work has been published in *Technical Communication Quarterly, Computers and Composition, Computers and Education,* the *Journal for Universal Computer Science,* and more.

Anastasia Salter is a Professor of English at the University of Central Florida, and the Director of Graduate Programs and the PhD in Texts and Technology for the College of Arts and Humanities. Dr. Salter is the author of *Playful Pedagogy in the Pandemic: Pivoting to Games-Based Learning* (Routledge, with Emily Johnson, 2022), *Twining: Critical and Creative Approaches to Hypertext Narratives* (Amherst College, with Stuart Moulthrop, 2021), *A Portrait of the Auteur as Fanboy* (University of Mississippi Press, with Mel Stanfill, 2020), *Adventure Games: Playing the Outsider* (Bloomsbury, with Aaron Reed and John Murray, 2020), *Toxic Geek Masculinity in Media* (Palgrave Macmillan, with Bridget Blodgett, 2017), *Jane Jensen: Gabriel Knight, Adventure Games, Hidden Objects* (Bloomsbury, 2017), *What Is Your Quest? From Adventure Games to Interactive Books* (University of Iowa Press, 2014), and *Flash: Building the Interactive Web* (MIT Press, with John Murray, 2014).